MISCANTHUS
FOR ENERGY AND FIBRE

MISCANTHUS
FOR ENERGY AND FIBRE

EDITED BY
MICHAEL B. JONES AND MARY WALSH

Published by James & James (Science Publishers) Ltd,
35–37 William Road, London NW1 3ER, UK

A catalogue record for this book is available from the British Library.

ISBN 1-902916-07-7

Printed in the UK by The Cromwell Press

Cover photos courtesy of Dr I. Lewandowski,
University of Hohenheim, Stuttgart.

Contents

Authors and Contributors

C. V. Beale
Writtle College
Chelmsford
Essex, CM1 3LG
England
CVB@writtle.ac.uk

M. Bullard
Arthur Rickwood (ADAS)
Mepal
Ely
Cambridgeshire, CB6 2BA
England
mike.bullard@adas.co.uk

D. G. Christian
Rothamsted Experimental Station
Harpenden
Hertfordshire, AL5 2JQ
England
dudley.christian@bbsrc.ac.uk

J. C. Clifton-Brown
Botany Department
University of Dublin
Trinity College
Dublin 2
Ireland
jcbrown@tcd.ie

S. Cosentino
Istituto di Agronomia generale e
Coltivazioni erbacee
Università degli studi di Catania
Via Valdisavoia 5
95123 - Catania
Italy
agronomi@mbox.fagr.unict.it

C. Dalianis
Agricultural University of Athens
75 Iera Odos
11855 Athens
Greece
cdalianis@aua.gr

P. Duarte
Grupo de Disciplinas de Ecologia da
Hidrosfera
Faculdade de Ciências e Tecnologia
Universidade Nova de Lisboa
Quinta da Torre, 2825-114 Caparica
Portugal

N. El Bassam
Institute of Crop Science
Federal Agricultural Research Centre
(FAL)
Bundesallee 50
D-38116 Braunschweig
Germany
NASIR.BASSAM@FAL.DE

A. Eppel-Hotz
Bayerische Landesanstalt für Weinbau
und Gartenbau
An der Steige 15
D-97209
Veitshoecheim
Germany

P. K. Farage
Department of Biological Sciences
John Tabor Laboratories
University of Essex
Colchester, CO4 3SQ
England
p_farage@lineone.net

A. L. Fernando
Grupo de Disciplinas de Ecologia da
Hidrosfera
Faculdade de Ciências e Tecnologia
Universidade Nova de Lisboa
Quinta da Torre, 2825-114 Caparica
Portugal
ala@mail.fct.unl.pt

E. Haase
Piccoplant GMBH
Brokhauser Weg. 75
D-26129 Oldenburgh
Germany
piccoplant@t-online.de

T. R. Hodkinson
Botany Department
University of Dublin
Trinity College
Dublin 2
Ireland
trevor.hodkinson@tcd.ie

W. Huisman
Department of Agricultural
Engineering and Physics
AGROTECHNION
Bomenweg 4
6730 HD Wageningen
Netherlands
Willem.Huisman@User.AenF.WAU.NL

S. A. Humphries
The Old Forge
Langley St, Hardley
Norwich
Norfolk, NR14 6DA
England
steve@humphries1000.fsnet.co.uk

M. B. Jones
Botany Department
University of Dublin
Trinity College
Dublin 2
Ireland
jonesm@tcd.ie

U. Jørgensen
Department of Soil Science (DSS)
Research Centre Foulum
P.O. Box 23
8830 Tjele
Denmark
Uffe.Jorgensen@agrsci.dk

S. P. Long
Department of Crop Science and Plant
Biology
190 Edward R. Madigan Laboratories
1201 West Gregory Drive
Urbana, IL 61801-3838
USA
stevel@life.uiuc.edu

H.-J. Muhs
Federal Research Centre for Forestry &
Forest Products
Institute for Forest Genetics & Forest
Tree Breeding
Sieker Landstr. 2
22927 Grosshansdorf
Germany
wuehlish@holz.uni-hamburg.de

J. F. Santos Oliveira
Grupo de Disciplinas de Ecologia da
Hidrosfera
Faculdade de Ciências e Tecnologia

Universidade Nova de Lisboa
Quinta da Torre, 2825-114 Caparica
Portugal
jfso@mail.fct.unl.pt

C. Petrini
A. Biotec
Via Pisciatello 213
47042 Cesenatico
Italy

V. Pignatelli
Inn Bioag. Prim., C.R. Casaccia
Via Anguilliarese 301
00060 S. Maria di Galeria
Rome
Italy
pignatelli@trisaia.enea.it

L. Scally
Botany Department
University of Dublin
Trinity College
Dublin 2
Ireland
mscally@tcd.ie

H. Schwarz
Agricultural University Vienna
Institute of Mathematics and Statistics
Gregor Mendelstr. 33
A-1180, Vienna
Austria

K.-U. Schwarz
Department of Soil Science (DSS)
Research Centre Foulum
P.O. Box 23
8830 Tjele
Denmark
kaiuwe.schwarz@agrsci.dk

P. Visser
Biomass technology group B.V.
c/o University of Twente
P.O. Box 217
7500 AE Enschede
The Netherlands
Visser@btg.ct.utwente.nl

M. Walsh
Hyperion Energy Systems Ltd
Main Street
Watergrass Hill
Co. Cork
Ireland
mm_walsh@corkcorp.ie

Preface

Miscanthus x *giganteus* is a woody rhizomatous C_4 grass species which originated in south-east Asia and was initially imported to Europe as an ornamental plant. It is a perennial plant with an estimated productive life time of at least 10–15 years, and both the stems and leaves of the crop can be harvested annually. *Miscanthus* is a promising non-food crop, yielding high quality lignocellulosic material for both energy and fibre production. It is characterised by relatively high yields, low moisture content at harvest, high water and nitrogen use efficiencies and an apparently low susceptibility to pests and diseases.

This book is a review of the state-of-the-art of *Miscanthus* in Europe. The information it contains is sourced from trials and experiments which have been carried out by different European research organisations and institutions. Many of these investigations were carried out as part of the *Miscanthus* Productivity Network. This network was established under the Agro-Industry Research (AIR) programme of the European Union's Directorate General for Agriculture (DG VI) in 1992 and its main objective was to generate information on the potential of *Miscanthus* as a non-food crop in Europe. The specific areas of interest were potential productivity, low temperature limitations on growth, water requirements, genotype screening, environmental impact assessment, harvesting, storage and utilisation. The genotype which was examined in the field trials by the partners was *Miscanthus* x *giganteus*. This is a naturally occurring interspecific hybrid which, like all *Miscanthus* species, is an unimproved plant, but which exhibits considerable yield potential under European conditions.

The European *Miscanthus* Productivity Network had 17 partners located in 10 countries throughout Europe.

- Hyperion, Ireland
- TCD (Trinity College, Dublin), Ireland
- FAL (Federal Research Centre for Agriculture), Germany
- CRES (Centre for Renewable Energy Sources), Greece
- LWG (Bayerische Landesanstalt für Weinbau und Gartenbau), Germany
- UNINOVA (Universidade Nova de Lisboa), Portugal
- ESSEX (University of Essex), UK

- BTG (Biomass Technology Group), The Netherlands
- ENEA (Ente per le Nuove Tecnologie, l'Energia e l'Ambiente), Italy
- IACR (Institute of Arable Crops Research), UK
- ADAS (ADAS Consulting Ltd), UK
- IAGCE (Istituto di Agronomia generale e Coltivazioni erbacee, Universita di Catania), Italy
- USC (Universidade de Santiago de Compostela), Spain
- BFH (Bundesforschungsanstalt für Forst-und Holzwirtschaft, Institut für Forstgenetik), Germany
- SORGHAL (Sorgham Organisation and Research Group for High Altitude or Latitude), Belgium
- A. Biotec, Italy
- INRA, (Institut National de la Recherche Agronomique, Thirerral-Grignon), France

Its objectives were to:

- determine the sustainable yield and quality of *Miscanthus* as a low input agricultural crop at different locations in the EC, with particular emphasis on northern Europe
- assess the limitations which low temperatures and other stress factors place on the growth of *Miscanthus* under European climatic conditions
- determine which genotypes of *Miscanthus* are most suitable for growth in the EC across its range of ambient temperatures, rainfall and soil conditions
- assess the environmental constraints of growing *Miscanthus* in the EC
- evaluate and test different technologies for harvesting, storage and drying the crop
- identify, evaluate and test selected end-uses of *Miscanthus*.

This book had its origins in a '*Miscanthus* Handbook' which was completed as part of a Concerted Action (Contract No. FAIR 3-CT96-1707) funded by the European Commission (DEVI) as part of the Food Agro Industry Research (FAIR) Programme.

Michael Jones, Dublin
Mary Walsh, Cork
2000

Commodity code: 49019900

£45.94

Payment by world pay received with
thanks 12 September 2005

VAT Reg. No 614 6453 48

VAT @ 17.5%	
VAT @ %	
Zero Rated	£45.94
Total	£45.94
Payment	(£45.94)
Total Due	£0.00

SALES INVOICE

CPL Scientific Publishing Services Ltd trading as CPL Press

Liberty House, The Enterprise Centre
New Greenham Park, Newbury RG19 6HW, UK
Phone +44 (0) 1635 817408   Fax +44 (0) 1635 817409
Email info@cplpress.com   http://www.cplpress.com

INVOICE N°.	TAX POINT
C7888JXJ	12-Sep-05

INVOICE TO:

MILLTOWN, TURE, MUFF
CO.DONEGAL 1, IRELAND

OUR REF.	ORDER N°.
	1501

FAO: Mr COLM CROSSAN,

SERVICES OR PRODUCT DESCRIPTION	ZERO RATED	SUBJECT TO VAT
Miscanthus - For Energy and Fibre [Hardcover 1902916077]	£40.00	
Shipping	£5.94	

1 Origins and Taxonomy of Miscanthus
by L. Scally, T. Hodkinson and M. B. Jones

1.1 Introduction

Since Andersson's first description of *Miscanthus* (Andersson, 1885), more than eighty different synonyms have been applied to the genus (The Plant Names Project, 1999). At present, it is estimated that *Miscanthus* comprises about fourteen species (Hodkinson *et al.*, 1997). Interspecific hybridisation is common and this has given rise to a large number of hybrids, many of which are sterile. In addition to natural hybridisation, a large number of *Miscanthus* cultivars have been produced by the horticultural industry for their ornamental value. *Miscanthus* also hybridises with other genera, especially *Saccharum*. *Saccharum* is closely related to *Miscanthus*, the only tangible differences between the two being the disposition of spikelets on the flowering panicle and the fragility of the rachis. Interest in the potential of certain *Miscanthus* hybrids as biomass crops has necessitated a review of the taxonomy of the genus in recent years. This chapter looks at the current status of *Miscanthus* taxonomy.

1.2 Origins of the Genus

The genus *Miscanthus* belongs to the family Poaceae. It has a wide ranging distribution, with natural boundaries extending from south-eastern Asia, through China, Japan and into Polynesia, with a few species occurring in Africa. Today, however, *Miscanthus* can be found naturalised throughout much of Europe, where it has been introduced, largely for its ornamental value. Its distribution is largely tropical or sub-tropical, and it grows from sea level to altitudes of at least 3000 m. Throughout these regions *Miscanthus* is generally considered to be a weed of disturbed areas, but it also forms extensive grassland communities.

One hybrid which has generated considerable interest in recent years is *M.* x *giganteus* Greef et Deu. This hybrid was first collected in Yokohama, Japan by Olson in 1935 from where it was taken into cultivation in Denmark by Karl Foerster and named *Miscanthus sinensis* 'Giganteus' hort. (Greef & Deuter, 1993). This plant was subsequently distributed throughout Europe. Some evidence suggests that this hybrid is a result of a cross between *M. sinensis* and *M. sacchariflorus* (Greef & Deuter, 1993; Linde-Laursen, 1993; Hodkinson *et al.*, 1997). However, this evidence is still not fully substantiated and the taxonomy of this individual and the genus *Miscanthus* has not been fully resolved. Many of the complications involved in *Miscanthus* taxonomy are due to its polyploid nature. Some believe that the high basic chromosome number of *Miscanthus* indicates that it may be derived from two ancestors, one with ten chromosomes and the other with nine (Adati & Shiotani, 1962; Linde-Laursen, 1993). Further complications arise from the fact that *Miscanthus* species hybridise both with other species within the genus and with other related genera such as *Saccharum*.

1.3 Collection of *Miscanthus* Gene Pool

The first step in a study of *Miscanthus* taxonomy was to obtain as wide a range of species, hybrids and cultivars as possible. Most of the material obtained by Trinity College, Dublin (TCD) was donated by various botanic gardens throughout the world and from other research institutes which were interested in *Miscanthus* as a biomass crop. All of the material obtained was taken into cultivation at the Trinity College Botanic Garden in Dublin and planted out in one area of the garden in the spring of 1996. Surprisingly, almost all the species, hybrids and cultivars produced viable seed, thus proving that many of these individuals, previously thought to be sterile, were in fact fertile. This led the TCD research team to conclude that the lack of seed production which was previously observed was partly due to an insufficient gene pool available for successful fertilisation and partly to variations in climatic conditions.

1.4 Assessment of Genetic Variation

The measurement of genetic variation within species is critical for their conservation, utilisation and management. It is essential that the diversity within *Miscanthus* is measured, both as an aid to the conservation of the genus and also to allow valuable traits (e.g. cold tolerance and pest resistance) to be bred into species which may be of commercial value. Traditionally, morphological measurements of various characters were the only way in which estimations of diversity could be made. However, these estimations of diversity are not precise as they measure phenotypic variation as well as genotypic variation. Molecular data, on the other hand, allows a direct measurement of diversity as the DNA itself is being analysed as opposed to its estimation from phenotype (Schaal *et al.,* 1991). The best possible method of measuring genetic diversity is the direct sequencing of DNA. Unfortunately, this method is both expensive and time-consuming, and, as relatively few individuals can be analysed in this way, it is often impractical with current technology. Morphological and molecular techniques vary in the type of data they produce and hence the way in which they resolve genetic differences and the taxonomic levels to which they can be applied (Karp *et al.,* 1996). The following sections examine the methods which TCD applied in order to measure diversity within *Miscanthus*.

1.4.1 Assessment of Morphological Characters

Morphological taxonomy of *Miscanthus*, as in many grasses, has proved rather difficult. This is because most of the diagnostic characters are derived from the inflorescence. Most taxonomic treatments consider the length of the inflorescence axis, the length of the racemes, the disposition of the spikelets on the axis, nerves of glume, dorsal hairs of glume and the presence or absence of awns as being the most useful characters for delimiting species, sections and subsections of *Miscanthus* (Lee, 1964; Clayton & Renvoize, 1986; Hodkinson *et al.*, 1997). However, none of these studies present an extensive review of all possible characters available to classical numerical taxonomy (Table 1.1). During the course of the *Miscanthus* Productivity Network, TCD decided to carry out such a review of all possible characters.

Table 1.1. Characters of Miscanthus *measured for morphological analysis.*

Character	Character
Awn – present/absent	Fertile lemma width
Awn length	Sterile lemma width
Callus hairs longest length	Palea length
Pedicel hairs longest length	Palea width
Pedicel length (1)	Lodicule length
Pedicel length (2)	Lodicule width
Fertile glume hair – present/absent	Leaf width
Sterile glume hair – present/absent	Leaf mid rib width
Fertile glume hair longest length	Leaf margin (no. of spines/10mm)
Sterile glume hair longest length	Upper leaf hairs – present/absent
Fertile glume length	Lower leaf hairs – present/absent
Sterile glume length	Hairs on main axis of inflorescence – present/absent
Fertile glume width	Inflorescence main axis length
Sterile glume width	Inflorescence total length
Fertile lemma length	Inflorescence width
Sterile lemma length	

A total of 31 characters were scored on individual flowers from 83 specimens with additional characters being scored on the inflorescence and the leaf (Table 1.1). The initial choice of characters was largely subjective, although some characters which had been shown by others to be useful in *Miscanthus* identification were used in the analysis. All measurements were carried out on herbarium specimens from the Royal Botanic Garden, Edinburgh, the Royal Botanic Garden, Kew, the Natural History Museum, Paris and the School of Botany, Trinity College, Dublin. Unfortunately, it was not possible to include all species currently estimated to belong to the genus in the analysis due to difficulty in obtaining herbarium specimens. However, they will be included in later analyses. The species included in TCD's analysis were *M. sinensis*, *M. sacchariflorus*, *M. floridulus*, *M. condensatus*, *M. transmorrisonensis*, *M. nepalensis* and *M. fuscus*. However, *M. condensatus* is considered a synonym of *M. sinensis* by Hodkinson and Renvoize (pers. comm.). Five individuals from the genus *Saccharum* were also included.

The characters scored were analysed by Principal Component Analysis (PCA, see Figure 1.1) and Detrended Correspondence Analysis (DCA, see Figure 1.2). Both methods provide a multivariate ordination of all the characters scored (Parnell & Waldren, 1996). However, PCA does not allow the use of bi-state characters in the data matrix. In addition to ordination, PCA also produces summary data on individual characters which provides information on their relationship to each other. The correlation matrix indicates which variables are highly correlated with each other. This allows one variable of a highly correlated pair to be eliminated from subsequent analysis of specimens, thus reducing the size of the character set.

The results of the PCA (Figure 1.1) demonstrate the clear separation between *M. sinensis* and *M. sacchariflorus* on axis 1 of the plot. It can be seen that most of the other species and genotypes (listed in Table 1.2) cluster closer to the *M. sinensis* group, but are largely unresolved. The results of the DCA show a similar situation, with a clear separation between *M. sinensis* and *M. sacchariflorus*. Again, the other species and cultivars fall into loose clusters closer to *M. sinensis*. DCA analysis has allowed the

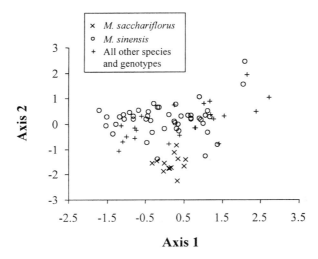

Figure 1.1. Principal Component Analysis (PCA). PCA of M. sacchariflorus *(✗),* M. sinensis *(○) and all other species and cultivars listed in Table 1.2(+), showing the separation between* M. sacchariflorus *and* M. sinensis *on axis 1 of the PCA.*

Table 1.2. Species and cultivars examined for morphological and molecular variation.

Species	Cultivars and hybrids
	Giganteus
M. condensatus	Goliath
M. floridulus	Gracillimus
M. fuscus	Grosse Fontäne
M. nepalensis	Poseidon
M. sacchariflorus	Rotsilber
M. sinensis	Silberspinne
M. transmorrisonensis	Silver feather
	Variegatus
	Zebrinus

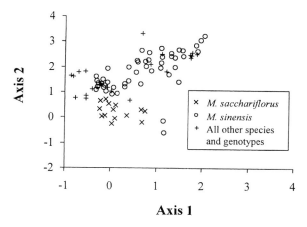

Figure 1.2. Detrended Correspondence Analysis (DCA). DCA showing separation between M. sinensis *and* M. sacchariflorus *on axis 1. All other species, as listed in Table 1.2, are largely unresolved.* M. sacchariflorus *(×),* M. sinensis *(○), other species and cultivars (+).*

overall shape of the inflorescence to be included in the analysis and a schematic representation of the inflorescence shape in relation to the *M. sinensis* cluster and the *M. sacchariflorus* cluster is shown alongside these groupings in the DCA figure.

The results of this study show that morphology may be of some use in delimiting species but is of little use below the species level. It has demonstrated the huge range of morphological variation present within the genus, especially within *M. sinensis*, and from this analysis it appears that most of the cultivars are derived from this species. Based on the morphological characters scored, *M. sacchariflorus* separates as a discrete group, easily distinguished from *M. sinensis* (Figure 1.2). None of the other species separate as such well defined groups. It is noteworthy however, that the only character which separated species of the genus *Saccharum* from *Miscanthus* in the analysis was the sessile nature of one of the spikelet pairs on the raceme. This would appear to be a rather weak character to split an entire genus from another and further investigation of *Saccharum* in relation to *Miscanthus* is recommended.

Correlation matrix data indicated that the characters of most use in delimiting species are:

- the presence or absence of an awn
- the presence or absence and the length of glume hairs
- the disposition of the spiklets on the inflorescence
- the length of the main axis of the inflorescence

This evidence would agree with the findings of other workers (Lee, 1964; Clayton & Renvoize, 1986).

The results indicate that morphological analysis would not be a practical method for screening genotypic variation in *Miscanthus* due to the low level of information that it provides and the time-consuming nature of the analysis.

1.4.2 Molecular Methods

Molecular methods have revolutionised the study of taxonomy in recent years. Before their development and introduction many taxonomic problems were left unresolved. They have been of particular value to the study of groups where morphological methods were not adequate or not always possible (e.g. species which seldom or never flower). Since the start of the *Miscanthus* Productivity Network in 1993, new developments in molecular systematics have occurred at such a rate that TCD have had to constantly alter or change their methods in order to incorporate the most recent advances. The most obvious advantage of using molecular data, especially DNA data, is that, unlike morphological data which can be prone to phenotypic variation, they provide a direct assessment of genetic diversity. In addition, molecular data reveals far more scorable characters than morphological data.

The first challenge in any molecular technique is the extraction of DNA. TCD have developed a mini-scale DNA extraction technique in their laboratory which successfully yields high-quality DNA from small amounts of plant material (*c.* 0.5 g fresh weight). This technique is a modified version of that described by Hillis *et al.* (1990). The technique, which is rapid and relatively inexpensive, has consistently yielded high molecular weight DNA in sufficient quantities for TCD's investigations. Once extracted, the DNA may be stored frozen for long periods (at least five years). This DNA can subsequently be used in a variety of molecular screening techniques and provides a reference bank of DNA for future work within the laboratory at TCD and also for exchange with other laboratories.

Restriction Fragment Length Polymorphism (RFLP) was the original method chosen for screening of *Miscanthus* accessions. The technique was initially applied to a number of *Miscanthus* species and polymorphisms between some species were found. However, as the *Miscanthus* Productivity Network project developed, the technique of Random Amplified Polymorphic DNA (RAPD), which was developed simultaneously by Williams *et al.* (1990) and Welsh & McClelland (1990), became more widely used for the screening of genotypes. This technique, although not the most suitable for the construction of phylogenetic hypothesis, is very well suited to the molecular screening of genotypes. The technique is based on the Polymerase Chain Reaction (PCR) and involves the amplification of random segments of genomic DNA with single primers of arbitrary nucleotide sequence. This technique has a number of distinct advantages over RFLP analysis in that it is faster, less laborious and cheaper to carry out and a large number of samples may be processed in a short time once the initial conditions have been determined.

However RAPD also has a number of disadvantages; one such is that RAPD bands are treated as dominant markers, unlike the co-dominant bands of RFLP analysis. This means that RAPD bands are scored as presence/absence polymorphisms (due to mutations in the DNA within the specified primer sites or variation in sequence length between primer sites) and segregate as dominants (3:1) in F_2 families (Williams *et al.*, 1990). Because of this, heterozygotes cannot be directly detected, and for this reason RAPD should not, in general, be used in the construction of phylogenetic hypothesis. However, part of the aim of this study was to screen and characterise different genotypes of *Miscanthus* which could not be differentiated by their morphological characteristics and for this purpose RAPD analysis is very suitable. Another disadvantage of RAPD analysis is that it can sometimes be difficult to obtain reproducible results between different laboratories and even within the same laboratory using the same DNA. This necessitates the use of very strict laboratory controls and great care on the part of the researcher. A third disadvantage of the RAPD technique is the difficulty of assessing the homology of the bands. Co-migrating bands on a gel may simply have migrated at the same rate because they contain the same number of base pairs. They may, however, have a completely different DNA sequence. The only way of testing the homology of bands is to isolate them from the gel and characterise them further using techniques such as DNA sequencing, restriction site analysis or DNA hybridisation using a probe of known sequence. This, however, negates the beneficial simplicity of the RAPD technique.

The final technique used by TCD was Amplified Fragment Length Polymorphism (AFLP), which is the most recently developed tool for molecular taxonomy. The AFLP technique, which was developed by Vos *et al.* (1995), combines the reliability and robustness of RFLP with the ease and powerfulness of RAPD. The AFLP technique has some of the limitations of the RAPD technique but the results are extremely reproducible. AFLP can provide a vastly increased character set and thus increases the number of potential polymorphisms. The increased number of markers increases the statistical reliability of the technique, even though, as with RAPD, the homology of co-migrating bands cannot be ascertained without analysis and further characterisation. The technique is especially useful for genetic mapping and fingerprinting and genetic distances can be calculated between genotypes.

Initially, all of TCD's accessions were screened by RAPD analysis and a single primer was identified which was capable of distinguishing between all genotypes, cultivars and species examined (Table 1.3). In most cases it is necessary to use a combination of primers to cover all genotypes (Graham *et al.*, 1994; Marshal *et al.*, 1995). The results of the RAPD analysis were very encouraging, allowing differentiation of all species, hybrids and cultivars listed. The screening also helped determine the identity of some incorrectly named genotypes.

One of the limitations of RAPD analysis is the difficulty in obtaining highly reproducible results. Although this did not present a problem within TCD's laboratory it must be appreciated that inter-laboratory reproducibility could present a problem. For this reason TCD chose to develop AFLP analysis for future screening of genotypes and also to assess the inter-relationships of the species.

As AFLP is a relatively new technique, a considerable number of trials were required to implement the method. The technique is now running well and screening of *Miscanthus* has commenced, with initial results being very encouraging. A much larger number of polymorphisms are present than with RAPD or RFLP analysis and the reproducibility of the technique is excellent. TCD's results so far have allowed them to fingerprint approximately 20 of their accessions. It is hoped that all of their *Miscanthus* accessions will be screened by this method before the end of 2000.

Since the implementation of the AFLP analysis of *Miscanthus* in TCD's laboratory other workers have simultaneously had success with this technique for *Miscanthus* screening (Greef & Schondelmaier, 1997; Hodkinson *et al.*, 1997). Although the work of TCD and others has so far aided in the identification of accessions and allowed correct identification of some incorrectly named genotypes, much more data must be collected before a useful phylogeny can be constructed or any real assumptions on the genetic diversity within the genus can be made.

Table 1.3. Table of RAPD analysis indicating presence or absence of specific molecular weight markers for each of the accessions.

Molecular Weight of Bands	Accession																
	GI	G2	G3	SS	RS	SF	G	P	U	V	Z	SIN	SAC	CON	GRA	FLR	SA
1500	+	+	+	+	+	+	+	+	+	+	−	+	+	+	+	+	−
1400	−	−	−	+	−	−	−	−	+	−	−	+	−	−	−	−	−
1300	+	+	+	+	−	−	−	−	+	−	−	+	+	+	+	−	−
1200	−	−	−	−	−	−	−	−	−	−	−	−	−	−	−	−	−
1100	−	−	−	−	−	−	−	−	−	−	−	−	−	−	−	−	−
1000	−	−	−	−	−	−	−	−	−	−	−	−	−	−	−	−	−
900	−	−	−	−	−	−	−	−	−	−	−	−	−	−	−	−	−
800	+	+	+	−	−	−	+	+	−	−	−	+	+	+	−	−	+
700	+	+	+	+	+	+	+	+	+	+	+	+	+	+	+	−	+
600	−	−	−	−	−	−	+	+	−	−	−	−	−	−	−	−	−
550	+	+	+	−	+	−	+	+	+	+	−	−	+	+	−	−	+
500	+	+	+	+	+	−	+	+	+	−	−	+	+	+	+	+	+
400	−	−	−	−	−	−	−	−	−	−	−	−	−	−	−	−	−
300	+	+	+	+	+	−	+	+	−	−	−	−	+	+	+	−	−
200	+	+	+	+	+	−	+	+	+	−	+	+	+	+	+	+	+
100	−	−	−	−	−	−	−	−	−	−	−	−	−	−	−	−	−

GI = M. x giganteus　　　　　　　U = M. sinensis cv. Undine　　　　SA = Saccharum sp.
G2 = M. x giganteus　　　　　　　V = M. sinensis cv. Variegatus
G3 = M. x giganteus　　　　　　　Z = M. sinensis cv. Zebrinus
SS = M. sinensis cv. Silberspinne　SIN = M. sinensis
RS = M. sinensis cv. Rotsilber　　SAC = M. sacchariflorus
SF = M. sinensis cv. Silberfeder　CON = M. condensatus
G = M. sinensis cv. Goliath　　　GRA = M. sinensis cv. Gracillimus
P = M. sinensis cv. Poseidon　　FLR = M. floridulus

As previously mentioned, sequence data, although not always practical, is the most direct way of assessing genetic diversity. To the knowledge of the present authors, the only research on this method for *Miscanthus*, has been carried out by Hodkinson, Renvoize and Chase at the Royal Botanic Gardens, Kew, UK (Hodkinson *et al.*, 1997). Their work on sequencing of the nuclear and plastid regions (ITS, 5S and *trn*L-F) has provided some information at the species and generic level. Their results from the sequencing of the ITS (Internal Transcribed Spacer of nuclear ribosomal DNA) region have shown that *Miscanthus* taxa *(M. sinensis, M. floridulus, M. oligostachyus* and *M. sacchariflorus)* from south-eastern Asia form a clear monophyletic group and that African *Miscanthus* species and *M. fuscus* from Assam-Thailand are separated from this monophyletic group. The authors have also shown that lack of sequence divergence within this region has made it impossible to differentiate between the more closely related *Miscanthus* species and that other molecular techniques (RAPD and AFLP) are required for this. All of the genetic material from this study is held at Kew, who, along with ADAS Consulting Ltd, are currently collecting in Japan and Korea.

One way of determining the origin of certain *Miscanthus* taxa and of ascertaining the identity of hybrids is to carry out artificial breeding experiments and to examine the progeny of such breeding experiments by molecular methods. This has been attempted but has proven to be extremely difficult as different species flower at different times of the year under the same climatic conditions. In order to carry out crosses between species it is essential to force the late-flowering varieties to flower earlier. It is also essential that all inflorescences are covered by a bag to prevent pollination by unknown individuals. The 'bagging' of such large inflorescences has proved to be difficult as it appears to interfere with the normal development of the inflorescence. A large experiment of this type was attempted at Trinity College Botanic Garden, Dublin, in the summer of 1996, but this experiment was unsuccessful, largely for the reasons outlined above. Others (Greef & Schondelmaier, 1997) have similarly attempted to carry out artificial crossing but have also failed. To conclude, it is anticipated that our combined morphological and molecular data (once complete) will be able to accurately differentiate species, assess inter-relationships and characterise infra-specific variation, and in doing so will advance our understanding of *Miscanthus* genetic resources.

2 | *Resource Capture by* Miscanthus

by S. P. Long and C. V. Beale

with contributions from P. K. Farage

2.1 Introduction

Plants, in order to grow, possess a set of structures and mechanisms for 'capturing' resources from the environment. The four main environmental resources are light, water, nutrients and CO_2. In this chapter, the capture of light, water and nitrogen resources by *Miscanthus* are reviewed.

2.2 Light Use Efficiency

The broad physiological processes determining yield may be summarised in an equation based on the principles developed by Monteith (1977):

$$W_h = S_t.\varepsilon_i.\varepsilon_c.\eta/k$$

where W_h is the dry matter at final harvest (g m^{-2}), S_t is the integral of incident solar radiation (MJ m^{-2}), ε_i is the efficiency with which the radiation is intercepted by the crop (dimensionless), ε_c is the efficiency with which the intercepted radiation is converted into biomass energy (dimensionless), η is the amount partitioned into the harvested components (dimensionless) and k is the energy content of the biomass (MJ g^{-1}). S_t is dependent on the site, while k varies little between species (Roberts *et al.*, 1993). In theory therefore, the dry matter at final harvest depends on ε_c and ε_i. The ability of a crop to maintain a closed canopy, particularly through the period of peak solar insolation, determines ε_i while Monteith (1978) noted that for healthy crops, ε_c varies little within each photosynthetic group. Thus, the potential dry matter productivity of a biomass-fuel crop, at a given site, will be determined primarily by the ability to form and maintain a closed canopy and by photosynthetic type.

The maximum conversion efficiency of intercepted light into biomass (ε_c) for C_4 plants is 40% higher than that of C_3 species, which constitute most of the vegetation and current crops of western Europe (Monteith, 1978). However, C_4 plants are susceptible to damage at low temperatures and their poor growth during the cool weather of spring and early summer in areas such as north-west Europe may reduce their potential as biomass crops. In $Z\,mays$, for example, exposure to low temperatures may result in a 50% (or greater) reduction in ε_i during the first two months of growth (Long *et al.*, 1992). Despite this disadvantage, $Z.\,mays$ can still achieve dry matter yields of 0.95–1.35 kg m^{-2} (9.5–13.5 t ha^{-1}) in southern England (Leaver, 1991). This compares well to herbage yields of up to 1.8 kg m^{-2} for the C$_3$ grass *Lolium perenne* (Lazenby, 1988).

Within the *Miscanthus* Productivity Network, light use efficiency was determined and analysed by means of:

- a replicated plot field experiment. Annual productivity was assessed over a four year period, with seasonal changes in growth and development being determined over the first three years. Conversion efficiency was assessed by determining crop radiation interception and the energy content of the biomass.
- controlled and field environments were used to assess the effects of low temperature on photosynthesis and differences between genotypes by measurement of leaf gas exchange and leaf spectroscopy.

In the following sections the factors affecting light use efficiency are identified and quantified in order to determine the light use efficiency of *Miscanthus*.

2.1.1 *Conversion Coefficient and Conversion Efficiency*

During the main period of vegetative growth, the dry matter production of many crops is linearly related to the quantity of intercepted photosynthetically active radiation (PAR) (Biscoe & Gallagher, 1977; Monteith, 1977). Conversion coefficients (P_p), expressed as dry matter production per unit of intercepted PAR (g MJ^{-1}), are calculated as the gradient of dry matter production against cumulative intercepted PAR, estimated by least-squares linear regression.

The conversion efficiency (ε_c) is the chemical energy accumulated per unit of intercepted PAR. This is the product of the mean energy content of the dry matter (k: MJ g^{-1}) and the conversion coefficient (P_p: g MJ^{-1}), i.e. dry matter produced per unit of intercepted PAR.

2.1.2 *Leaf Area Development and Light Interception*

Leaf growth at Writtle College Farm in Essex, UK, was found to begin at about 10°C which corresponds to air temperatures in late April in the southern UK and similar latitudes in western Europe. Leaf area growth was rapid, and in the second year following establishment reached a photosynthetic surface area index (SAI) of *c.* 6–8, depending on treatment (Beale, 1996; Beale & Long, 1995).

Light interception during the second growing season was calculated from 24 April when the first green leaf blades appeared. Canopy closure (efficiency of PAR interception; $\varepsilon_i = 0.9$) was achieved by June 1 at an SAI of approximately 4. The average value of ε_i for irrigated plots over the growing season (i.e. from emergence to late-September) was 0.83 ± 0.006 (i.e. 83% of the available solar radiation was trapped). When measured over the full 1993 growing season, from canopy emergence to complete senescence of the *M.* x *giganteus* crop on 30 November, the total interception of PAR (S_i) was 881 MJ m^{-2}, equivalent to a seasonal ε_i of 0.83 (Table 2.1). This was about 5% higher than another cool temperature C_4 grass, *Spartina cynosuroides* which showed slightly slower canopy development in the spring and earlier canopy senescence. It was observed that irrigation is necessary to obtain the maximum SAI (Beale, 1996; Beale & Long, 1995).

Table 2.1 Efficiencies of radiation interception and conversion in the three years following planting at Writtle College Farm, Essex, UK. Source: Beale, 1996.

Year of growth	1	2	3
Radiation			
S_t (MJ m^{-2})	787	1061	1030
ε_I	0.32	0.83	0.88
S_i (MJ m^{-2})	252	881	905
Above-ground[a]			
W_a (kg.m^{-2})	0.68	2.87	3.27
P_p (g MJ^{-1} PAR)	2.7	3.3	3.6
k_a (MJ kg^{-1})	18.50	18.28	18.24
ε_{ca}	0.050	0.060	0.066
Total[t]			
W_t (kg m^{-2})	1.07	3.85	3.59
P_p (g MJ^{-1} PAR)	4.3	4.4	4.0
k_t (MJ kg^{-1})	18.15	17.88	18.22
ε_{ct}	0.077	0.078	0.072

Year 1 = the year of planting

ε_I = PAR interception efficiency

W = Dry matter production

k = Average energy content

$W = S_t.\varepsilon_i.\varepsilon_c / k$

S_t = Accumulated incident PAR

S_i = Intercepted PAR

P_p = Conversion coefficient

ε_c = Conversion efficiency of PAR

$W = S_t.\varepsilon_i.\varepsilon_c.P_p$.

[a] – values based on above-ground biomass   [t] – values based on total biomass

The ε_i value was highest in year 3 when ε_i between emergence and 20 September was 0.88 (total interception of PAR [S_i] value of 905 MJ m^{-2}). Over three years of testing, it was observed that nitrogen fertilisation had no effect on light interception. However, measurement of N removal in the crop suggested that, in the longer term, reductions in light interception would occur in the absence on N-fertilisation (Beale & Long, 1997b).

The PAR interception efficiency value ε_i of 0.88 measured at the Writtle College Farm site (Beale, 1996), is in line with the value of 0.86 which was measured at a trial site at ADAS Arthur Rickwood in Cambridgeshire, UK. (Bullard, Heath & Nixon, 1995). *Miscanthus* appears exceptional among C_4 plants in its ability to form and maintain a canopy through most of the growing season in cold temperate climates. Nevertheless, earlier leaf area development at a threshold temperature of 8°C would increase the total amount of radiation intercepted by 10%.

The role of climate variables (temperature, light and humidity) in the control of leaf development of *Miscanthus* genotypes was studied in controlled environment conditions by Clifton-Brown (1997). Temperature was found to be the most important factor in the regulation of leaf expansion when plants were grown with optimal water and nutrient supplies, although high vapour pressure deficits do have the ability to cause transient reductions in leaf expansion rate (Clifton-Brown & Jones, 1997). Differences in the thermal response of leaf expansion rate of 32 genotypes of *Miscanthus* were determined by calculating the threshold temperature for leaf growth. This temperature ranged between 5.0°C and 7.7°C for the genotypes examined. An estimate of the effect of differences in the thermal response of leaf extension rate on the potential yield of the *Miscanthus* genotypes was calculated for Irish climatic conditions using a simple growth model. Potential yield varied between 3 and 23 t ha^{-1} year^{-1} (ibid), thus demonstrating the critical role which differences in leaf extension rate can play in the selection of more productive genotypes.

The ability of *Miscanthus* x *giganteus* to form a tall closed canopy early in mid-spring may explain why weed control was unnecessary after the first year of growth. In the wild, the similar species *Miscanthus sinensis* may occur in monotypic stands, because, once established, there is insufficient heterogeneity to allow other species to establish in any gaps (Tang & Washitani, 1995). The excellent light interception observed for trials of *M.* x *giganteus* in Europe may in part reflect the current absence of foliar diseases and pests, however, BYDV (Barley Yellow Dwarf Virus) has affected some stands and significantly decreased leaf area growth (Christian *et al.*, 1994).

In summary, leaf area development and light interception efficiency can vary between genotypes and are limited by low temperatures at the beginning of the growing season and water limitation in mid- to late summer. Light interception may be limited by foliar diseases, which as yet have not emerged, however, *M.* x *giganteus* is a single genotype, and past experience has shown that large-scale plantations of single genotypes are liable to devastating damage if a disease becomes established.

2.1.3 Energy Content of the Dry Matter

The overall energy content of the harvested crop will depend upon the quantity and energy content of the individual plant organs. The energy released on complete combustion of the dry plant matter was found to vary only slightly between species and plant organs, ranging between 16.0 ± 0.1 MJ kg^{-1} for roots to 19.0 ± 0.1 MJ kg^{-1} for the leaves. The mean energy content of the above-ground dry matter of *M.* x *giganteus* was 18.4 MJ kg^{-1}. Energy values for the total crop, inclusive of roots and rhizomes, were slightly lower at 18.1 MJ kg^{-1} (Beale & Long, 1995; Beale, 1996).

2.1.4 Efficiency of Conversion of Intercepted Energy into Biomass

It can be seen from Table 2.1 that the conversion coefficient of above-ground dry matter production per unit of intercepted PAR (P_p) as determined from regression analysis was 2.76 ± 0.04 g MJ^{-1} in year 1, rising to 3.29 ± 0.43 g MJ^{-1} in year 2 and 3.61 ± 0.22 g MJ^{-1} in year 3. A study by Bullard, Health & Nixon (1995) calculated a conversion coefficient (P_p) of 1.7–2.3 g MJ^{-1} in year 1 (corrected to the photosynthetically active part of the spectrum) for *M.* x *giganteus* grown in parallel trials in Cambridgeshire, UK. This lower conversion coefficient was attributed to a transplanting check and unusually dry summer. Nevertheless, it was still sufficient to provide a dry matter yield of >20 t ha^{-1} (Bullard, Heath & Nixon 1995). Similar conversion coefficients to those found by Beale & Long (1995) were observed in the INRA trials near Paris, allowing dry matter yields to approach 40 t ha^{-1}.

Table 2.1 reveals that the conversion efficiency of intercepted PAR into biomass (ε_c) was calculated as 0.050, 0.060 and 0.066 (dimensionless) in the first, second and third years following planting, respectively, at Writtle College Farm. However, these values only refer to above-ground biomass and do not take account of the accumulation of below-ground biomass. In late September of the establishment year, below-ground dry matter production was 0.36 ± 0.02 kg m^{-2}. This rose to 0.98 ± 0.04 kg m^{-2} and 0.96 kg m^{-2} for years 2 and 3, giving conversion efficiencies (into total biomass) of 0.078 and 0.072 (Table 2.1). These conversion efficiencies are comparable to the best figures for C$_4$ plants growing in warm climates, where conditions are considered optimal for this group of plants.

2.1.5 Photosynthesis

High conversion efficiencies require both high PAR interception efficiencies (ε_i) and high conversion efficiencies of the intercepted PAR into biomass energy (ε_c). This will only occur if leaf photosynthesis is efficient. Most C$_4$ plants are incapable of photosynthesising at temperatures below about 12°C. Even maize cultivars bred for western Europe are capable of little photosynthesis at 12°C, show impaired development of the photosynthetic apparatus in leaves at temperatures below 17°C and are subject to light damage (photoinhibition) during low temperature periods (Long, 1999). Research was carried out within the *Miscanthus* Productivity Network in order to determine whether *M.* x *giganteus* was different.

Controlled environment studies showed that *M.* x *giganteus* was very different from even the best western European maize cultivars. Plants grown continuously at day temperatures of 8°C, 12°C and 25°C were compared for their photosynthetic capacity. Remarkably, and in contrast to all previously examined C$_4$ species (Long, 1983; Nie *et al.*, 1992), leaves of *M.* x. *giganteus* grown at 12°C show the same photosynthetic capacity as leaves of plants grown at 25°C. Growth at 8°C results in a *c.* 50% reduction in photosynthetic capacity, suggesting that the threshold for impairment of the photosynthetic apparatus lies between 8 and 12°C. Examination of photoinhibition of photosynthesis showed that *M.* x *giganteus* exposed to high light at 5°C lost about 50% of its maximum quantum yield and showed a >50% reduction in maximum efficiency of photosystem II.

It was concluded that leaf photosynthesis in *M.* x *giganteus* continues down to a temperature of <5°C, while plants can form photosynthetically competent leaves down to 8°C and photosynthetic capacity is unaffected by growth temperatures down to 12°C. This suggests that the threshold for photosynthesis and the development of the photosynthetic apparatus is 3–5°C below the threshold of maize.

Field assessments of mid-day CO$_2$ uptake were made at regular intervals from May to December 1994 in order to ascertain seasonal changes in the maximum daily rate of leaf photosynthesis. Measurements were taken within one and a half hours either side of solar noon, on days with no cloud cover. Typical midday values in early and mid-season ranged between 20 and 27 µmol m^{-2} s^{-1}, but declined to 5 µmol m^{-2} s^{-1}

by 1 December with the highest mid-day mean value (35.3 μmol m^{-2} s^{-1}) recorded on 28 June. Measurements were made under light saturating conditions (photon flux >1,400 μmol m^{-2} s^{-1}) on each of the dates except 15 October and 1 December, when the photon fluxes at mid-day were 1180 and 690 μmol m^{-2} s^{-1} (Beale, 1996) respectively.

2.1.6 Conclusions of Light Use Efficiency

Light use efficiencies (dimensionless) of a third year *M.* x *giganteus* crop grown at the Writtle College Farm were calculated as 0.066 for the above-ground biomass and 0.072 for the total biomass. These values, which are in agreement with values obtained in other EU *Miscanthus* trials, are comparable to the best figures for C$_4$ plants grown under optimum growing conditions. The high light use efficiency of *M.* x *giganteus* in temperate conditions is attributable to the remarkable ability of the plant to carry out photosynthesis at low temperatures. This is in contrast to all previously examined C$_4$ plants which show a definite impairment of photosynthetic capacity at such temperatures (Long, 1999).

2.2 Nitrogen Use Efficiency

Although increases in productivity of agricultural crops have been obtained by increasing inputs of nitrogen fertiliser, this can result in a number of environmental problems, including potential water pollution from leachates and run-off. Furthermore, the energy cost of fertiliser production is high. The perceived environmental benefits of biomass energy crops could be negated if large quantities of fertiliser inputs were required for their production. Consequently, it is environmentally desirable that biomass energy crops should be selected from species that exhibit a high nutrient use efficiency and minimal losses to the environment.

M. x *giganteus*, as a rhizomatous perennial grass producing an annual crop of stems, has the potential to translocate nutrients to the rhizomes at the end of each growing season, so that the dead stems, when cropped, will have a low mineral nutrient content. This minimises nutrient offtake and the pollution resulting from combustion of nutrient-rich material, while returning nutrients to the rhizomes for the support of the next year's growth.

Theoretically, *M.* x *giganteus* should have the benefit of the higher nitrogen use efficiency which is associated with the C$_4$ photosynthetic pathway (Long, 1983). The *Miscanthus* Productivity Network examined the seasonal variation in the above- and below-ground N content of established crops of *M.* x *giganteus* in order to determine the nitrogen use efficiency of *Miscanthus* and the nitrogen translocation, accumulation and offtake characteristics of the crop.

2.2.1 Seasonal Variation in Nitrogen Concentrations

At the Writtle College Farm, UK and LWG, Germany (Jodl *et al.*, 1996; Beale & Long, 1997b) *M.* x *giganteus* trials, the highest nitrogen concentrations occurred at the start of the growing season. Thereafter the nitrogen concentrations in the above-ground material appeared to dilute as the above-ground dry matter increased, and then declined further as the canopy senesced. At the Writtle College Farm the mean N concentration of the above-ground dry matter declined by 83% during the growing season, from a value of 29.1 mg g^{-1} in July to 5.0 mg g^{-1} in February. Very similar nitrogen contents of 5.9 mg g^{-1} and 6.1 mg g^{-1} were observed in *M.* x *giganteus* and *M. sinensis* at the time of harvest in trials in western Denmark (Jørgensen, 1997). It was found that nitrogen concentrations were significantly lower in the dead leaf tissue than in the green leaves, presumably a consequence of translocation from the senescing tissue. Stem tissue showed a greater seasonal variation in nitrogen concentration than that of other organs, with a steep decline between June and September coinciding with rapid increases in stem dry matter. Nitrogen concentrations in the rhizomes varied less than in the leaf or stem, and showed a general pattern of decline from emergence until mid-summer followed by an increase through to February. Nitrogen concentrations in the roots were generally lower than those in the rhizomes (Beale & Long, 1997b).

Between emergence and July, the nitrogen content of the above-ground *M.* x *giganteus* crop increased from zero to 25.3 g m^{-2}, of which 9% could have been supplied by rhizome reserves with the remainder from the soil. The percentage of the total plant N found in the rhizome at the final harvest, and hence the percentage potentially available for the following year's growth, was 58%. Nitrogen use efficiency of approximately 200 g g^{-1} was observed for the above-ground harvested material of *M.* x *giganteus*, compared to a very much higher nitrogen use efficiency value of 310 g g^{-1} for the C$_4$ species *S. cynosuroides*. Nitrate losses through leaching were negligible at just 0. 1 g m^{-2} (Beale & Long, 1997b).

The nitrogen concentrations observed in above-ground *M.* x *giganteus* material were as little as 15–30% of those reported for the C$_3$ crops wheat and ryegrass, and 20–50% of those reported for the C$_4$ crop maize. The relatively low nitrogen concentrations in the shoots of *M.* x *giganteus* harvested in the winter could be explained by translocation. This suggests that efficient internal recycling of nitrogen occurred.

The results suggest that high *M.* x *giganteus* yields can be attained without high inputs of fertiliser. It was calculated that the N requirement of a *M.* x *giganteus* crop producing an above-ground harvest of 25 t ha^{-1} dry matter would be 93 kg ha^{-1} (calculated on the basis of the annual nitrogen accumulation values in the Writtle College Farm trials (Beale & Long, 1997b)). Mineralisation and atmospheric nitrogen deposition will provide part of this requirement. The total nitrogen requirement could be expected to decline after a few years once the crop has achieved its maximum net rhizome biomass. Nitrogen would be only required to compensate for the annual crop offtake.

Nitrate leaching was found to be negligible, which can be attributed to several factors. Crop nitrogen demand was found to be high at the start of the growing season shortly after fertiliser was applied, and crop growth continued through the summer and early autumn when mineralisation of soil nitrogen reserves was high. The extensive rhizome network of *M.* x *giganteus* ensures that roots can intercept nitrogen across the whole plot, without the gaps that may be present between plants of an annual crop at this stage in the growing season (Beale & Long, 1997b). An experiment carried out on a *M.* x *giganteus* crop at Rothamsted, Herts, UK (Christian, Poulton *et al.*, 1997) indicated that the crop only assimilated 38% of the N fertiliser which had been applied to the crop (Table 2.2). It can be seen that most of the N taken up during growth was unlabelled and would therefore have been obtained from the mineralisation of soil organic matter and from atmospheric deposition. It is unclear why the

Table 2.2 Yield and nitrogen content of harvested M.x giganteus *(60 kg ha⁻¹ labelled N was applied in spring). Source: Christian, Poulton et al., 1997.*

Dry matter yield (t ha⁻¹)	N content (kg ha⁻¹)		
	N content (labelled)	N content (unlabelled)	Total
15.56	23.0	139.4	162.8

crop only utilised 38% of the N fertiliser. However, one possible reason is that the plant has a low nitrogen demand during early growth when the fertiliser was applied. Recent studies using nutrient culture techniques show that nutrients stored in the rhizomes influence growth more than external sources of N at the beginning of growth (Wiesler *et al.*, 1997). If the plant initially utilises internally stored N in preference to external sources of N then the application of N fertiliser at the start of growth may not be appropriate except in the planting year.

A nitrogen budget for a one-year old crop was calculated using various measurements taken in a crop grown at Rothamsted, UK. The budget (given in Table 2.3) shows that the harvested crop contained 170 kg N ha⁻¹ of which fresh uptake during the growing phase was 125 kg ha⁻¹ (45 kg ha⁻¹ was contained in the roots and rhizomes at the beginning of the growing season). The balance shows that nearly 38% of the N in the crop (64 kg ha⁻¹) was acquired from unidentified sources.

Table 2.3 N budget for Miscanthus *grown during 1994. Crop received 60 kg N ha⁻¹ fertiliser in spring. Source: Christian and Riche, 1997.*

	Nitrogen content (kg N ha⁻¹)
In crop at harvest:	
Leaves and stems	57
Litter	15
Roots and Rhizomes	98
Total N content at harvest	+170
Sources of nitrogen:	
N in roots and rhizomes at start of growth	45
N from soil	38
N from fertiliser	23
N from other sources	64

2.2.2 Conclusions of Nitrogen Use Efficiency

It has been shown that high *Miscanthus* crop yields can be obtained without high inputs of nitrogen fertiliser, in that a crop producing an above-ground harvest of 25 t ha⁻¹ dry matter would require a nitrogen input of 93 kg ha⁻¹ yr⁻¹. The nitrogen use efficiency of above-ground *M. x giganteus* harvested material has been calculated as 200 g g⁻¹ (Beale & Long, 1997b). This is considerably lower than the value of 310 g g⁻¹ which was calculated for another C_4 perennial, *S. cynosuroides*. The nitrogen use efficiencies which were measured at all of the sites of the *Miscanthus* Productivity Network are reported in Chapter 3.

One possible explanation for the lower nitrogen use efficiency of *M.* x *giganteus* may be the inability of this genotype to complete shoot senescence in the autumn. The result of this is that frosts kill the shoots before re-translocation of nitrogen to the underground rhizomes is complete (Jørgensen, 1997). Selection of genotypes that do complete shoot senescence in the autumn is therefore likely to improve nitrogen use efficiency and decrease nutrient contamination of the harvested product. Also, as discussed earlier, improvements in nitrogen use efficiency may be obtained by timing of fertiliser application.

2.3 Water Use Efficiency

Efforts have been made to maximise the productivity of energy crops as their economic feasibility is strongly related to their yield. However, increases in productivity will result in increases in water demand, and consequently water may become a limiting factor to both crop productivity and economic viability. Since the potential economic return from energy crops is currently low relative to other arable enterprises, farmers are more likely to consider growing energy crops on their less productive land than on the better land. In many cases the low productivity of such land is a result of poor water availability. The problem of low water availability could be alleviated by irrigation, but investment in irrigation could further reduce the economic viability of the crop. It is therefore highly desirable to select potential energy crops from species that exhibit a high water use efficiency (WUE), i.e. that can attain maximum productivity with minimum water use.

In theory, C_4 species exhibit a higher WUE than C_3 species (Long, 1983). The *Miscanthus* Productivity Network carried out experiments in various trials in order to determine a number of factors relating to the water use efficiency of the crop, including the water demand per annum, the timing of the peak water demand, the relationship between WUE and rainfall, etc. Seasonal water use was measured with drainage lysimeters, and changes in soil water content measured with soil moisture capacitance probes.

The total water use of a *M.* x *giganteus* crop was calculated by the University of Catania (Italy) according to the following equation:

$$\text{Water used (ET)} = \Delta U + P + I - R - Dp$$

where:

- ΔU = change in soil water content (obtained by measuring soil moisture at crop emergence and at November, down to a depth of 100 cm)
- P = rainfall during growing season
- I = irrigation
- R = runoff
- Dp = deep percolation (negligible in Mediterranean conditions).

It was concluded from the study that *M.* x *giganteus* is able to utilise large quantities of water (9329 m^3 ha^{-1}) in order to produce maximum yields (31.6 t ha^{-1}). It was observed that reductions in the level of irrigation supplied to the crop resulted in crop yield decreases. However, these decreases were not proportional to one another.

At the Writtle College farm site, most of the water abstracted by both irrigated and non-irrigated crops was taken from the upper 0.6 m of the soil. The proportion of the total moisture deficit drawn from soil depths of 0.6–1.2 m was small in the irrigated crops, but greater in the non-irrigated crops. A progressive drying of the soil profile and increasing depth of water extraction occurred through the summer. The daily rates of water extraction, averaged over the five-month period from 26 April to 30 September, were *c.* 2.2 mm d^{-1} for non-irrigated *M.* x *giganteus* with 3.3 mm d^{-1} for the irrigated crop (Beale *et al.*, 1999).

The non-irrigated crop of *M.* x *giganteus* attained a water use efficiency of 0.0075 ± 0.0005 (dimensionless) compared with 0.0061 ± 0.0003 in the irrigated crop (Table 2.4). It was concluded that irrigation reduced the water use efficiency of the *M.* x *giganteus* crop by 18% (Beale, 1996). This was also found to be the case in the study carried out by the University of Catania where higher irrigation rates were associated with lower water use efficiencies.

Table 2.4 Water use efficiency of irrigated and non-irrigated crops of M. *x* giganteus *over the main growing season (emergence until September) at the Writtle College Farm.*

Crop	Dry matter (kg m^{-2})	WUE ($\times 10^{-3}$) (dimensionless)
M. x *giganteus* (non-irrigated)	2.44 ± 0.17	7.5 ± 0.5
M. x *giganteus* (irrigated)	3.08 ± 0.17	6.1 ± 0.3

Although the complexities of plant/soil water relations make it difficult to obtain clear explanations for the observed responses to water, it has been shown that C_4 plants are able to attain high water use efficiency values in cool temperate climates (Table 2.5 compares the water use efficiencies of some C_3 and C_4 grass species). Despite the high water use efficiency, *M.* x *giganteus* responds to additional water supply because of the high production of biomass. Analysis of WUE shows that over 500 mm of water would be required to achieve the maximum yield of *c.* 30 t ha^{-1} during the growing season. This amount is well in excess of the average growing season precipitation for eastern England (Beale *et al.*, 1999).

2.3.1 *Conclusions of Water Use Efficiency*

While *M.* x *giganteus* achieves a high water use efficiency, it nevertheless will require irrigation at most sites to achieve its maximum potential yield (Beale & Long, 1997a; Bullard *et al.*, 1997). However, the use of irrigation may affect the economic viability of the crop.

Table 2.5 Review of water use efficiencies (WUE) of C$_3$ and C$_4$ grass species. Source: Beale, 1996.

Crop	WUE	Notes	Reference
Zea mays (C$_4$)	0.0027	mean of 4 years	3
	0.0042	California, mean of 2 years, T$_l$ only	4
	0.0041	Colorado, mean of 2 years, T$_l$ only	4
	0.0035	Utah, mean of 2 years, T$_l$ only	4
	0.0019	Arizona, mean of 2 years, T$_l$ only	4
Setaria spp. (C$_4$)	0.0064	glasshouses, Nottingham	1
	0.0039	Hyderabad, dry season, irrigated	1
	0.0046	Hyderabad , dry season, drying soil	1
	0.0021	Naimey, dry season, drying soil	1
	0.0035		2
Sorghum spp. (C$_4$)	0.0037	Philippines, rain-watered	1
	0.0032		2
	0.0038	mean of 4 years	3
Triticum aestivum (C$_3$)	0.0020	mean of 4 years	3
Hordeum vulgare (C$_3$)	0.0019	mean of 4 years	2
Oryza sativa (C$_3$)	0.0015		2
Lolium perenne (C$_3$)	0.0023	well-watered, controlled environment	5
	0.0037	well-watered, pot, glasshouse	5
	0.0019	droughted, pot, glasshouse	5
Festuca arundinacea (C$_3$)	0.0016	mean of watered and droughted	6
	0.0027	mean of watered and droughted	6

1 Squire (1990)
2 Hay & Walker (1989)
3 Fitter & Hay (1987)
4 Tanner & Sinclair (1983)
5 Thomas (1994)
6 Johnson (1994)
T$_l$ – leaf transpiration

3 | *Agronomy of* Miscanthus

by D. G. Christian and E. Haase

with contributions from H. Schwarz, C. Dalianis, J. C. Clifton-Brown and S. Cosentino

3.1 Climatic Preferences

The origins of the genus *Miscanthus* are in the tropical and subtropical parts of south-eastern Asia (Greef & Deuter, 1993), which is characterised by warm temperatures and heavy and well distributed rainfalls. This suggests that the natural climatic preference of *Miscanthus* would be mild temperatures and high water availability. However, the naturalisation of *Miscanthus* in more temperate climates suggests that it is relatively tolerant in terms of temperature and water availability. One of the aims of the *Miscanthus* Productivity Network was to identify the climatic constraints on harvestable yield at the trial sites which were established throughout Europe.

3.1.1 Temperature Requirements

Although plants like *Miscanthus* which use the C_4 pathway of photosynthesis have the potential to significantly outyield those with C_3 photosynthesis, most C_4 species are best suited to tropical and subtropical climates. In fact, the majority of C_4 species have very low growth rates in temperate climates and often the perennial C_4 species cannot survive winter temperatures below freezing. There are, however, a very small number of C_4 species which are known to occur naturally in northern Europe or in climatic conditions which are very similar. Among these are several Spartina species, *Cyperus longus* and *Miscanthus* species, all of which have been identified recently as potentially high-yielding biomass crops.

It was found in the trials of the *Miscanthus* Productivity Network that the growth of *Miscanthus* in northern Europe is limited by low temperatures despite the fact that *Miscanthus* is better adapted to temperate climates than most other C_4 crops. Third-year yields of over 24 t ha^{-1} d.m. (dry matter) were recorded in southern Europe (with irrigation) compared with Irish and British third-year yields of between 11 and 16 t ha^{-1} d.m., and third-year yields of 18.3 t ha^{-1} d.m. in northern Germany (FAL). However, these yield differences may not be entirely due to temperature, as several northern European countries experienced abnormally dry springs and summers in 1995 and 1996; these had a negative effect on yields. Dry matter yields of over 24 t ha^{-1} (second year) have been reported in northern European sites when climatic conditions have been more favourable (e.g. Bullard & Kilpatrick, 1997).

It was also observed in the trials of the Network that ambient temperatures influence the growth and development of the *Miscanthus* crop and regulate the length of the growing season. The start of the *Miscanthus* growing season is determined by the date of the latest spring frost, while the end of the growing season is determined by the date of the first autumn frost. It was also shown that the rate of canopy development is controlled by ambient temperatures; this is because temperature strongly limits leaf expansion of *Miscanthus* with a threshold for growth at between 5 and 10°C.

Experiments investigating the thermal response of leaf extension of a number of genotypes have shown that the response of absolute leaf extension rate to temperature varies widely between genotypes.

In summary, the rates of leaf expansion and canopy development, the dry matter yields and the length of the *Miscanthus* growing season were found to be influenced by ambient temperatures. The yields of *Miscanthus* were found to be limited by low temperatures in northern Europe and were lower than yields recorded in southern Europe when water was not a limiting factor. Nevertheless, the northern European yields compare very favourably with the annual dry matter production from short rotation coppice which is a typical energy crop in these countries. There are indications that genotype screening would lead to the selection of *Miscanthus* genotypes which are capable of producing higher yields in northern European sites. The subject of winter survival and frost tolerance are addressed below.

3.2 Soil Preferences

Research has been carried out by the University of Agricultural Sciences, Vienna, to determine the effect of soil type on yield, water content and stem number of *M.* x *giganteus* (H. Swartz, pers. comm.). Trials were established in Austria on five sites with four different types of soil (Table 3.1). They were established in April 1989 from rhizomes (planting density – 1 per m^2).

Fertiliser was applied annually (N: 60 kg ha^{-1}; P$_2$O$_5$: 36 kg ha^{-1}; K$_2$O: 150 kg ha^{-1} and MgO: 22.5 kg ha^{-1}) to all sites, in addition, the Markgraf and Steinbrunn sites were irrigated (90 mm year^{-1}). The number of stems, yield and water content were recorded each year.

The results are given in Table 3.2. It can be seen that the yield, water content and number of stems of *M.* x *giganteus* varied between the sites. The water content also varied quite significantly from year to year.

The study concluded that, in addition to temperature and water supply during the growing period, soil type and quality are determinants for the productivity of *M.* x *giganteus*. Under good growing conditions for roots, the form of soil aggregate (determined by the volume and size distribution of pores) has a more significant effect on productivity than soil type or soil pH. The physical characteristics of the soil determine the efficiency of fertilisation and water supply to the crop.

Research was also carried out by LWG to determine the soil preferences of *Miscanthus* (Hotz *et al.*, 1996), with the following conclusions.

Table 3.1 Soil and climate characteristics of the five trial sites, Austria.

Sites	Soil depth	St Florian	Atzenbrugg	Markgraf	Steinbrunn	Ilz
Type of soil		dystric Cambisol	calcaric Cambisol	Chernozem	calcaric Cambisol	dystric Fluvisol
Humus (%)	15 cm	1.8	2.3	1.9	2.3	2.6
	35 cm	0.6	1.2	1.6	1.8	1.0
	80 cm	0.4	0.4	0.8	0.7	0.5
pH (nKCl)	15 cm	5.7	6.8	7.5	6.8	4.4
	35 cm	5.6	6.8	7.6	6.9	4.9
	80 cm	5.6	7.2	7.6	7.3	4.7
Annual mean temperature (°C)		9.0	8.8	9.4	10.0	9.1
Duration of the vegetation period (days)		229	234	239	239	229
Sum of temperature (°C days)		3248	3156	3385	3481	3285
Annual mean precipitation (mm)		844	620	520	504	874

Table 3.2 Number of stems, yield (t ha^{-1} dry matter) and water content (%) of M. x giganteus grown at the different sites.

		St. Florian	Atzenbrugg	Markgraf	Steinbrunn	Ilz
1990	No. of stems	43	32	37	29	27
	Yield (t ha^{-1} d.m.)	15.7	8.8	14.8	8.0	12.1
	% H$_2$O	48.4	41.3	33.8	38.8	44.6
1991	No. of stems	49	55	55	35	43
	Yield (t ha^{-1} d.m.)	24.9	22.1	21.3	17.5	23.0
	% H$_2$O	35.0	28.8	35.3	31.0	40.6
1992	No. of stems	49	53	56	38	59
	Yield (t ha^{-1} d.m.)	22.7	19.8	21.6	20.9	28.9
	% H$_2$O	36.8	36.1	28.0	30.4	38.1
1993	No. of stems	55	50	62	40	52
	Yield (t ha^{-1} d.m.)	23.0	18.0	23.0	19.3	26.1
	% H$_2$O	28.0	30.1	24.1	35.5	36.1
1994	No. of stems	48	52	56	42	54
	Yield (t ha^{-1} d.m.)	20.3	19.6	21.4	17.3	25.8
	% H$_2$O	27.4	38.8	22.5	31.4	38.5
1995	No. of stems	46	44	54	42	50
	Yield (t ha^{-1} d.m.)	18.0	17.6	22.7	18.7	27.6
	% H$_2$O	34.2	30.2	26.7	30.5	37.2

- Soil that is suitable for growing maize is also likely to be suitable for *Miscanthus*.
- The most suitable soil for growing *Miscanthus* is a medium soil such as a sandy or silty loam (brown earth or para brown earth) with a good air movement, a high water-holding capacity and organic matter content.
- Maximum yields are not achievable when the crop is grown on shallow soils in

combination with long dry spells during summer although establishment and survival are possible.

- Cold and heavy waterlogged soils (e.g. clays) are not suitable for growing *Miscanthus*. This was demonstrated in experimental trials on clay soil where full establishment was not achieved up to the fifth year and all plants were characterised by a low tiller number and plant height (maximum plant height was about 1.5 m).
- It is possible to grow *Miscanthus* in sand soils with a low water capacity but yields are low in these circumstances.

3.3 Planting and Establishment

The first phase of *Miscanthus* production is planting and establishment of the crop. This section outlines the different planting propagules which may be used, as well as the planting dates and planting mechanisms which may be employed.

3.3.1 Propagation Method

One step in the production of a *Miscanthus* crop is the establishment of plantlets in the field. *Miscanthus* has been proven to be a low-input crop because of its favourable water, nutrient and radiation use efficiencies, however, the high investment required for planting needs to be reduced. In order to do this, highly mechanised, cost-effective methods of plant propagation need to be developed. The sections below present the state-of-the-art of different *Miscanthus* propagation methods in a short overview, as well as results of research which has been carried out on different propagation techniques.

Seed

The commercial propagation of *Miscanthus* by seed in Europe is not likely for a number of reasons which are outlined below:

- The growing period in middle and northern Europe is too short for *Miscanthus* to produce ripe, fertile seeds (El-Bassam *et al.*, 1992; Lewandowski & Kahnt, 1993).
- *M.* x *giganteus* is a triploid interspecific hybrid and is therefore practically sterile (Linde-Laursen, 1993). In situations where fertile seeds are produced (e.g. southern Europe, greenhouses in middle and northern Europe), the morphology of the progeny is highly variable (Linde-Laursen, 1993). Therefore, even a specimen with fertile seeds would have to be stabilised in the desired genotype by inbreeding and long-term screening for target properties before commercial production would be possible.
- Even if fertile and genotypically stable seeds could be obtained, direct sowing of seed in the field in spring seems to be inefficient for middle and northern Europe because of the lack of winter-hardiness in very young plantlets (El Bassam *et al.*, 1992). The Danish Institute of Agricultural Science (DIAS) report that, when seedlings survive, they take several years to become established and will thus require high herbicide inputs during these years in order to facilitate weed control during the establishment phase.

Because of the above reasons, only vegetative propagation is foreseen for the commercial production of *Miscanthus* in middle and northern Europe. The following sections outline the different options for vegetative propagation of *Miscanthus*.

Rhizomes / Rhizome Cuttings

Rhizomes can be used for the establishment of a *Miscanthus* crop by the direct planting of rhizomes (or rhizome pieces) in the field. Research has been carried out (some as part of the *Miscanthus* Productivity Network) in order to investigate the establishment of a *Miscanthus* crop from rhizomes.

LWG began an investigation in 1996 on the effect of rhizome size and planting depth on crop establishment and winter survival. Good establishment rates were recorded for the planting of big rhizome pieces at soil depths of 100 mm, however, a planting soil depth of 200 mm was found to result in increased winter survival in the first year. It was concluded that successful establishment is only possible when big rhizome pieces (*c.* 200 mm length) with a lot of buds are planted at soil depths of at least 200 mm (Eppel-Hotz *et al.*, 1997).

DIAS carried out an investigation on planting of rhizome pieces at a trial site in Hornum in 1991. The rhizome pieces were divided into two groups (smaller and larger than 100 mm) and planted by hand at a soil depth of 50–100 mm. The size of the rhizome piece was found to have a major effect on plant emergence, with 34% emergence being recorded from the small rhizome pieces (<100 mm) in comparison to 82% emergence from the larger rhizome pieces (>100 mm). Of the plants which had been established from the small rhizome pieces survived 91% the winter, while 94% of the plants established from the larger rhizomes survived (Jørgensen, 1995). In addition, DIAS found that the winter survival of plants established from rhizome pieces depended to a large extent on whether the rhizomes were stored prior to planting. Only 9% winter survival was recorded in the plants established from stored rhizome pieces. Similar results were obtained by Huisman & Kortleve (1994) who reported emergence rates of 70–95% from rhizome pieces planted immediately after harvesting from the mother plant compared with emergence rates of 50–60% from rhizome pieces which were stored before planting. Research carried out in The Netherlands by Wageningen University (WA) and the Institute for Agricultural and Environmental Engineering, Wageningen (IMAG-DLO) showed that planting of rhizomes of weight >50g, within a short time after harvesting resulted in successful establishment (emergence rates of 91–98%).

DIAS also carried out an investigation comparing mechanical rhizome establishment to establishment of propagated plantlets of *M* x *giganteus* and *M. sinensis* 'Goliath' at Foulum in 1993. The meristematic propagated plantlets were 25–30 cm high and had been grown in 60 mm pots while the rhizomes were obtained from rotary cultivation of a mother crop (see section 3.3.3. for method) and were ploughed in to a depth of 150–200 mm. At the end of the growing season the height of the crop established from mechanised rhizome planting was 2.9 and 2.2 times higher than the crops established from plantlets of *M.* x *giganteus* and *M. sinensis* 'Goliath' respectively, while dry matter production of the rhizome-established crop was found to be 6.4 and 12.8 times higher than the dry matter production of the crop established from plantlets of *M.* x *giganteus* and *M. sinensis* 'Goliath' respectively. Winter survival of the plants established from rhizome pieces was observed to be significantly higher than that of the plants established from plantlets (Table 3.3). The clone *M. sinensis* 'Goliath' survived well, even though the plantlets were weaker at planting than those of *M.* x *giganteus*. However, in general, good survival of *M. sinensis* has been observed in Denmark and also in Germany (Hotz & Kuhn, 1994).

Table 3.3. Winter survival of M. x giganteus *established by different methods.*

Propagation method	% survival
Mechanical propagation-small plants (< 5 shoots)	28
Mechanical propagation-large plants (> 5 shoots)	74
Meristematic plantlets – *M.* x *giganteus*	0
Meristematic plantlets – *M. sinensis* 'Goliath'	86

In summary, the research which has been carried out by LWG and DIAS has indicated that successful establishment of a *Miscanthus* crop from rhizomes or rhizome pieces is possible. The factors which were found to affect establishment and winter survival were rhizome size, planting depth and the storage prior to planting. The results from the different trials indicate that best results can be achieved when large healthy rhizomes/rhizome pieces (*c.* 200 mm length) which have not been stored are planted at soil depths of 200 mm. The results also indicate that rhizomes are more favourable than micropropagated plants as planting propagules for crop establishment in terms of growth, dry matter yield and winter survival in the first year.

Micropropagation / Tissue Culture

Conventional micropropagation is considered to be too expensive to make commercial production of *Miscanthus* economically viable. However, in order to establish a cost-efficient propagation system a method was developed by Piccoplant for somatic embryogenesis of *Miscanthus*. The experiments carried out by Piccoplant (in association with Veba Oel) investigated the use of different propagation materials and genotypes for somatic embryogenesis and is outlined below.

Methods

Apical shoot sections (*c.* 60–90 mm length and including apical meristems and immature inflorescences) of several *M.* x *giganteus* clones were used as explants in the experiments. The explants were surface-sterilised by immersing them in 3% NaOCl solution for 30 minutes and washed three times in hormone-free liquid culture medium. The immature inflorescences were prepared by removing the outer leaves and cutting them into pieces 1–2 mm long). Rhizomes from *in vitro* propagated shoots were also used as explants.

Callus induction was carried out on culture medium (D. Daniel pers comm) which contained M+S medium (pH = 5.8) with added 2,4-D (2.5 mg l^{-1}), BAP (0.5 mg l^{-1})

and agar (0.8%). The explants were placed in petri dishes (diameter 90 mm) which contained 25 ml culture medium and were sealed with parafilm. The explants were cultured at 23°C in darkness, the calli which developed were transferred to new culture medium at four- to six-week intervals. Callus induction and growth were monitored continuously using a stereo-photomicroscope.

Embryogenic suspension cultures were started by placing embryogenic calli (0.5 g fresh weight) in erlenmeyer flasks containing culture medium (10 ml). The suspension cultures were maintained in flasks containing 40 ml of culture medium which were kept on a shaker (frequency of 100 rpm) and transferred to new media at three-week intervals. Calli from the suspension cultures (1–2 mm in size) were used for the regeneration of shoots.

Results

Four to six weeks after placing the inflorescence explants on the callus induction medium, the main axis began to swell and by eight to ten weeks the explants had developed non-morphogenic and morphogenic callus types. The different callus types were separated and further cultivated (Haase & Hunsinger, 1995). It was observed that when apical shoot tissue was used as explant material, morphogenic callus was induced at the basal part of the meristem. The induction frequency was found to vary according to genotype (Table 3.4).

Table 3.4. Induction rates (%) of morphogenic callus from apical shoot explants of two M. *x* giganteus *clones.*

Clone	% induction of morphogenic callus
4104	57
4152	100

Genotypic variation in the frequency of induction of morphogenic callus was also observed when rhizomes from *in vitro* propagated shoots were used as explants. Table 3.5 gives the induction frequency of different *Miscanthus* clones (50 rhizomes from *in vitro* propagated shoots were used as explants for each clone).

The morphogenic capacity was found to vary according to the type of callus material being used (Table 3.6). When callus of type 1 or 3 was used for regeneration, somatic embryos were produced while callus types 4 and 5 formed organogenic tissues as well as somatic embryos.

Regeneration rates were found to vary between 500 and 1500 shoots per gramme of callus, depending on genotype, the culture medium and the hormone applications. Multiplication rates of 8.2 to 10 fold were observed during the three-week culture intervals. The morphogenic capacity of calli did not decrease even with long-term cultivation of up to 44 months.

Table 3.5. Induction rates (%) of morphogenic callus from rhizome explants of different M. x giganteus *clones.*

Clone	4100	4101	4104	4118	4121	4122	4123	4124	4125	4126	4127	4128
Induction rate (%)	35.5	43.4	46.8	39.8	28.3	22.5	33.3	31.6	42.1	36.7	26.9	40.0
Clone	4129	4130	4131	4132	4335	4136	4138	4139	4140	4141	4151	
Induction rate (%)	45.4	38.0	48.6	43.9	36.6	31.6	30.4	40.0	34.5	50.0	30.7	

Table 3.6. Morphogenic callus types from rhizome explants of different M. x giganteus *clones.*

Callus type	Callus description	Morphogenic capacity
1	soft, nodular, white callus	morphogenic (embryogenic)
2	rough, nodular callus	non morphogenic
3	translucent, nodular callus	morphogenic (organogenic and embryogenic)
4	compact, green callus	morphogenic (organogenic and embryogenic)
5	semi-friable callus with reddish spots	morphogenic (organogenic and embryogenic)
6	soft, brownish callus	non morphogenic
7	soft, white callus with small reddish points	rhizogenic

The plants which were regenerated were uniform and morphologically identical to the mother plants. The only exception to this was the regeneration of albino plants during the induction phase from pure embryogenic calli. The young regenerated plants appeared more juvenile and vigorous than classically micropropagated material.

The potential of callus types 1, 4 and 5 for the induction of suspension cultures was assessed. Long-term morphogenic suspension cultures were established from callus types 1 and 5, the multiplication rate of these cultures reached 8 fold after a culture period of 5 weeks. The regeneration rate of the suspension cultures reached 486 shoots per gram of callus.

Conclusion

The experiments on micropropagation which were carried out in Piccoplant indicate that *M. x giganteus* can be used to establish morphogenic callus and suspension cultures: this confirms the results of Petersen & Holme (1994). The high rates of morphogenic callus induction and subsequent shoot regeneration rates from callus which were reported indicate that these methods may be commercially applied. However, the manual transfer steps might have to be mechanised in order to reduce costs and time.

Stem Segments

It is possible to propagate *Miscanthus* by using cuttings of stem segments. The use of this method for the propagation of *Miscanthus* has been investigated in Germany by LWG and BFH.

Experiments carried out by LWG in Germany between 1988 and 1992 showed that the best time to cut the stem segments was from late July until the end of August. The stem segments must contain well-developed nodal buds with the best results being recorded from the first two nodes at the base of the stem. About 80% of the cuttings taken by LWG rooted and developed young plantlets after 4–6 weeks. As stem cutting and plantlet induction is done in the summer it is necessary to store the plants during the winter, in a frost-free environment such as a cold greenhouse (additional heating is not necessary).

The feasibility of *Miscanthus* propagation via stem cuttings was also investigated by BFH. In this trial, stem cuttings were taken from six-year old plants in September and October and also from one- and two-year old plants which had been grown in a greenhouse. The cuttings were planted into a mixture containing peat and sand (2:1 v/v) and lime (1 kg m^{-3}). Induction of rooting was done in a greenhouse at a temperature of 18–22°C. The cuttings were covered with plastic sheets, watering and anti-fungal treatments were carried out as necessary. The cuttings were lifted in January when development of roots and shoots was scored. Afterwards the rooted cuttings were potted and maintained in order to observe their subsequent growth and development.

The plants resulting from the stem cutting propagation method were found to produce few but strong shoots and seemed to develop in a similar way to plants propagated from rhizomes. It was found that high rooting frequencies of up to 100% could be achieved and that six to seven plants could be produced per stem, and stem cuttings of larger diameters and lengths were generally found to develop better than smaller cuttings. Stems originating from the younger one- or two-year old greenhouse-grown plants did not develop as well as those from the six-year old plants. This was attributed to the larger diameter of the older plants. It was also found that basal cuttings rooted earlier than apical cuttings. This result, which agrees with the findings of LWG, might be due to the different states of differentiation of these cuttings (the apical cuttings might be in a state of induction of inflorescence rather than roots and would therefore root later than the basal segments). It was found that the timing of stem cutting influenced plantlet development; of the two harvesting dates used (15th September and 11th October), the first one gave significantly higher plantlet numbers. This also agrees with the findings of LWG who recommend that cuttings should be taken up to the end of August.

3.3.2 *Planting Date*

The planting date should be late enough in the year to avoid severe late spring frosts but early enough to allow good establishment, growth and translocation of reserves to the rhizome prior to the winter frosts. In general, rhizomes or rhizome pieces can be planted earlier than microplants or plants which have been established in pots, as the latter will be quite susceptible to frosts. Typical planting dates for rhizomes would be from March until May, depending on the climate, while planting dates for microplants or pot-grown plants are later (late April–May) in order to avoid frosts and thus increase establishment rates.

3.3.3 Planting Equipment

The planting equipment which should be employed is dependent on the planting propagule used; these can be either seed, rhizomes or plantlets (produced either from micropropagation or stem cuttings). The equipment may already exist for planting of other crops, adapted from already existing components, or specially designed for *Miscanthus* planting. The use of specially designed equipment will be expensive and will have a negative effect on the economics of crop production.

Planting of *Miscanthus* seed can be carried out by using existing equipment such as that used for planting of sugar beet. However, as discussed earlier, the use of seed for *Miscanthus* crop establishment is unlikely. It is possible to plant *Miscanthus* microplants or plantlets by using machinery which would normally be used for planting vegetable plantlets (e.g. cabbages).

Rhizomes have been identified as the most likely planting propagule to be used for *Miscanthus* crop establishment. Research has been carried out by DIAS and Wageningen University in order to investigate methods for rhizome planting.

Rhizome planting was carried out by Wageningen University by means of a semi-automatic machine with planting tubes. This machine was operated by four people. A rhizome was dropped by hand into a planting tube (150 mm diameter) on a light signal which was proportional to the travelled distance. The distance between rows was 750 mm while the distance within rows was dependent on the required planting density. The machine used was specially designed but standard planting machines could be adapted for *Miscanthus* rhizome planting by altering the planting tube size.

A method for rhizome harvesting and planting has been developed by DIAS. This involves rotary cultivation of an established *Miscanthus* crop followed by lifting the rhizome pieces into a trailer using a stone picker. The rhizomes were transported to the field for planting where they were spread either in beds or broadcast, either by hand or by using a farmyard manure spreader: both methods have been carried out on test fields in Denmark. The rhizomes were immediately ploughed in to a depth of 150–200 mm and, finally, the area was rolled to ensure good contact between rhizomes and soil. It is recommended that the operation is performed as quickly as possible, as it is crucial that the rhizomes (and the roots on the rhizomes) do not dry out during transport and spreading. The method developed in Denmark has also been used in The Netherlands where a lilybulb or potato harvester was used instead of a stone picker and the rhizomes were planted by a potato planter (Huisman & Kortleve, 1994).

A new machine for rhizome planting has been developed by Hvidsted Energy Forest, Denmark, and was successfully tested in October 1997. This machine facilitates the mechanisation of propagation. The planting capacity of the machine varies from 0.3 to 0.5 ha hr^{-1} depending on the planting density. Hvidsted Energy Forest now offer a *Miscanthus* planting service on a contractual basis, excluding the cost of the rhizomes and transport to the field.

Research carried out by DIAS indicates that rotary cultivation of the mother crop followed by planting of the rhizome pieces reduces the costs of establishment to about

20% of the costs of planting plantlets. However, they also concluded that the method needs to be optimised with respect to planting dates and depth of planting. Also, further research is required to investigate the use of this method for planting of different *Miscanthus* species which may have different rhizome morphologies and also to assess the risk of transferring soil-borne diseases during planting. At present, it is recommended that only 10 to 20 ha of new *Miscanthus* be planted from 1 ha of mother plants. However, when the method has been optimised, these propagation recommendations may be doubled.

3.3.4 *Factors affecting Establishment – Winter Survival*

Many of the factors which affect establishment of a *Miscanthus* crop have been described. These include the water availability and ambient temperatures at the site, the type of planting propagule used, the planting date, whether or not the rhizomes are stored before planting, etc. However, it has been observed that one of the biggest obstacles to crop establishment is the ability of the crop to survive the first winter. This problem has been observed to a greater extent in middle and northern European trials. Research has been carried out as part of the *Miscanthus* Productivity Network to investigate the problem of winter mortality in the first year of crop growth in an effort to improve establishment rates.

TCD's trial site at Cashel, Ireland, is the second most northerly of the trials of the *Miscanthus* Productivity Network. Trials were established in Cashel in 1990 from rhizomes and micro-propagated plantlets and in 1993 and 1994 from micro-propagated plantlets. It was observed that 95% of the rhizome propagated plants from the 1990 trial survived. Following planting of micro-propagated plantlets in the June 1993 trial, less than 0.6% of the plants died during the first three months up to September 1993, however, by April 1994 most of the plants (99%) had died. The winter survival of the micro-propagated plantlets established in June 1994 was also very low (17%). Similar mortality rates of micro-propagated *M.* x *giganteus* during the first winter and spring were observed at other sites in The Netherlands, Belgium and Germany.

It was assumed that the high level of winter failure in these trials was due to low winter temperatures. However, investigations carried out by TCD have shown that plants remain viable until the following spring, but if the first shoots produced are killed by late spring frosts the plants do not resprout (i.e. they cannot survive the setback of death of the first shoots, which may be due to a lack of rhizome reserves). It is noteworthy that late spring frosts did occur in the whole of northern Europe in spring 1994. A possible explanation is that the small micro-propagated plants, established in mid-summer, did not produce sufficient metabolic reserves in their rhizome system to enable them to survive the winter and retain enough reserves for the early shoot growth in the following spring. Winter survival may therefore be dependent upon the sequestering of a critical amount of metabolic reserves in the rhizomes at the end of the previous growing season. Rhizome production in autumn has also been shown to be vital for winter survival of a similar C_4 species, *Sorghum halepense* (Warwick *et al.*, 1986).

It has also been suggested that the ability of *Miscanthus* plants to survive extended frost periods is a result of dormancy (Greef, 1994; Jørgensen, 1995; Eppel-Hotz *et al.*,

1997). Dormancy is induced at the end of the vegetation period by the increasingly colder temperatures and night lengths in autumn and early winter. A sequence of processes such as the translocation of reserves to the rhizomes, the dying of leaf and stem cells and the increasing dehydration of the rhizome lead to dormancy. Young, recently propagated plants and especially micro-propagated plantlets are not able to acquire the degree of dormancy necessary to survive frost temperatures. This is confirmed by the observation that micro-propagated plantlets steadily produce new sprouts, irrespective of the ending vegetation period (Boelke, 1995). It is presumed that the micro-propagation reduces dormancy in plants because of the application of hormones to induce shoot production. It has been found that micro-propagated plants produce 15–20 small shoots in comparison to rhizome-propagated plants which produce an average of three shoots. Observations show that it takes three to five years before this habit is overcome and the usual type of shoots develop. LWG assessed the use of *Camposan* to increase winter survival, an agent containing the growth hormone 2-chlorethyl-phosphorous-acid, intended to induce dormancy. It was found that the application of *Camposan* could improve winter survival rates if it were applied during a dry, warm period (i.e. *c.* 20°C). However, it was concluded that it is extremely difficult to determine the correct time for application due to the unpredictability of the climate (Eppel-Hotz *et al.*, 1997).

Experiments carried out in TCD by Clifton-Brown (1997) indicate that there is a sharp and total decline in rhizome viability after exposure to temperatures of –5°C and below; it was also demonstrated that the failure rate of *Miscanthus* rhizomes is strongly influenced by duration of frost. Susceptibility of the plant material to damage from low temperatures has also been found to depend on rhizome size and age, planting depth and planting density. Soil quality has also been found to influence viability, with survival being lowest on moist soils which drain badly.

In Germany, BFH assessed a number of frost protection measures including fleece, polythene sheets, straw and ridging. It was reported that both straw covering and ridging were the least expensive measures against frost impact, however, the survival rate may be reduced in mild winters from the effects of increased soil wetness in these treatments. In such winters it would be preferable to use fleece or polythene sheets, however their efficiency in frost-protection has yet to be proved. LWG also investigated the effect of frost protection by straw covering and ridging, and found that straw covering and undersowing of mustard or rapeseed might improve winter survival. However, further research is required to confirm these results and to validate the parameters used for scoring of winter survival.

In conclusion, the factors which affect the establishment of a *Miscanthus* crop include water availability, ambient temperatures, the type of planting propagule used, the planting date and whether or not the rhizomes are stored before planting. However, it has been found that crops which have established in middle and northern Europe sometimes fail to survive the first winter, thus making winter survival in the first year a significant obstacle to establishment in these areas. Winter survival in the first year has been found to depend on:

• the state of dormancy of the plant; younger plants are generally not able to achieve dormancy until the first frosts occur, whereas adult plants (and some other genotypes) are able to complete growth earlier.

- the ability of the plants to sequester a critical amount of metabolic reserves in the rhizomes at the end of the previous growing season.
- the propagation method used; rhizome-propagated plants exhibit higher winter survival rates than micro-propagated plants, which has been attributed to the fact that micro-propagated plants do not produce sufficient metabolic reserves in their rhizome system to enable them to survive the winter, and that they are not able to acquire the degree of dormancy necessary to survive frost temperatures.
- the severity and length of winter frosts; rhizome viability decreases after exposure to temperatures of −5°C and below; the failure rate of *Miscanthus* rhizomes is also strongly influenced by duration of frost.

There are indications that winter survival rates may be improved by using frost protection measures such as straw covering, etc. However, these methods need to be validated through further research and development.

3.4 Fertiliser Requirements

Miscanthus is a perennial herbaceous rhizomatous grass and has the ability to mobilise and re-mobilise nutrients between various organs of the plant. Although its life span can be many years, its stems and leaves function for only one season. The only permanent organ is the rhizome which functions in vegetative propagation and the storage of nutrients. The internal cycling of nutrients between above- and below-ground organs allows the harvesting of biomass with a low nutrient content, but complicates the quantification and optimisation of fertiliser applications.

The *Miscanthus* Productivity Network investigated three different nitrogen fertiliser rates (0, 60 and 120 kg ha^{-1} year^{-1}) in order to define the crop's N requirement. Phosphorus (100 kg ha^{-1}) was applied at planting and 140 kg ha^{-1} of potassium was applied each year to ensure that the supply of these nutrients would not limit growth or the uptake of nitrogen. Two partners, ACR, UK and LWG, Germany, carried out additional experiments to measure nutrient uptake during growth. All partners measured the net annual primary production (harvestable biomass) and many partners measured the N content of harvested biomass. The following sections outline the results of these investigations.

3.4.1 Growth and Nutrient Uptake

Miscanthus shoots are produced from buds on the rhizomes at the beginning of active growth in the spring. The rhizome is the source of nutrients which supports the initial growth until the stems and leaves start to produce assimilates and support new growth (Figure 3.1).

Maximum nutrient uptake probably occurs slightly before maximum biomass is produced; the time when this occurs is affected by growth conditions. Measurements taken at Rothamsted in 1994 (Figure 3.2), show that peak P uptake occurred in July while peak N and K uptakes occurred in September. In 1995, peak uptakes of all three nutrients in the same plots occurred in July. However, there was a drought in that summer which may have restricted growth and nutrient uptake.

Miscanthus requires several years' growth before maximum productivity is reached,

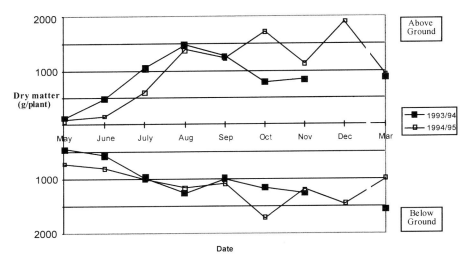

Figure 3.1. Development of M. *x* giganteus *biomass (g plant⁻¹ d.m.) from May 1993 to March 1995, Veitshöchheim, Germany. Source: Jödl et al., 1996.*

and the demand for nutrients increases during this period. In 1994 the maximum average nutrient uptake at the Rothamsted site was 111 kg N ha⁻¹, 11 kg P ha⁻¹ and 107 kg K ha⁻¹, while in 1995 this increased to 177 kg N ha⁻¹, 19 kg P ha⁻¹ and 223 kg K ha⁻¹ (Figure 3.2). In 1995 the amount of N and K taken up in stem and leaves was greater than the supply of these minerals as fertiliser.

It can be seen from Figure 3.1 that below-ground biomass increases rapidly during the summer and continues as long as aerial growth increases. Figure 3.3 shows that the nutrient content (g plant⁻¹) rises in parallel to the growth pattern. It can be seen from Figure 3.3 that there was a second increase in the below-ground nutrient content in September, probably a result of the replenishment of reserves and the growth of new roots and rhizomes. By October the nutrient content was found to be the same as it was in the previous March (9.5g N, 2.1g P, 16.3g K and 1.2g Mg per plant).

Figure 3.4 shows that nutrient content (%) in roots and rhizomes changed very little during the year, with the measurements in March being similar to the measurements in the previous May (0.9% N, 0.09% P, 0.8% K and 0.08% Mg).

Figures 3.3 and 3.4 show that the nutrient content of the above-ground biomass declines after maximum uptake has been reached. Some of this decline is the result of re-mobilisation from senescent leaves and stems. Himken *et al.* (1997) studied nutrient uptake in an established crop and found that the amount which could be mobilised and re-mobilised was in the range of 21–46% for N, 36–50% for P, 14–30% for K and 27% for Mg.

3.4.2 The Effect of Nitrogen on Biomass Production

Trials of the *Miscanthus* Productivity Network have revealed that the effect of nitrogen fertilisation rates on biomass yield is generally small. This has also been found in some other experiments (Eghbal, 1993; Hotz *et al.*, 1993; Lewandowski & Kahnt, 1994;

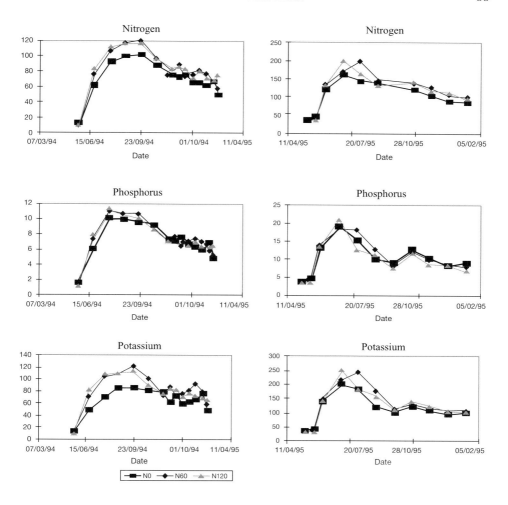

Figure 3.2. Nutrient uptake (kg ha^{-1}) in 1994 and 1995 in Rothamsted, UK. Crop received either 0, 60, or 120 kg N ha^{-1} y^{-1}.

Himken *et al.*, 1997). Experiments carried out at two sites in Austria by Schwarz and Liebhard (1995) revealed significant effects of nitrogen fertilisation rate on biomass yield in some years but not others. The Austrian trial results show that highest yields were not recorded at the highest N fertiliser levels every year, but that highest yields were consistently recorded at the site receiving the most rainfall (844 mm y^{-1}).

Trials in Greece recorded highest yields on sites with the highest rate of irrigation and similarly, in Italy, yields were highest at the site with the greater water supply. In Catania (Italy), significant interactions were found between nitrogen fertilisation rates and irrigation rates (see section 3.5.5), with the highest yields recorded in treatments which had the highest N fertilisation rate combined with the highest irrigation level (100% of evaporation). No interaction was found for N treatments at lower levels of

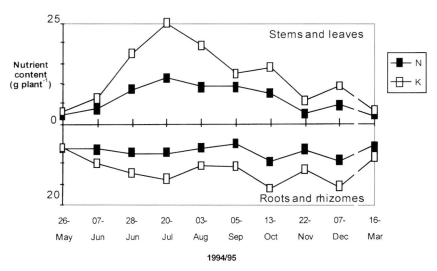

Figure 3.3. Changes in the nutrient content (g plant⁻¹) of M. x giganteus *from May 1994 to March 1995, Veitshöchheim, Germany. Source Jodl et al., 1996.*

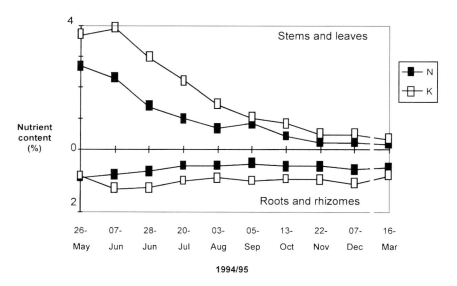

Figure 3.4. Changes in the nutrient content (%) of M. x giganteus *from May 1994 to March 1995, Veitshöchheim, Germany. Source Jodl et al., 1996.*

irrigation (25% of maximum evaporation). This experiment also found that water use efficiency declined with increasing rates of N fertilisation. Significant responses to N rate with irrigation were also recorded at the University of Essex in the UK.

3.4.3 Nutrient Content of Harvested Biomass

It has been mentioned earlier that nutrient uptake increases with crop maturity. It is frequently stated that *Miscanthus* requires 3–4 years growth to reach maturity, therefore it is uncertain if yields from mature crops were reported in the *Miscanthus* Productivity Network project. The N contents of crops from the later years of the project were used in order to calculate a reasonable estimate of nitrogen offtake at harvest.

LWG in Germany calculated the nutrient offtake in the third, fourth and fifth years of crop growth as a percentage of the dry matter content of the crop; the calculated nutrient offtakes were 0.5% N, 0.04% P, 0.55% K and 0.05% Mg. Rothamsted (RES) calculated the nutrient offtake in the second and third year of growth (Table 3.7). It can be seen that in the third year of growth each tonne of dry matter contained 8.14 kg N, 0.69 kg P and 8.74 kg K. These offtakes (except for phosphorus) were slightly greater than in the previous year and higher in terms of concentrations than at LWG in Germany.

Table 3.7. Nutrient content of harvested biomass at Rothamsted, UK (averaged for nitrogen treatments, 0, 60, 120 kg ha⁻¹).

	2nd year	3rd year
Average yield (t ha^{-1})	7.66	10.78
Nutrient content (kg ha^{-1})		
Nitrogen	59.46	87.70
Phosphorus	5.43	7.41
Potassium	56.60	94.27
Content per tonne dry matter		
Nitrogen	7.76	8.14
Phosphorus	0.71	0.69
Potassium	7.39	8.74

N offtake at harvest was found to be higher at RES than at eight other sites of the *Miscanthus* Productivity Network (Table 3.8), however yield and N content were found to vary greatly between these sites. Differences in N content may be attributed to the amount of leaf present in the harvested crop as leaf material has a higher N content than stem material. The low N offtakes recorded at FAL and UNINOVA, Lisboa resulted in very high nitrogen use efficiencies compared to the other sites.

3.4.4 Conclusions of Fertiliser Requirements

While the dynamics of nutrient flows within the *Miscanthus* production system are not completely resolved, some general conclusions can be drawn. The ability of the plant to acquire and conserve large quantities of nutrients implies that once the crop is established it requires relatively low fertiliser applications to support growth. The amount of P and K exported in the biomass at harvest (i.e. 7.4 and 94.3 kg ha^{-1} respectively in the third year) can be replaced by fertiliser applied at compensatory rates but with adjustments to support increased growth as the crop increases in maturity.

Table 3.8. Yield, nitrogen content and nitrogen use efficiency of Miscanthus crops at different sites (all received 60 kg N ha⁻¹).

				Country and partner					
	IE	DE	DE	PT	GB	GB	GB	ES	BE	Mean
	TCD	FAL	LWG	UNINOVA	UE	RES	ADAS	USC	SORGHAL	
Year	1993	1992	1993	1994	–	1995	1995	1996	1995	
Yield										
(t ha⁻¹ d.m.)	15[a]	13.50	9.28	35.58	19.4	9.84	12.2	13.6	16.3	16.1
N content										
(kg)	106	25	40	58	97	78	76	76	54	67.7
N content										
(kg t⁻¹)	7.1	1.8	4.3	1.6	5	7.9	6.2	5.6	3.3	4.3
Nitrogen use										
efficiency [b]	143	540	232	613	200	126	160	179	302	277

[a] Predicted offtake
[b] calculated as yield (kg ha⁻¹) / N content (kg ha⁻¹)

No clear conclusion was made regarding the effects of different rates of N fertilisation on crop yield and this requires further investigation. In some cases the low response to N fertiliser applications may have been due to the return of mineralised N to the soil (mineralised from decomposing litter), while in other cases the low response may have been due to insufficient water supply at the trial site. It is not possible to carry out a regression analysis when investigating only two or three N fertiliser rates. Multi-rate studies such as those conducted in Austria are required to establish the relationship between N and biomass yield. It is probable that the optimum economic nitrogen fertilisation rate will be lower than the fertilisation rate which produces maximum yield. The timing of nitrogen application to meet crop demand also needs to be investigated in order to minimise losses.

3.5 Irrigation Requirements

Although *M.* x *giganteus* can be successfully grown without irrigation in northern and middle European regions, irrigation seems to be necessary for substantial growth and biomass yields in southern Europe. However, southern EU regions face considerable water irrigation shortages and recent irrigation practices have shown a shift from obtaining highest yields per unit area of land towards obtaining highest yields per unit volume of applied water. The effect of irrigation rate on *Miscanthus* growth was studied in two sites in Greece: Kopais (central Greece) and Kefalonia (western Greece), and in southern Italy (Catania). The results are outlined in the following sections.

3.5.1 Effect of Irrigation Level on Miscanthus Plant Height

Under southern EU conditions, it was observed that *Miscanthus* resprouted from the middle to the end of April, depending on the climatic conditions. Initial plant growth was very rapid with plants reaching heights of up to 2.5 m by the end of June and final heights of 3–3.2 m (with irrigation) from mid-August to mid-September. Figure 3.5 shows plant height development in field trials carried out in Catania. It was observed that there was no significant effect of irrigation rate on plant height during the initial growing period, attributable to the high moisture content of the soil at this time. However, irrigation rates were found to have an effect on plant height development from late June to the end of the growing season.

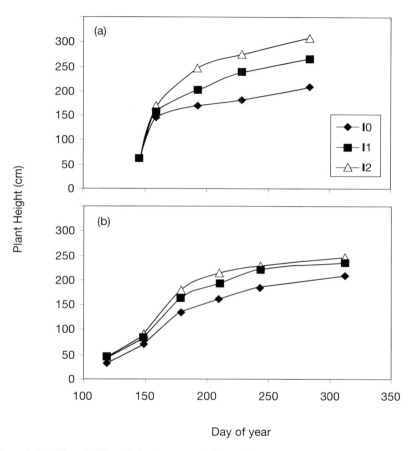

Figure 3.5. Effect of different irrigation rates on Miscanthus *height in the second (a) and third (b) growing period, in Catania, southern Italy, where IO = 25%, I1 = 50% and I2 = 100% potential evapotranspiration.*

3.5.2 *Effect of Irrigation Level on* Miscanthus *Shoot Production*

High shoot numbers per plant (up to 64 shoots of 60 mm or more in length) were recorded in *Miscanthus* at the beginning of the second growing period in Kopais and Catania. The high planting density of the crop (500 x 500 mm) resulted in the formation of a very dense canopy after the second growing period, in which individual plants could not be distinguished. In the third and following growing periods in Greece shoot densities of up to 260 per m^2 were counted during the initial growing stages.

This high shoot density resulted in severe competition for nutrients and light, especially in the lower canopy layers. A large number of shoots died back in late May–early June and the shoot number per plant or per square metre was sharply reduced to about 38 per plant in Catania and 30 per plant in Greece. This sharp decrease occurred within 10 to 15 days (Figure 3.6). Shoot density continued to decrease until the end of the growing season, when the shoot density was 19–26.8 per plant in the Greek trials and 24.8–34.8 per plant in the Italian trials.

Under these competitive conditions the effects of irrigation rates on shoot number were almost negligible. However, shoot production, in some cases, was slightly differentiated with irrigation rates late in the growing season.

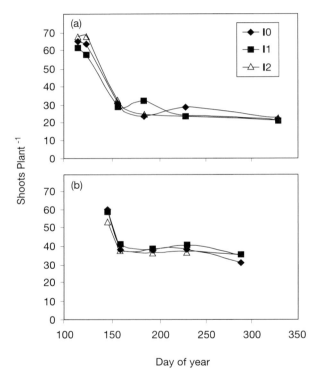

Figure 3.6. Effect of different irrigation rates on Miscanthus *shoot production in the second growing period, in (a) Kopais, central Greece and (b) Catania, southern Italy, where IO = 25%, I1 = 50% and I2 = 100% potential evapotranspiration.*

3.5.3 *Effect of Irrigation Level on* Miscanthus *Leaf Area Index*

Leaf area index (LAI) development followed a one-peak curve in all trials carried out in Greece and Italy. No effects of the irrigation rate on LAI were recorded in any of the Greek trials except during the peak LAI values in June–July (Figure 3.7). A significant effect of irrigation rates on LAI was observed in both growing periods in Italy (Figure 3.8).

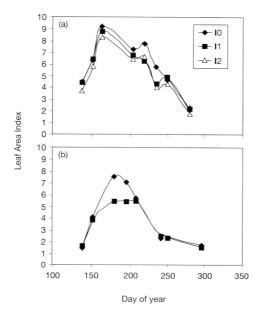

Figure 3.7. Effect of different irrigation rates on Miscanthus *leaf area index in the third (a) and fourth (b) growing periods in Greece. Third growing period refers to trials carried out in Kopais, central Greece, while fourth growing period refers to trials in Kefalonia, western Greece, where IO = 25%, I1 = 50% and I2 = 100% potential evapotranspiration.*

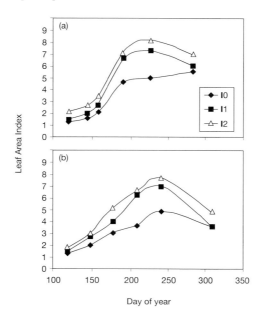

Figure 3.8. Effect of different irrigation rates on Miscanthus *leaf area index in the second (a) and third (b) growing period in Catania, southern Italy, where IO = 25%, I1 = 50% and I2 = 100% potential evapotranspiration.*

3.5.4 *Effect of Irrigation Level on Number of Leaves per Shoot*

The leaves produced by *Miscanthus* are elongated, coriaceous and ciliate along the margins, with flat blades. Under Greek conditions, an average of 15–17 leaves developed from each shoot until the inflorescence emerged. The leaves started to die back in the summer months (June–July) and continued so that by mid-August the number of leaves per shoot was reduced to between 5 and 7 (central Greece, third growing period). The reduction in leaf number may be attributed to the high density of the plantation which induces senescence of the lower leaves.

In the second growing period in southern Italy the number of leaves per shoot was found to be affected by irrigation rates. The final number of leaves per shoot was 13.6 for the higher irrigation rate, 11.5 for the medium and 10.7 for the lower. Similarly, in the third growing period, leaf numbers per shoot ranged from 9.2 to 13.4 according to irrigation rate.

3.5.5 *Effect of Irrigation Level on* **Miscanthus** *Yields*

M. x *giganteus* grown both in western-central Greece and southern Italy showed rapid initial growth and high dry matter accumulation rates. Peak biomass yields occurred in August (Greece) and October (southern Italy) and were followed by a decline in biomass production until the end of the growing period.

Dry matter yields were found to be affected by irrigation rates in Greece and southern Italy. The lower irrigation rates resulted in significantly reduced dry matter yields which were more evident after July. The medium irrigation rates also resulted in lower dry matter yields than the higher irrigation rates.

The results indicate that doubling the irrigation rate (water per unit area of land), may result in a dry matter yield increase of only 10.4–30.4%. Therefore, in areas of the southern EU which are facing water shortages it could be recommended that *Miscanthus* be grown under moderate irrigation rates, thus saving irrigation water for other uses while not dramatically reducing yields.

It was observed that the effects of different irrigation rates were almost negligible in fields with a high underground water table. In these fields *Miscanthus* could be successfully grown without irrigation with only slightly less dry matter yields than the fully irrigated plots. These findings indicate that *Miscanthus* has the ability to draw water from underground water tables.

Finally, an interaction between irrigation and nitrogen fertilisation rates was highlighted in the fully irrigated plots in southern Italy from the second growing period (Figure 3.9). At the highest irrigation rate, there were differences between different nitrogen fertilisation rates (31, 25 and 17 t ha^{-1} respectively for the higher, medium and lower rates), while at the lowest irrigation rate, no differences were found. Significant differences were only found between the highest and the lowest nitrogen fertilisation rates with the medium irrigation rate.

3.5.6 *Conclusions of Irrigation Requirements*

It was found that growth characteristics such as plant height, number of leaves, leaf area index and yield were dependent on irrigation rates when *Miscanthus* was grown

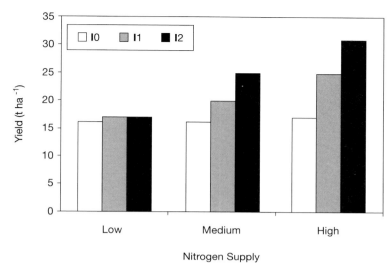

Figure 3.9. Effect of nitrogen rates on dry matter yields for each irrigation rate in Catania, southern Italy, where IO = 25%, I1 = 50% and I2 = 100% potential evapotranspiration.

in sites where there was a low water supply (e.g. southern EU areas or sites with low water table). One exception was the 'number of stems' character which was found to be more dependent on planting density than irrigation rate. *Miscanthus* yields were dependent on irrigation rates, but it has been found that doubling irrigation rates may increase dry matter yields by as little as 10%. Therefore, in view of the water shortages in areas of the southern EU, it may be more economically and environmentally favourable to grow *Miscanthus* using moderate irrigation rates, thus saving irrigation water for other uses while not dramatically reducing yields. This would ensure highest yields per unit volume of applied water rather than the more conventional highest yields per unit area of land.

3.6 Weed Control

Weeds, if not controlled, will compete with the crop for light, water and nutrients and thus reduce yields. The level of weed interference will depend on the stage of maturity of the crop (i.e. its ability to out-compete weeds), the degree of weed infestation at the site and the diversity of weed species (affected by site location, season, climate and previous land use).

Weed control is essential during the establishment phase of the crop because the slow initial growth of *Miscanthus* reduces its ability to compete. The planting process causes soil disturbance which promotes seed germination. Furthermore, the low planting densities which are used result in large unoccupied spaces where weed growth can occur. At this stage the young *Miscanthus* plantlets can easily become overwhelmed by weeds. It may not be possible to use herbicidal weed control directly after planting as the newly transplanted plants often endure transplant stress. Consequently, mechanical weed control may be the only option at this stage; as the crop is widely spaced and evenly distributed, mechanical weed control is feasible.

As the *Miscanthus* crop becomes more established, a range of selective herbicides can be used for weed control. Table 3.9 gives a list of herbicides which have been successfully used for weed control in *Miscanthus*. Bullard, Nixon and Heath (1995) report that any active ingredient which is appropriate for cereals should also be suitable for *Miscanthus* (with the possible exception of some graminicides) and that C_4 specific herbicides such as atrazine could also be used.

Table 3.9. Herbicides used for weed control in Miscanthus. *Source: Bullard* et al., *1995b.*

Active ingredient(s)	Data source[1]	Notes
atrazine	1	Gesaprim @ 2.5 l/ha
bromoxynil / ioxynil	1	Briotril @ 2.5 l/ha
bromoxynil / fluroxypyr / ioxynil	1	Advance @ 2 l/ha
clopyralid	2	(100 g/l a.i.) 2.4 l/ha
dichlorprop	2	(667 g/l a.i.) 5 l l/ha
diflufenican / isoproturon	2	(100:500 g/l a.i.) 3 l/ha
fluroxypyr	1, 2	Starane 2 @ 2 l/ha
glyphosate[2]	1, 2	Roundup @ 3 l/ha
isoproturon	2	Tolkan @ 4 l/ha
metsulfuron methyl	1, 2	Ally @ 30 g/ha
metsulfuron methyl + bromoxynil / ioxynil[3]	1	Ally @ 30 g/ha + Deloxil @ 1 l/ha
metsulfuron methyl + fluroxypyr[3]	1	Ally + Starane 2 + (20 g/ha + 0.5 l)
MCPA	2	(750 g/l a.i.) @ 5 l/ha
MCPA + MCPB	1	Trifolex-Tra @ 7.7 l/ha
mecoprop – P	2	Duplosan @ 6 l/ha
paraquat[2]	1	Gramoxone @ 4 l/ha
tribenuron methyl	2	75%

[1] ADAS, Georg Noyé Institute of Weed Control 'Flakkebjerg', Denmark
[2] Herbicides for use before emergence
[3] tank mixtures

Once the full canopy develops, the germination of new weed seedlings is dramatically reduced, and only shade-tolerant species such as *Fallopia convolvulus* and *Stellaria media* or particularly mature individuals will survive. Autumn-germinating species such as *Poa annua* may present problems after crop senescence has occurred in the establishment year.

In the first season after establishment early emerging weeds can be successfully controlled with pre-emergence applications of glyphosate or paraquat applied before shoots emerge. Applications at this time are most likely to be necessary to control grass weeds such as *Elytrigio repens* and *Poa annua*. Once the *Miscanthus* shoots have emerged, selective herbicides must be used for the control of vigorous annual dicotylenonous weeds. A weed wiper may be used to apply post-emergence gramoxone to the taller, more persistent weeds such as thistles.

In subsequent seasons, weed interference is effectively suppressed, initially by the leaf litter layer on the soil surface and subsequently by the closure of the crop canopy which reduces the light penetrating into the understorey. Weeds that do survive are etiolated and offer little competition to the crop. Spraying of herbicides around the edges of the plantation may be all that will be required in the established crop.

The market price which is obtained for *Miscanthus* grown as a biomass fuel is likely to be quite low and consequently the gross margins will be low. The expenditure on weed control will therefore have to be carefully calculated and minimised (Speller, 1993).

It is possible that the long-term cultivation of *Miscanthus* will promote the development of a new weed fauna which would include perennial competitive species, spring-germinating species and stress-tolerant species which are adapted to low light conditions, or opportunistic species which can take advantage of gaps within the canopy.

In summary, weed control is likely to be relatively intensive after planting and during the establishment phase. However, once the crop has become established, the demand for weed control is low. The development of new weed fauna in long-term plantations must be monitored in order to identify any 'new' weed species which will pose a threat to the crop.

3.7 Diseases

There have been no reports of diseases that significantly risk production of *Miscanthus*. However the crop can be affected by a range of diseases known to occur in graminaceous plants. These include *Fusarium* which has been observed on *Miscanthus* in Ireland (J. Clifton-Brown, pers. comm.), and the aphid-transmitted Barley Yellow Dwarf luteovirus (BYDV) which has been reported in the UK (Christian *et al.*, 1994; Huggett, 1996).

Some diseases have been identified elsewhere but they have not been reported in Europe, possibly due to the fact that European climatic conditions are less favourable for their development. In Japan, *Miscanthus* streak virus has been reported but the insect vector was not identified (Yamashita *et al.*, 1985). A fungus which attacks *Miscanthus* foliage was identified in the United States, found in a commercial planting of horticultural stock and caused the death of plants at the seedling stage. The fungus was found in *Miscanthus spp.* and five varieties exhibited severe symptoms. These were *Miscanthus sinensis* Anderss, *Miscanthus sinensis* Var *gracillimus* Hitch., *Miscanthus sinensis* var. *variegatus* Beal, *Miscanthus sinensis* var. *Zebrinus* Beal and *Miscanthus sinensis* var. *Strictus*. The name proposed for the disease is *Miscanthus* blight (O'Neill & Farr, 1996).

If the area of *Miscanthus* grown in Europe increases, a greater risk of disease may arise. The present situation is that few disease problems exist but the long-term disease risks may only be assessed by monitoring large-scale plantations. The possibility of disease spread from other crops such as *Saccharum* spp. cannot be discounted and strict quarantine of plants imported from countries where both *Miscanthus* and *Saccharum* are indigenous would be a wise precaution.

4 | Miscanthus *Productivity*

by J. C. Clifton-Brown, S. P. Long and U. Jørgensen

with contributions from S. A. Humphries,
K.-U. Schwarz and H. Schwarz

4.1 Introduction

This chapter deals with the estimates of theoretical and practical yields of *M.* x *giganteus*. The yield potential of *Miscanthus* is described as well as some productivity models which have been developed for the prediction of yields. The observed yields which have been reported in field trials are presented.

4.2 Yield potential of *Miscanthus*

The yield potential of *Miscanthus* is set by the equation adapted from Monteith (1977), by Beale and Long (1995):

$$W_h = S_t.\varepsilon_i.\varepsilon_c.\eta \ / \ k \ (1)$$

As already mentioned in Chapter 2:

- W_h is the dry matter at final harvest (g m^{-2})
- S_t is the integral of incident solar radiation (MJ m^{-2})
- ε_i is the efficiency with which the crop intercepts that radiation (dimensionless)
- ε_c is the efficiency with which the intercepted radiation is converted into biomass energy (dimensionless)
- η is the amount partitioned into the harvested components (dimensionless)
- k is the energy content of the biomass (MJ g^{-1}).

The energy content of *M.* x *giganteus* harvested shoots (k) is assumed to be a constant of *c.* 18 MJ kg^{-1}, and the total amount of biomass partitioned (η) into these shoots was estimated at 0.6 (Beale & Long, 1995); yield potential (W_h) will therefore depend on ε_i and ε_c. Beale and Long (1995) estimated ε_i at 0.85 for years 2 and 3 after planting: this appears typical for healthy stands. They estimated ε_c at 0.065, which appears close to a maximum. The yield potential for a site is therefore:

$$W_h = S_t . 1.84 \times 10^{-3} \ (1a)$$

Total photosynthetically active radiation (PAR) ranges from an annual receipt of 1500 to 3200 MJ m^{-2} in the EU, giving a range of potential yields from 27 t ha^{-1} in Ireland, Scotland and Scandinavia to 59 t ha^{-1} in the Mediterranean. Practical yields, even under optimal conditions of cultivation, are lower. The primary reasons are, firstly, that there is no canopy for part of the year, so at least 20% of radiation is lost, and secondly, that the crop can run out of water even in western Europe so ε_i (the efficiency with which the crop intercepts radiation) and ε_c (the radiation use efficiency) are reduced before temperatures become low enough to cause canopy senescence.

4.3 Productivity Models

This section introduces productivity modelling and its use for the prediction of *Miscanthus* yields. Firstly, simple productivity models are introduced. Following this, an example is given where a productivity model was used for the prediction of yields and the compilation of a productivity map for *Miscanthus* in Ireland. Finally, a complex mechanistic productivity model (WIMOVAC) which has been developed by the University of Essex is described in terms of its structure and implementation.

4.3.1 Simple Productivity Models

Productivity models can be both simple and complex. Simple models have the advantage of transparency and are effective when combined with a Geographical Information System (GIS). However, they cannot deal with complexities of interactions and weather variation within the growing season, and they cannot use the mechanistic information necessary for assessing approaches to plant breeding.

Equation (1a) illustrates a simple but effective model of potential crop yield. This could be adapted to actual yield by taking account of temperature, soil moisture and nitrogen input. Temperature affects the crop by determining the period over which a canopy can be present. Analysis of leaf growth suggests that there will be no canopy when temperatures are below 10°C, and this could be incorporated into equation (1a) by replacing S_t by S_t' (the integral of photosynthetically active solar radiation for the period of the year when mean temperature is >10°C). It has been estimated that 1 mm of water is required for every 0.07 t of biomass yield ($\varepsilon_w = 0.7 \times 10^{-3}$) while 5 kg of added nitrogen (N) is required for each tonne of biomass yield. Therefore at a steady state the actual yield (W_h') achieved at a site could be approximated by:

$$W_h' = \min \{S_t' . 1.84 \times 10^{-3}; 5 \times 10^{-3}/N; 0.7 \times 10^{-3}/M\} \ (1b)$$

where:

- N = the mass of added nitrogen (kg m^{-2})
- M = the soil moisture available to the plant in the growing season (kg m^{-2}).

4.3.2 Development and Application of an Empirical Productivity Model

An empirical climate-driven growth model was parameterised using measurements made at a field trial in central Ireland. In this model, rainfall was assumed to be non-limiting for growth, therefore air temperature and solar radiation were the only climatic variables which were needed to make predictions of *Miscanthus* productivity. The potential productivity of *M.* x *giganteus* at 20 meteorological stations around Ireland was predicted by running the parameterised model using mean climatic data from the different stations as inputs. The results were incorporated into a GIS in order to interpolate the yield predictions and to produce a productivity map for Ireland. This section describes the modelling procedures used and the results obtained from application and implementation of the model.

Development of the model

Air temperatures have two important effects. Firstly, as *M.* x *giganteus* leaves are frost-sensitive, the start and end of the growing season are determined by the last frosts in spring and first frosts in autumn. Secondly, air temperature has been shown to be the most important environmental determinant for leaf expansion rates which affect canopy development (Clifton-Brown, 1997). Consequently, it was considered that canopy development could be predicted for the model by calculating the thermal time which the crop experiences using a threshold temperature of 10°C for the start of leaf growth (Clifton-Brown *et al.*, 1996).

A four-year-old field trial of *M.* x *giganteus*, consisting of eight 100m^2 plots, established at Cashel, Ireland, was used to parameterise the model. Fertiliser was applied at rates sufficient to ensure that the growth of the crop was not nutrient limited. During the growing seasons of 1994 and 1995 measurements of percentage radiation interception, leaf area index (LAI) and standing aerial dry matter, were made every two weeks. Degree days above 10°C were calculated from air temperatures recorded 1 km from the site. Daily incident radiation values were calculated from the mean radiation received at two meteorological stations located 62 km north (Birr) and 43 km east (Kilkenny) from the site.

Two relationships were established between climate and crop growth in both years which provided the empirical parameters for the productivity model. Firstly, a thermal leaf area coefficient was obtained by regression of LAI on degree days above 10°C. Secondly, an estimate of the conversion coefficient (ε_c) was obtained from the regression of the standing aerial dry matter on the intercepted radiation. Figure 4.1 shows the model modules and their linkages for a *Miscanthus* productivity model.

A GIS was used to carry out surface interpolation of predicted yields using the model and meteorological data obtained from 20 Met Éireann stations in Ireland (ten years of daily weather data, from 1984–93, were obtained from each of the meteorological stations).

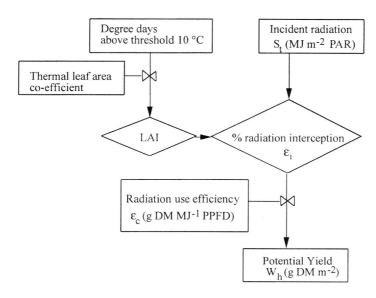

Figure 4.1. The Miscanthus *productivity model – modules and linkages.*

Application of the model

Figure 4.2 shows the relationship between leaf area index (LAI) and degree days above 10°C (DD_{TB10}) for the two growing seasons. This indicates that canopy development, in terms of LAI, can be predicted from a knowledge of thermal time above a threshold of 10°C. In both years, a LAI of above 3.2 was sufficient to intercept 95% of the incident radiation. The radiation use efficiency (ε_c) of the crop was derived from the relationship between aerial dry matter and intercepted radiation (Figure 4.3).

Because this model, in its present form, assumes that rainfall is non-limiting, this relationship was established for times when the soil moisture deficit was less than 100 mm. In 1994 there was no indication of water stress developing, and a linear relationship between intercepted radiation and aerial dry matter was maintained throughout the growing season. However, 1995 was unusually hot and dry at the trial site and this led to the development of drought conditions which arrested the leaf area expansion during the latter part of July and throughout August. Soil moisture deficit in August exceeded 250 mm in 1995 compared to 50 mm in 1994. The conversion coefficient value of 2.4 g (dm) MJ^{-1} (PAR) obtained was consistent for both years, and is close to the value of 2.6 g (dm) MJ^{-1} (PAR) reported by van der Werf *et al.* (1993) for *Miscanthus* grown in The Netherlands.

Using the parameters derived from the trials in 1994 and 1995 the *Miscanthus* growth model was run using the meteorological data for 20 stations in Ireland. A surface interpolation routine in a GIS was applied to the yields predicted for each of the meteorological stations and the results are presented in the form of a potential yield map for *Miscanthus* in Ireland (Figure 4.4).

The productivity model predicts that annual Irish *Miscanthus* dry matter yields can range from 16 to 26 t ha^{-1} y^{-1}. However, these are the maximum harvestable yields at

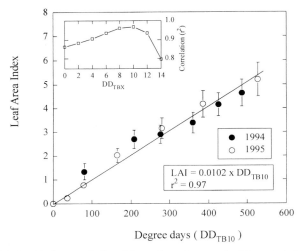

Figure 4.2. Relationship between LAI and degree days above 10°C (DD_{TB10}) for M. x gigagnteus in 1994 and 1995 at Cashel, Ireland. Error bar = ± 1 sem (n=40). Inset graph shows the influence of base temperate on the correlation coefficient (r^2) of the relationship.

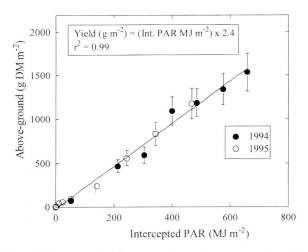

Figure 4.3. Relationship between aerial dry matter of M. x gigagnteus and cumulative intercepted radiation at Cashel, Ireland. Note: The slope of the regression is the average radiation use efficiency (ε_c) for the crop for both the 1994 and 1995 growing seasons. Data for 1995 excluded measurements when soil moisture deficit exceeded 150 mm.

the end of the growing season, *Miscanthus* is normally harvested later in the year when the dry matter yields will be lower due to translocation of assimilates to the rhizomes and senescence and loss of leaf and shoot material. The dry matter yields predicted by the model for the trial site in 1994 and 1995 were 17.3 and 18.4 t ha^{-1} respectively. These are considerably higher than the actual harvested dry matter yields (December harvest) of 13.6 and 14.0 t ha^{-1} which were recorded at the site. These results suggest that losses and translocation between the time of peak yield and the time of harvest were approximately 20–30%. It is necessary to quantify the dry matter loss before the time of harvest at more sites so that the model can be developed in order to predict final harvestable yields of *Miscanthus* on a regional basis. The model also needs to be developed in order to take account of the effects of soil moisture deficits or limited soil nutrient supply.

However, despite its present limitations, it is possible to use this empirical model to identify the areas in Ireland with the most suitable temperature and radiation conditions for growing *Miscanthus.*

4.3.3 *Mechanistic Productivity Model (WIMOVAC)*

WIMOVAC is a mechanistic Windows-based productivity model developed by the University of Essex. Its detail makes it less appropriate than the empirical model described in section 4.3.2 for GIS applications. Its value lies in its ability to predict the value of potential modifications in cultivation and genotype, i.e. as a guide to future experiments and breeding. For example, it may be used to address questions such as: what yield advantage could be obtained by breeding programmes for lowering the threshold temperature for leaf extension or for increasing resistance of the photosynthetic apparatus to chilling? Similarly it could address the issues of whether higher yields may result from the selection of a more vertical canopy architecture or from increased partitioning of assimilate into leaves, as opposed to stem and rhizome.

Briefly, WIMOVAC uses mechanistic sub-models for photosynthesis, transpiration, light interception and canopy microclimate, to predict carbon uptake, water balance and microclimate. Growth is predicted by partitioning net carbon uptake among the organs of the plant. Partitioning is governed by tables, which depend on the developmental stage, and temperature, water and nitrogen limitation on growth. Developmental stage is predicted by thermal time, i.e. the accumulated temperature above a threshold during the growing season. For example, partitioning is predominantly to leaf growth during the early season, shifting to rhizome as thermal time accumulates. WIMOVAC uses a simple Windows™ interface, which allows the user access to the model and its operation through the familiar Windows dialogue boxes. The model is therefore transparent, and equations, parameters and assumptions may be accessed without any knowledge of computer languages. The user may specify location, climate, and other site characteristics through a dialogue box. Similarly the user may open the Parameter database to change crop characters, such as photosynthesis, partitioning coefficients, temperature thresholds and canopy architecture.

Model System and Methods

WIMOVAC was written in Microsoft Visual Basic (version 2.0/3.0), an event-driven, pseudo object-orientated and visual programming language which provided the user interface design component necessary. Visual Basic gives most of the flexibility and discipline of other structured languages, such as PASCAL, C and C++, but allows the rapid development and prototyping of visual control elements. It is these visual

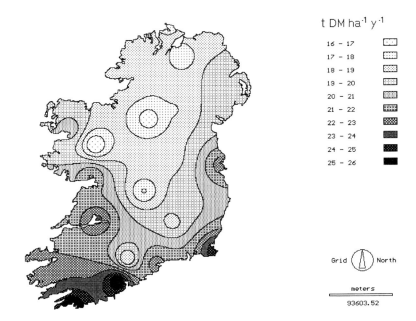

Figure 4.4. Potential productivity (t dm ha⁻¹ y⁻¹) of M. x giganteus *throughout Ireland, based on mean daily radiation and air temperatures from 1984 to 1993.*

control elements which are essential to providing non-computer expert access to the models in WIMOVAC.

Structure and Components of Model

The mechanistic model of leaf photosynthesis developed by Farquhar *et al.* (1980) has been widely used and validated (Long, 1985; Long & Drake, 1991; Harley *et al.*, 1992). Equations originally derived by Farquhar *et al.* (1980) and given in Long & Drake (1991) were modified to include a potential phosphate limitation arising from the failure of triose phosphate utilisation (starch and sucrose production) to keep up with triose phosphate production in the Calvin cycle (Sharkey, 1985). The principles developed by Farquhar *et al.* (1980) have been incorporated into a further model of one of the two known variants of C_3 photosynthesis, so-called C_4 photosynthesis, by Collatz *et al.* (1992). This sub-model of the biochemistry of C_4 photosynthesis is used for *Miscanthus*.

The biochemical model uses C_i (intercellular CO_2 concentration) rather than C_a (atmospheric CO_2 concentration) as a driving variable since C_i approximates to the concentration of CO_2 at the site of reaction. C_i is determined within the leaf from the interaction between assimilation of CO_2 and stomatal conductance to CO_2. Therefore the biochemical model of CO_2 assimilation must be integrated with a model of stomatal behaviour in order to be useful in predicting leaf response to varying environmental conditions. A mechanistic understanding of the control processes involved in regulating stomatal conductance remains incomplete, however Ball *et al.*

(1987) developed a phenomenological expression for the regulation of stomatal conductance which has proved very robust. The expression used in the WIMOVAC model is that of Harley *et al.* (1992) who modified the expression of Ball *et al.* (1987) to a more practical version requiring Ca and relative humidity in the air outside the boundary layer, rather than the values within the boundary layer which are difficult to estimate or measure. Because assimilation of CO_2 and stomatal conductance are inter-dependent, the value of C_i and assimilation rate have been solved numerically by iteration (Humphries & Long, 1995).

The direct effects of temperature on the kinetic properties of carboxylation and RuBP regeneration use the equations of Collatz *et al.* (1992), but are modified in WIMOVAC to account for changes in the solubility and Rubisco affinity for CO_2 and O_2 (Long & Drake, 1992). In addition, solubilities for O_2 and CO_2 were recalculated relative to their values at 25°C using polynomial relationships fitted to tabular values of solubility at different temperatures (Kaye & Laby, 1973; Linke, 1965). Jordan & Ogren (1984) provided data on the response of the kinetic constants of Rubisco to temperature which are used in WIMOVAC.

Effects of varying leaf nitrogen content on the biochemistry of leaf processes have been introduced into the model using procedures of Field (1983) and Harley *et al.* (1992) which propose linear relationships between leaf nitrogen content and the maximum rate of carboxylation, maximum rate of electron transport and dark respiration rate. All leaves, either singularly or as part of a canopy, are assumed here to have a leaf nitrogen concentration of 2 g m^{-2} unless otherwise specified by the user.

Although single leaf level analysis can provide many insights into plant adaptation to the environment, canopy level analysis is essential to predict crop productivity (Norman, 1980). WIMOVAC allows the user to specify one of three separate models of canopy microclimate. Which of these is selected depends on the detail that is available. In summary these are as follows:

- **Single Layer Model.** Here the canopy is divided into two populations of leaves, sunlit and shaded. From radiation geometry the proportion of the canopy that is sunlit at any point in the day is calculated and the mean light flux to the sunlit and to the shaded leaves is calculated. This information is then used to calculate leaf radiation balance, photosynthesis and transpiration. The only crop information required is leaf area index and leaf angular distribution. All leaves are assumed to have the same photosynthetic potential (Norman, 1980; Forseth & Norman, 1993; Long, 1991; Long & Drake, 1992).
- **Multiple Layer Model.** This is a development of the single layer model, that divides the canopy into a series of layers of equal leaf area. It allows for the fact that diffuse radiation diminishes with depth into the canopy (Reynolds *et al.*, 1992) and it allows specification of different photosynthetic properties and leaf angles for different canopy layers. Up to 10 layers may be specified, and the proportion of sunlit and shaded leaf area for each is calculated, as for the single layer model. It allows numerical experiments to determine the ideal canopy characteristics for maximising *Miscanthus* production in a given region.
- **Plant Spacing Model.** The above models assume a random distribution of foliage over the ground surface. The condition is approximated by *Miscanthus* stands once a dense canopy is achieved and for old stands. For new stands, where planting

is in rows, a different approach is needed to predict light interception, which takes acount of the regular orientation of the rows and cyclical distribution of leaf area perpendicular to the rows (Boote & Pickering, 1994). This sub-model allows experimentation with different row spacings and planting densities for *Miscanthus*. For example, this may be used to examine the trade-off between increased spacing to decrease establishment costs versus the additional time needed to obtain maximum yield after planting.

An expression (from Penman, 1948; Monteith, 1965 and 1973) has been introduced into the canopy models to calculate instantaneous evapo-transpiration. This expression has been combined with a boundary layer conductance model which describes the transfer of water vapour from the evaporating surface to the bulk air stream in terms of the aerodynamics of the turbulent air above the canopy (Campbell, 1977; Thornley & Johnson, 1990). Transpiration rates at both the sunlit and shaded leaves within the canopy are calculated according to the light and temperature microclimatic conditions within the canopy, and the effects of radiation on stomatal conductance via photosynthesis and leaf temperature. A derivation of the Monteith (1965 and 1973) and Penman (1948) equation is used to predict the difference between canopy leaf temperature and the ambient air temperature outside the canopy. Default parameter settings for both the transpiration and leaf temperature modules were as for Campbell (1977). Leaf transpiration and leaf temperature are not independent quantities so an iterative procedure is used to establish their respective equilibrium values.

WIMOVAC contains a database of standard soil types and the ability to input characteristics of other 'user-defined' soils. The soil database contains a description of soil appearance, volumetric field-holding capacity, volumetric wilting point and critical threshold value. The field-holding capacity is the maximum amount of water that a given soil is able to hold before runoff occurs, the wilting point is the soil water content at which plants growing on the soil are unable to abstract further water and the critical threshold value is the soil water content at which soil dry-down processes due to plant uptake within the model are switched. The model assumes that soil dry-down results from runoff and evaporation of water at the soil surface, percolation to lower layers and uptake by the plant canopy. If the soil water content is greater than the critical threshold value the canopy uptake of water is assumed to equal the canopy potential transpiration rate, assuming no stomatal resistance to leaf water loss. If the soil water content is less than the critical threshold value and greater than the wilting point value canopy water uptake is assumed to equal the actual canopy transpiration rate, which is limited by stomatal resistance. At a soil water content less than the wilting point value the canopy is assumed to be unable to extract further water from the soil. A multiple layered approach to soil dry-down (from Johnson, 1993) is used in WIMOVAC.

WIMOVAC allows the simulation of leaf or canopy microclimate, and water and CO_2 exchange over a diurnal, weekly or annual time course using climate records or generated macroclimate. Macroclimate conditions are obtained from inputs of latitude and mean precipitation and temperature. The daily course of solar radiation for a given latitude is predicted from the equations of Long (1991) or can be input from actual radiation records. WIMOVAC provides spreadsheet style data handling facilities for the input of climate records to the model. Finally, the plant growth module of

WIMOVAC allows the user to specify how the daily carbon gain by the crop will be partitioned between different organs and how this partitioning is affected by developmental stage, defined by degree days, temperature, soil moisture and nitrogen availability. For example, it would allow evaluation of the trade-off between senescence and retranslocation prior to a frost kill of the canopy versus lost photosynthesis during the autumn due to earlier senescence. The current version of WIMOVAC is free software which may be copied and redistributed under the terms of the GNU General Public License, published by the Free Software Foundation. The copyright is retained by the authors.

Example application of WIMOVAC

Figure 4.5a shows a WIMOVAC simulation of the progression of stem, leaf and rhizome dry mass for the average climate conditions of the Writtle College site in south-eastern England. Predicted maximum shoot dry mass is *c.* 25 t ha^{-1}, declining to *c.* 20 t ha^{-1} at the end of December. This is explained by the loss of leaf mass nd by some translocation to the rhizomes. These values are similar to those observed at this field site (Beale & Long, 1995).

Although *Miscanthus* x *giganteus* has proved highly productive in southern England, it nevertheless loses potential production because its canopy develops late, relative to many C$_3$ perennial grasses. Canopy closure typically occurs in May, yet radiation levels of *c.* 10 MJ d^{-1} are received in March and April, and are wholly or partially lost due to low interception at this time. The major barrier to intercepting this radiation appears to be the temperature threshold of leaf extension growth. Variation in the threshold temperature for leaf extension growth has been identified within *Miscanthus* germplasm. Would there be a significant theoretical benefit of selecting for a *Miscanthus* with the characteristics of *Miscanthus* x *giganteus*, but a 2°C lower threshold for growth? Figure 4.5b shows a test of this question with WIMOVAC. If the threshold temperature for growth could be lowered by 2°C, then dry matter production would commence about a month earlier and by day 230, *c.* 2 t ha^{-1} more shoot mass would have accumulated. However, a lower threshold temperature may also accelerate development, with the result that flower initiation and cessation of leaf growth will be earlier and the gain in dry matter could be lost (Figure 4.5b). If, however, a lower threshold leaf extension temperature could be coupled with a higher thermal requirement for flowering, such that flowering occurred at the same time regardless of the minimum threshold temperature for growth, then dry matter yield in December could be increased by *c.* 4 t ha^{-1}.

A key factor in the choice of *Miscanthus* as a biomass crop has been its use of C$_4$ photosynthesis. It is well known that C$_4$ photosynthesis increases light use efficiency in warm climates where photorespiration will represent a significant loss of production in C$_3$ photosynthesis. In colder climates photorespiration represents only a small loss of efficiency and the benefit of C$_4$ photosynthesis may be small or abolished. Is the high potential productivity in the cool climate of southern England of *Miscanthus* in any way a result of its C$_4$ photosynthesis, or is it a result of other characters? WIMOVAC is used here to examine this question. Figure 4.5c suggests that if C$_3$ photosynthesis is substituted for C$_4$, keeping all other plant characteristics constant, dry matter gain over the period of most active growth would be decreased by about

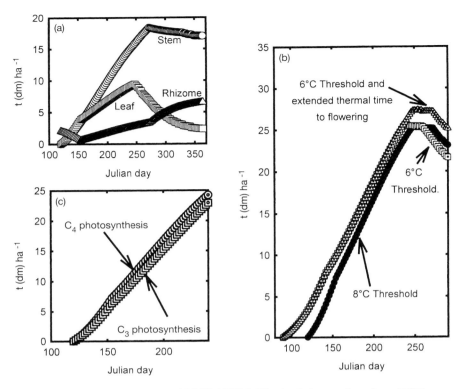

Figure 4.5. Some example simulations with WIMOVAC. The simulations are for a site at 52°N, assuming the mean temperature conditions for Writtle College, Essex, in south-eastern England. Initial rhizome mass, prior to spring regrowth, is assumed to be 2 t (dm) ha⁻¹. (a) The progression of leaf, stem and rhizome mass over the growing season. (b) Illustrates how simulated dry matter production would be affected if the threshold for growth was 6°C, as opposed to the assumed 8°C. Because the lower threshold would accelerate the development and the onset of flowering (where replacement of leaves ceases) a further line illustrates the effect of the lower threshold temperature coupled with a greater thermal time requirement for the onset of flowering. (c) A hypothetical simulation in which C₄ photosynthesis is replaced by C₃ photosynthesis.

1.5 t ha⁻¹, about 7%, suggesting that even at this relatively northerly location in Europe there is still a significant theoretical gain from C_4 photosynthesis in a biomass crop.

4.4 *Miscanthus* Yields Reported in Field Trials

M. x *giganteus* productivity trials started in Europe in Denmark and Germany in the 1980s. In 1990 a small European project (JOUB-CT90-0069) funded field trials in Denmark, England and Ireland. In 1993, the European *Miscanthus* Network (EMN) project funded 16 partners to make field trials across Europe. This section contains two sub-sections. The first sub-section outlines results from the EMN project. The second sub-section outlines yields obtained from field trials carried out in other projects in Germany, Denmark, Austria and Sweden.

4.4.1 *European* Miscanthus *Network Productivity trial*

The principle objective of EMN was to determine the sustainable yield of *M.* x *giganteus* as a low input agricultural crop over a wide distribution in the EU. To meet this objective 15 partner's sites were identified for trials throughout Europe (Figure 4.6). A common protocol for the establishment and management of these trials was drawn up. All the trials used the same source of plant material (micro-propagated plants from Piccoplant, Oldenburg, Germany). These were supplied as 20 cm tall plantlets in peat pots with 3 to 6 shoots and were hand planted into a ploughed and rotivated seed-bed at a planting density of 4 plants m^{-2} in May and June 1993. The protocol recommended three blocks containing three 10×10 m plots treated with 0, 60 or 120 kg N ha^{-1}. Plants were irrigated at most sites several times immediately following planting. Thereafter irrigation was used only at the more southern sites (partner nos 4, 6, 9, 12, 13, Figure 4.6). Weed control varied at different sites depending on the local weed pressure. Both chemical and mechanical methods were used. Harvest time was recommended as between December and February depending on local climatic conditions at the sites.

Establishment of the micro-propagated plants in the first year was successful at all sites, and plants grew until the first frost in autumn. However, at a number of northern sites re-growth from the rhizome was not observed in the following spring. These included sites at partners 2, 3, 5, 8, 14 and 15 (see Figure 4.6). Where winter failures occurred, trials were either replanted or, where available at the same site, yields were obtained from older *M.* x *giganteus* trials which had successfully over-wintered in the first winter following planting. These older trials were mainly established with rhizome propagated plantlets.

Harvestable yields for each of the sites are shown in Figure 4.7. In general, the yields from the plots receiving the highest nitrogen fertilisation (120 kg N ha^{-1}) were used, but at some sites the average of all fertilisation rates were used because of insignificant differences in the nitrogen affect. Differences in the growing conditions are given in the legend. At sites where over-wintering problems occurred, yields from older plantations were substituted. In northern Germany (BFH, partner 14), only two years of data were presented because the trials were re-established in 1994 and these survived better than the first planting in 1993.

It can be seen that, in general, the yield increased dramatically from year 1 (establishment year) to year 2 in all sites with more gradual yield increases in subsequent years. In Greece and Sicily where irrigation was used, ceiling yields of >26 t ha^{-1} were reached in the second year (Figure 4.7). In the UK ceiling yields of >15 t ha^{-1} were reached in Essex and at ADAS Authur Rickwood in two years without irrigation. In Lisbon and central Italy (with limited irrigation) ceiling yields reached 24 and *c.* 18 t ha^{-1} after three years. In southern Germany (LWG) ceiling yields of about 10 t ha^{-1} were attained after three years, but these low yields were attributed to poor site conditions locally and are not representative of the region. In northern Germany (FAL) and Ireland (TCD) ceiling yields reached after five years were 22 and 14 t ha^{-1} respectively. It is clear that ceiling *Miscanthus* yields are attained more quickly in warmer climates and that yields are higher than in cooler climates, especially when water supply to the crop is adequate.

In general, C_4 plants have a higher nitrogen use efficiency than C_3 plants.

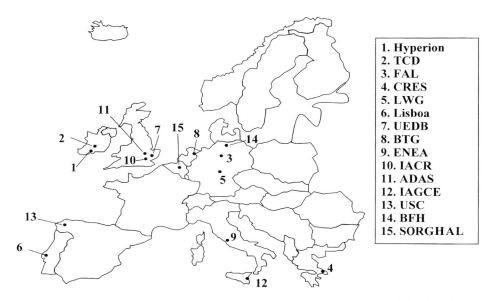

Figure 4.6. Geographical distribution of the trials in the European Miscanthus *Productivity Network. See Preface for key to acronyms*

Investigation of the effect of N on *Miscanthus* yields has produced inconclusive results. Most partners report no significant nitrogen effects in the early years of crop growth. It was postulated that the previous cropping history may have an impact on the nitrogen supply in the early years of the plantation, with plants utilising residual nitrogen which has been retained in the soil from previous crops. In the later years of the trial some partners noted that the crop performed better in the high nitrogen plots (120 kg ha^{-1}). As the crop gets older and yield increases, additional N fertilisation may be required; this is indicated by the fact that the nutrient offtake of *Miscanthus* increases as the crop gets older. Further research is required to establish the nutrient demand of the mature crop. A number of partners have linked irrigation levels to nitrogen uptake, reporting that where adequate soil water was maintained during the growth period the effects of nitrogen were increased. This again would appear to have a greater effect on older plantations. All partners reported that responses to fertiliser will vary according to soil type and nutrient supply capacity.

Moisture content at harvest ranged from 25–40% in southern countries and 30–60% in more northern countries. The lower moisture contents in southern European countries may facilitate the implementation of autumn harvesting. However, further research is required to define the timing of autumn harvesting in order to achieve the highest dry matter yields without adversely affecting survival ability and vigour of the resprouting plants. Genotypic variation in moisture content at harvest was observed in LWG's screening experiments where new cultivars had a moisture content at harvest of 20–30% compared with a moisture content of 44–50% for *M.* x *giganteus*.

The most important limitation to biomass production from *M.* x *giganteus* in northern Europe was poor over-wintering in the first year following planting. More

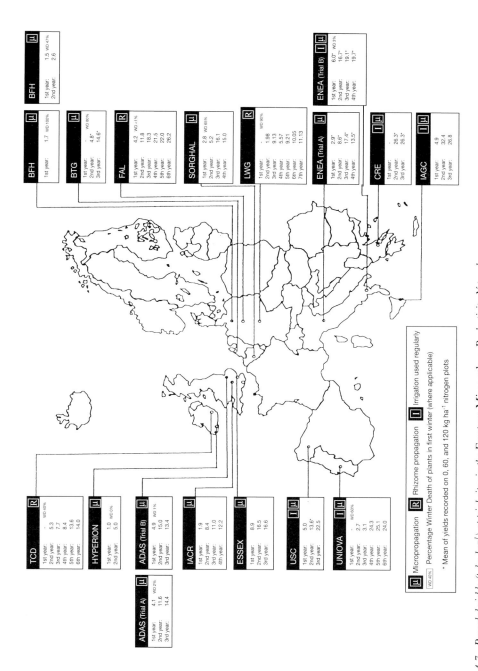

Figure 4.7. Recorded yields (t dm ha⁻¹) at trial sites in the European Miscanthus Productivity Network.

problems were encountered with the 1993 plantings in the EMN trials with micro-propagated plants than in earlier trials which used rhizome propagated plantlets. The reason for the poor over-wintering were not clearly identified. At some sites with low temperatures and or rainfall during the first growing season the small micro-propagated plants grew too slowly and produced practically no rhizome reserve from which new growth could start in the following spring. Sub-zero soil temperatures can also kill the shallow rhizomes. A particular problem for *M.* x *giganteus* in the first year is the lack of dormancy at the end of the growing season, and plants can re-grow when temperatures rise to about 10°C. In climates which have winter temperatures which fluctuate rapidly between sub-zero and +10°C it has been anticipated that death occurs in a cold spell immediately after a warm period. In the second and subsequent winters no over-wintering losses were reported, and these may be attributed to normal induction of dormancy in the autumn, and deeper rhizomes which are positioned in a more thermally stable environment than those of first year plants. The key factors which determine susceptibility to low temperatures need to be positively identified through further research.

In spring time, new shoot growth is limited to the frost-free period. In southern climates growth starts earlier than in more northern sites. With sufficient water, plants can utilise more radiation and therefore growth rates are higher. Here, at a plant density of 4 plants m^{-2}, a closed canopy forms in most climates during the second growing season. Self thinning of slower growing shoots occurs as the season progresses. Plant spacing influences the rate at which the ceiling yield is reached. Since canopy closure is reached more quickly in southern climates, low planting densities may be more economic.

Water availability to the crop during the growing season is the main limiting factor for growth in southern European countries and one important factor in yield determination at low rainfall sites in northern Europe. The extent of yield reduction through insufficient water depends not only on climate but also on soil type. Models that account for water restricted growth, such as WIMOVAC, need to be developed further. Genotypic variation in response to water deficit may be important to optimise water use efficiency.

In conclusion, the *Miscanthus* Network Productivity trials have shown that winter yields from *M.* x *giganteus* ranged between 7 and 26 t dm ha^{-1} following the third growing season. Highest non-irrigated yields were 15–19 t dm ha^{-1}. Ceiling yields can be reached in two years, but may take up to five years at some sites. Poor over-winter survival of newly established *M.* x *giganteus* plantations from micro-propagated plantlets were observed at many northern sites. More reliable establishment techniques need to developed for *M.* x *giganteus* or new genotypes bred with better over-wintering capacities.

4.4.2 *Yields Reported in Trials outside the* Miscanthus *Productivity Network*

This section outlines the *Miscanthus* yields which were measured in field trials which were not part of the *Miscanthus* Productivity Network.

Yields Reported in Germany

In Germany, a number of field trials were established from 1990–92 in sites with varying soil types and climatic conditions. The geographical distribution of the sites is shown in Figure 4.8 while soil types are shown in Figure 4.9. Plant development and dry matter yield were recorded at all sites using a standard protocol, done firstly by Veba Öel GmbH and subsequently by the Federal Research Centre of Agriculture (FAL). A description of methods and results is given by Schwarz K.–U. *et al.* (1994; 1995a).

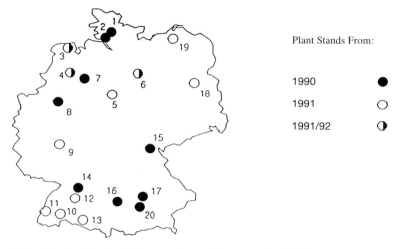

Figure 4.8. Experimental sites in Germany. Source: Schwarz et al., 1995a.

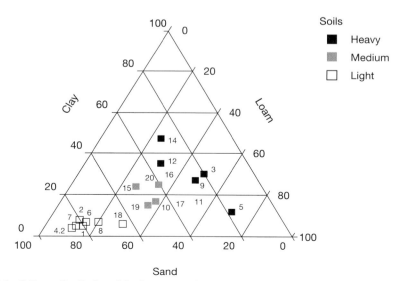

Figure 4.9. Soil type distribution of the German experimental sites. Source: Schwarz et al., 1995a

Yields were measured in November/December in order to determine the full biological yield after translocation of assimilates to the rhizomes but before significant leaf fall. Mean *Miscanthus* crop yield at the trial sites increased during the first few years until it reached an apparently stable level of 18–20 t dm ha $^{-1}$ in 1993; while shoot density and crop height showed a similar trend (Figure 4.10). There was significant variation in dry matter yield between sites for the first four years (Figure 4.11). Yields were found to increase faster on sandy soils than on clay, however clay soils gave higher mature yields. Ground water levels were also found to affect yields with higher yields being observed on sites which had a higher ground water table.

Climatic conditions were found to affect productivity. Figure 4.12 shows the correlation between yield, temperature sum and precipitation in 1992. The effect of planting density on yield was assessed at two sites. Initially it was found that planting density correlated positively with yield, shoot growth and plant height. However, after four years, the effect of different planting densities was insignificant (Figure 4.13). Finally, the effects of soil nitrogen levels were also investigated at the same two sites. A positive correlation between yield and soil nitrogen content was observed in only one out of the four years.

In conclusion, at maturity, yields of 18–20 t dm ha $^{-1}$ were observed in the German trials. It was observed that yields were dependent on soil type, water availability and climatic conditions, but independent of planting densities and soil nitrogen levels.

Yields Reported in Denmark

The first *Miscanthus* field trial in Denmark was established in 1983 at the research station in Hornum. In 1989, 10 large-scale *Miscanthus* plantations (each approx. 1 ha.) were established at sites under a variety of growing conditions. These plantations were managed using practical farming conditions and methods and harvested using commercially available machinery. The harvest of *Miscanthus* from the Danish field trials and large-scale plantations was generally carried out in April when the dry matter percentage was above 75%. Consequently, the yield results presented in this section do not represent the full *Miscanthus* biological yields due to the loss of leaves and stems during the winter period (Figure 4.14 shows the biomass accumulation over time).

Dry matter yields in the field trial which was established in 1983 in a loamy sand soil ranged between 8 and 15 t ha $^{-1}$ dm in most years. However during the 1990s, the yields were considerably lower. This may be partly due to unfavourable climatic conditions (drought and late spring frosts), however, it may also be due to an age effect (Jørgensen, 1996). Weeds normally present no problem in fully established plots of *Miscanthus* as the crop is very competitive. However, after the years of adverse climatic conditions, the crop was less competitive and herbicide applications were necessary after 1995.

The effect of planting density on yield was investigated by using four different planting densities in the field trial which was established in 1983. Initially, a significant positive correlation between planting density and yield was observed. However, as was the case in the German experiments, this relationship was eliminated with time (Jørgensen, 1996).

Yields from the larger plantations which were established in 1989, grown under practical farming conditions and harvested by commercially available machinery in

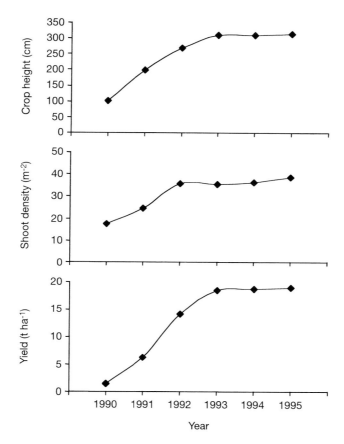

Figure 4.10. Crop height, shoot density and dry matter yields at German sites established in 1990. Source: Kai-Uwe Schwarz, pers. comm.

the spring are shown in Figure 4.15. As observed by Nielsen (1987a) and Schwarz *et al.* (1995a), production increases faster on sandy soils but long-term yields are better on loamy soils. Mean dry matter yield harvested in spring seems to have stabilised at 7–9 t ha^{-1} comparable to yields obtained in a field trial of similar age under low input research conditions in Hornum.

Yields Reported in Austria and Switzerland

Miscanthus production was investigated in Austria on four sites with three different soil types and in regions with different climatic conditions and altitudes of 200–300 metres. The trial was established in 1989, the planting density used was 1 plant per m^2 and the experimental area was 450 m^2. Further experimental details are available in Schwarz (1993, 1994) and Schwarz H. *et al.* (1994).

Hand harvesting was carried out in November/December and in February of each year. *Miscanthus* yields were found to stabilise at about 20 t ha^{-1} dm after the third growing season (1991–92). However, a wide variability in yield between the different

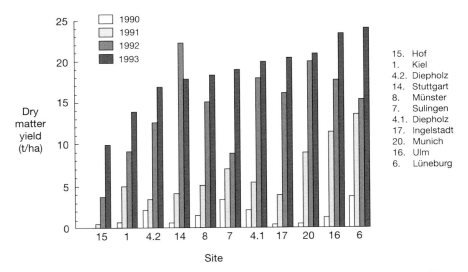

Figure 4.11. Dry matter yields in the first four growing seasons at different German sites. Source: Schwarz et al., *1995a*

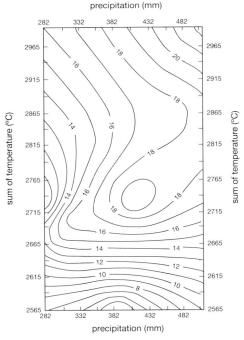

Figure 4.12. Dry matter yield (t ha⁻¹) in relation to the temperature sum and precipitation in the growing season, 1/5–31/10 (Schwarz et al., *1995a). At lower heat sums yield is largely affected by temperature and, to a lesser extent, by the amount of precipitation. Under higher temperature conditions the amount of rainfall has an increasing influence on the yield and there is an interaction between both factors. Highest yields of more than 20 t/ha DM were reached at temperature sums of over 2900°C and rainfalls of more than 430 mm during the vegetation period (May–October).*

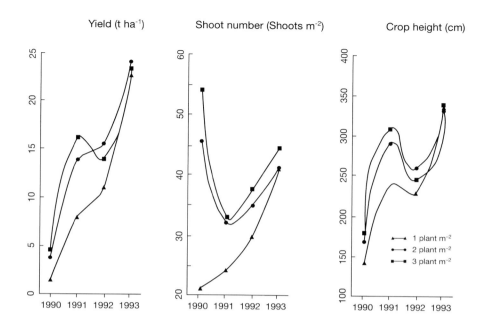

Figure 4.13. Yield, shoot number and crop height versus planting density at a site in Germany. Source: Schwarz et al., 1995a.

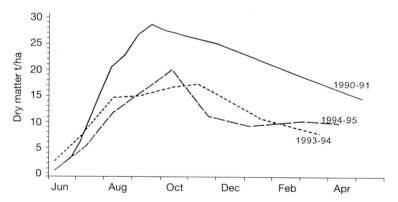

Figure 4.14. Biomass accumulation and loss of M. x giganteus *in three years. Source: Jørgensen, 1996.*

sites was observed (Figure 4.16). This was attributed to climatic factors, particularly rainfall. It was calculated that a precipitation of 700 mm was required in order to obtain higher yields.

Yield, water content and nitrogen content were found to decrease significantly during the 12 weeks from November/December to the end of February. The yield decrease from November to February was between 1.3 and 5.9 t ha^{-1} dm while the water content decrease was between 11 and 28% and the nitrogen content decrease was between 0 and 2 g kg^{-1} dm. There were no clear effects of climate and site on the

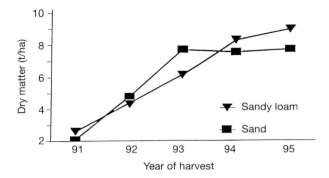

Figure 4.15. Spring yields of M. x giganteus *established in 1989, grown under farm conditions and harvested by machine. Source: Hansen, 1996.*

yield, water content and nitrogen content decreases which were observed during the 12 week period between November/December and the end of February.

Two *Miscanthus* trials were established in Switzerland in 1992. The first was on a sandy loam soil in Zürich while the second was on a brown soil in Anwill. Harvesting was carried out annually in March at dry matter contents between 60% and 80%. As was the case in Austria, plant establishment was faster than at German and Danish sites with yields of 6–12 t ha^{-1} dm being harvested after the second year of production (Figure 4.17). The highest yields were recorded in the sandy loam site at Zürich. Small but similar effects of planting density and fertiliser applications were observed at both sites. Yields were observed to be higher at high planting densities (1 plant m^{-2} compared to 0.7 plant m^{-2}), however, this effect was only observed in the first years of growth. Fertiliser levels (40–50 kg N ha^{-1}) were not found to influence yield in the first years of growth.

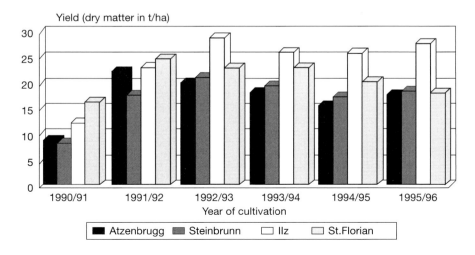

Figure 4.16. Yield (t dm ha^{-1}) on four sites in Austria from the second to the seventh year of growth. (Dry matter contents between 50 and 70%).

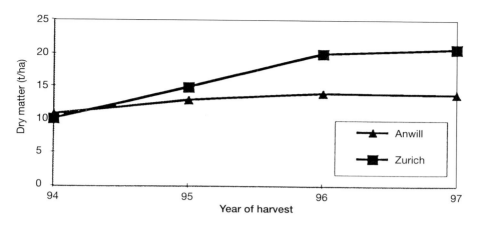

Figure 4.17. Yields at two Swiss sites (density of 1 plant m⁻²).

4.4.3 *Conclusions from* Miscanthus *yields*

This chapter has outlined the results of *Miscanthus* trials which were carried out as either (i) part of the European *Miscanthus* Productivity Network, or (ii) independent trials. The factors which were found to influence yields in these trials were also identified. It can be seen that the results of the independent trials agree to a great extent with the results of the *Miscanthus* Network in a number of areas. These are outlined below.

- Winter survival of newly established *M.* x *giganteus* plantations from micropropagated plantlets was successful in southern Europe but was found to be unreliable in northern Europe. The factors have not been identified but are most probably associated with insufficient growth rates in the first growing season to develop sufficient rhizome.
- Different nitrogen fertiliser applications were seldom reflected in crop yields. This is partly due to the efficient cycling of nitrogen in and out of the rhizome and the lower requirements of plants with C_4 photosynthesis for nitrogen.
- In northern Europe ceiling yields range from 15 to 25 t ha^{-1} y^{-1} at the end of the growing season. Higher productivity has been recorded in central and southern Europe where yields range from 25 to 40 t ha^{-1} y^{-1} but here irrigation is required.
- Moisture contents in autumn-harvested *Miscanthus* are higher than in spring but harvestable yields in spring are 30–50% lower than in autumn. Optimum harvest time depends on the climatic conditions at the site.
- Higher planting density increases the rate at which the ceiling yield is attained. At northern sites this requires longer because growing seasons are cooler (typically 3–4 years), while at southern sites ceiling yields are reached in two years. Yield crashes due to plant overcrowding are possible, but as yet little concrete evidence for this exists.

5 | Miscanthus *Breeding and Improvement*

by U. Jørgensen and H.-J. Muhs

with contributions from N. El Bassam,
A. Eppel-Hotz, C. Petrini and J. C. Clifton-Brown

5.1 Introduction

Although *M.* x *giganteus* has been attracting much attention as a high-yielding biomass crop in recent years, further development of the crop is required in order to improve characters such as yield, cold tolerance and other features related to its industrial use.

This chapter outlines the current state-of-the-art of *Miscanthus* crop breeding and improvement in Europe. The chapter is divided into three parts. The first part describes research which has been carried out on *Miscanthus* crop breeding as part of a European research project, EMI (European *Miscanthus* Improvement). The second and third parts of the chapter describe the laboratory and field screening of *Miscanthus* genotypes, which was carried out as part of the *Miscanthus* Productivity Network.

5.2 Breeding Techniques

Very little information exists on the relevant techniques for *Miscanthus* crop breeding. This is due to the fact that it is a new crop and therefore, until now, there has been little interest in crop breeding and improvement. However, two projects are currently being funded by the EU (DG VI). The first is 'EMI: broadening the genetic base, testing genotypes and development of breeding methods' (1997–2000), coordinated by the University of Hohenheim, Germany, and aims to develop methods to enable more efficient breeding of improved *Miscanthus* varieties. The second is 'Reduction of fouling, slagging and corrosion characteristics of *Miscanthus* for power and heat generation using biotechnology (BIOMIS)' (1998–2002), coordinated by Plant Research International, Wageningen, The Netherlands, and aims to improve *Miscanthus* genotypes for combustion quality traits using molecular techniques.

5.2.1 Background and Objectives

Future *Miscanthus* varieties will need to have improved characteristics such as higher yields, resistance to biotic and abiotic stress factors and other specific characters relating to its use for industrial and energy-related purposes. In addition, varieties will need to have a high overwintering rate and produce non-viable seeds to prevent

Miscanthus from becoming a pest plant. Much of the work of EMI is focused on the production of varieties with non-viable or sterile seeds.

Sterility or decreased fertility can be achieved by triploidy, interspecific hybridisation or a combination of both. The sterility is due to irregular chromosome pairing during meiosis as several chromosomes will be present as trivalents (in triploids) or as monovalents (in interspecific hybrids). Thus, gametes with different numbers of chromosomes are produced during meiosis, resulting in decreased gamete fertility.

Out of more than 20 *Miscanthus* species, only *M. tinctorius*, *M. sinensis* and *M. sacchariflorus* are of interest for biomass production or industrial uses. *M. tinctorius* is used for thatching in Japan, but no growing experience is available in Europe. *M. sinensis* is diploid ($2n=2x=38$) while *M. sacchariflorus* is di- or tetraploid ($2n=4x=76$). The most abundantly grown clone in Europe is *M.* x *giganteus*, a pollen sterile triploid ($2n=3x=57$) hybrid between the diploid *M. sinensis* and tetraploid *M. sacchariflorus*. Problems with overwintering during establishment have been observed with *M.* x *giganteus*, especially in northern Europe, and results in Denmark have shown comparable biomass yields from plantations of *M.* x *giganteus* and selected *M. sinensis* clones (Jørgensen, 1997).

The EMI project hypothesised that Europe may be divided into several ecological zones and varieties with different genome compositions may have to be developed for these zones, e.g. *M. sinensis* may be more suited in northern Europe, whereas *M. sacchariflorus* requires warmer temperatures and may be better adapted to the Mediterranean area while hybrids like *M.* x *giganteus* may perform better in central Europe. The main effort in the EMI project was to produce either vegetatively or seed propagated sterile varieties for large-scale plantations.

5.2.2 *Plant Production*

Sterility can be attained with both seed production and vegetative propagation. Seed production is normally less expensive than vegetative propagation, however, seedlings need to be genetically homogeneous and fast-growing in the field with a high number of seeds or seedlings having to be planted per hectare. Whether this is possible depends on the cost of seed production and establishment.

In order to choose between propagation methods, different parameters such as the combining ability of clones, seed set, genetic variation of important characters and the efficiency of propagation techniques have to be evaluated. The method of propagation chosen will influence the choice of breeding strategy.

5.2.3 *Hybridisation*

To obtain varieties suited for the different ecological zones in Europe a number of *M. sinensis* and *M. sacchariflorus* clones at different ploidy levels were used as parents in crosses carried out within the EMI project. The parents in such crosses have to be compatible with each other and also need to flower at the same time to facilitate crossing. Good seed setting and seed germination rates are important factors that determine the economic feasibility of a breeding programme.

Flowering

Control of flowering is necessary in order to make specific crosses. Clones of *M. sinensis* are day-neutral and relatively easy to get into flower. *M. sacchariflorus* flowering was difficult to control, and was expected to be a short-day plant but other parameters may also affect flowering. The environmental conditions which induced flowering in *M. sacchariflorus* were investigated by the EMI project in controlled environments (with controlled temperature and photoperiod) and in the field in Portugal, Spain, Crete and Bulgaria, which should resemble the natural habitat of the species in Japan and China.

Seed Setting

Production of seeds in numbers high enough for large-scale plantations requires high seed-setting rates. Seed setting is affected by the parental combination of the cross as well as the environmental conditions under which the plants are grown.

Seed setting under conditions comparable to those of commercial seed production was investigated as part of the EMI project by growing selected parents either in greenhouses or in the field. The seed produced was sown under optimal conditions in order to determine the germination rates. The work with intraspecific hybrids mainly focused on the production of triploids by crosses of di- and tetraploid clones.

Seed Germination

In addition to good seed setting, adequate seed germination is also required for an efficient seed-based cropping system. Temperature and light conditions normally affect seed germination but this has not been thoroughly investigated for *Miscanthus*. Conditions that ensure optimum seed germination were determined in the EMI project by experiments in which light and temperature were controlled. The method developed was subsequently used to test seed quality produced under field conditions and germination percentages after controlled crosses. In addition, the effects of seed storage period on seed survival and germination rates were investigated.

5.2.4 Polyploidisation / Chromosome Doubling

An efficient method to produce tetraploids was necessary in order to produce intraspecific triploids. Antimitotic chemicals (e.g. colchicine and oryzalin) can be used to double the number of chromosomes, but the success of these methods varies according to plant species. Ploidy levels can be verified by flow cytometry.

Rhizome tips, axillary buds, immature inflorescences, shoot apices, leaf explants or embryonic callus may serve as targets for chromosome doubling. The tetraploid plants produced were to be used in crosses so the gamete-producing cells had to be tetraploid. Chimerism, though, may cause problems if it arises. Although generally considered true to type, plants produced from axillary buds are derived from many cells and the risk of chimeras is increased if axillary buds are used as targets for chromosome doubling.

Experiments carried out within the EMI project evaluated different explants and antimitotic chemicals, as well as their concentrations and exposure times. The ploidy level of plants produced was examined by flow cytometric analyses. Only one genotype was used in the initial development of the methods for polyploidisation but a number of genotypes were used later as starting material.

5.3 Genotype Screening

This section outlines the genotype evaluations which have been carried out as part of the *Miscanthus* Productivity Network, in order to determine genotypic variability in characters such as low temperature effects, frost tolerance, mineral content and biomass yield. New screening techniques were developed for the assessment of some characters and are described in the sections below.

5.3.1 Low Temperature

As detailed in earlier chapters, the length of the *Miscanthus* crop growing season is regulated by the occurrence of below 0°C air temperatures. In addition, ambient temperatures control the rate at which the canopy develops during the growing season. This is because temperature limits leaf expansion of *Miscanthus* with a threshold for growth between 5 and 10°C (Figure 5.1).

TCD have investigated the effect of temperature on leaf growth of a large number of genotypes. The screening method developed by TCD initially involved potting and maintenance of rhizome-propagated plants of the different genotypes in a growth

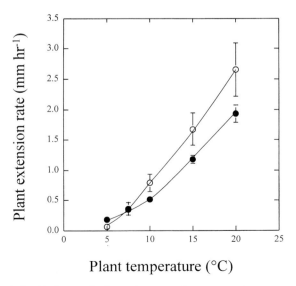

Figure 5.1. The relationship between leaf extension rate and temperature for two genotypes of Miscanthus. *Source: Clifton-Brown & Jones, 1997.*

room (20 ± 3°C) with optimum supply of water and nutrients. The genotypes were exposed to a temperature treatment of 18 h at 20°C and 11.5 h at 15, 10, 7.5 and 5°C. Plant expansion rates were measured using auxanometers and a mean plant expansion rate was calculated for each genotype at a given temperature.

It was found that the rates of plant extension of different genotypes varied widely at different temperatures, with plant expansion rates measured between 10 and 20°C for the genotypes varying between 3.0 and 4.7. It was observed that the genotypes with the highest expansion rates at 20°C did not have the highest expansion rates at 5°C. TCD also report that genotypes with lower threshold temperatures for leaf expansion are unlikely to have higher productivities than genotypes which have more rapid expansion rates at temperatures greater than 10°C. Breeding offers the potential to combine these characters. However, earlier canopy development will only result if the mechanisms in the fast-growing and low-temperature tolerant genotypes are compatible.

5.3.2 Frost Tolerance

Winter losses of young plantings of *Miscanthus* in the field is a fundamental problem during establishment. Proper field management can improve establishment (see Chapter 3) and thus reduce winter losses. Another approach to increase winter survival is the selection for frost-tolerant *Miscanthus* genotypes. However, no data relating to the development of screening methods or their application for the selection of frost-tolerant genotypes are available. BFH have carried out some investigations to test the Differential Thermal Analysis (DTA) method for screening frost tolerance. Their investigations (described below) were divided into two sections, these were (a) determination of the frost tolerance of different plant parts (i.e. leaves, shoots, rhizomes and buds), and (b) determination of the frost tolerance of different genotypes.

Differential Thermal Analysis (DTA)

The exact moment of freezing of a tissue sample can be determined by using the DTA to measure the temperature difference between a tissue sample and the surrounding receptacle. The ambient temperature around the sample was constantly reduced (cooling rates of 30 to 60°C per hour). There is a small rise in temperature due to the crystallisation warmth (exothermic reaction) at the moment when the sample freezes and the water in the tissue changes from the liquid to the solid phase. This peak in the temperature curve can be recorded precisely. The ambient temperature of the receptacle and the temperature of the tissue sample is assumed to be the same, when the cooling rate is slow enough.

The volume of the sample seems to influence the result, because in small samples the temperature at the start of the exothermic reaction is lower than the results from tests on the whole respective plant part. Therefore, the freezing temperatures of the sample tissue can only be estimated by a comparison within a series of samples tested or by using a standardised reference sample (e.g. wet tissue paper). The validity of the value of the reference sample needs to be rechecked from time to time.

The drawback of this method is that the used apparatus only allows measurement of small pieces of tissue at rapid cooling rates, which gives lower freezing temperatures and implies a higher frost tolerance than under field conditions. The method needs to be improved to get unbiased exothermic reaction temperatures.

Frost Tolerance of Different Tissue Types

Different tissue types of four *Miscanthus* clones were assessed by using a differential thermal analyser. The tissues analysed by BFH were from the roots, rhizomes, buds (dormant and flushing) stems, and leaves. Figure 5.2 gives the results of the DTA screening tests. As mentioned earlier, the temperatures given are the ambient temperatures prevailing around the tissue samples at the time of their freezing.

It can be seen that there is some variation between the different tissues but there is no indication of the existence of any trends between the different tissues analysed. BFH suggest that the variation between different tissues may be due to the fact that the samples had to be cut into small pieces of about 0.25 to 0.5 cm^3. The surface area of the sample and the period between preparation and testing of the sample varied, which led to the evaporation of different amounts of water from the samples. In general, a lower water content decreases the freezing temperatures, therefore the frost tolerance may have been over-estimated in some samples due to water loss prior to sampling. The actual freezing temperatures of the tissue are expected to range between –2°C and –5°C.

The rhizomes and appending buds would be expected to have a higher frost tolerance as they are the overwintering organs, however this was not found to be the case. BFH suggest that survival of rhizomes and buds of *Miscanthus* crops in the field during frost periods may be due to the fact that they are protected and insulated by the typical micro-structure of the plant stock and the surrounding soil rather than

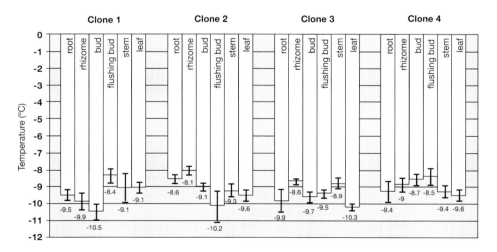

Figure 5.2. Differential Thermal Analysis (DTA) in different plant tissues of four Miscanthus *clones in August, 1995. As reference a sample of moist tissue paper was used, which froze at –7.5°C. The absolute values given have to be put in relation to the freezing temperature of the reference.*

their inherent frost tolerance. Alternatively, frost tolerance may only develop in these organs after dormancy has been induced in autumn or early winter. If this was the case, frost tolerance would not have been detected in the tests described here, as screening was carried out on young plants which had been grown in the greenhouse for some months (this represents a state usually reached by August when grown under field conditions).

Frost Tolerance of Different Genotypes

The results given in Figure 5.2 not only show that there are no significant differences in frost tolerance between the tissues tested, but also that there is no difference between the four clones. In another experiment the four clones were tested as well as the *M.* x *giganteus* 'Hornum' clone. This test was done in the spring on leaf tissue (4–5 leaf stage) of three-year-old plants. The results are given in Figure 5.3. The freezing temperatures were found to be much higher than those recorded in the earlier experiment (Figure 5.2), which can be explained by the younger state of the tissues tested in the second experiment. Figure 5.3 indicates that there is very little variability in frost tolerance between the different clones. Other investigators agree that frost tolerance doesn't vary much between clones of *M.* x *giganteus* (J. C. Clifton-Brown, pers. comm.). However, distinct differences in frost tolerance are reported to have been found between different accessions of *M. sinensis* and *M. floridulus*. It may be possible to use cross-breeding to combine the high growth potential of *M.* x *giganteus* with frost tolerance of either *M. sinensis* or *M. floridulus* (M. Deuter, pers. comm.).

A third differential thermal analysis compared the frost tolerance of six horticultural *Miscanthus* cultivars and *M.* x *giganteus* (clone Hornum). This was done in August on leaf tissue of five- to eight-year old field-grown plants. The frost tolerance levels which were recorded are the highest of the three experiments which were carried out (Figure

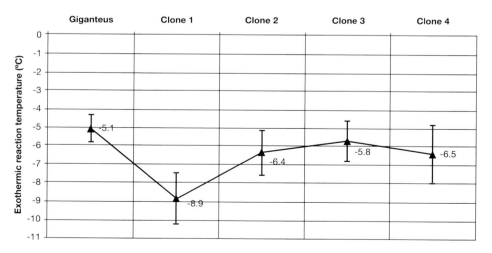

Figure 5.3. Temperature analysis on leaves of four Miscanthus *clones and* M. x giganteus *clone 'Hornum', grown in the greenhouse and measured at spring (May 1997, cooling rate 60°C h⁻¹).*

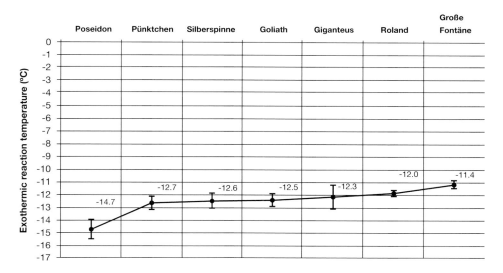

Figure 5.4. Differential temperature analysis of leaf tissue of different field-grown Miscanthus *cultivars measured in August, 1996. ('Giganteus' refers to the clone 'Hornum', cooling rate 60°C h⁻¹, exothermic reaction temperature of wet tissue paper = –8.6°C).*

5.4). BFH attribute this to the fact that the plants were older and they had been growing in the field rather than the greenhouse. 'Poseidon' exhibits a significantly higher frost tolerance than any of the other cultivars, but there is no significant difference in frost tolerance between any of the other cultivars.

5.3.3 Biomass Yields

A large number of *Miscanthus* genotypes have been evaluated for their yields and other productivity-related characteristics. This section describes the evaluations which were carried out by FAL and LWG in Germany, A. Biotec in Italy and DIAS in Denmark.

Genotype Evaluations Carried Out in Germany by FAL

Genotype evaluations were carried out to investigate the productivity of a range of *Miscanthus* genotypes. Two evaluation trials were set up in 1989 and 1991 respectively. In the first trial, three evaluation plots (planting density of 1 plant m⁻²) were established (one at Braunschweig and two at Veitshöchheim). No establishment or winter losses were observed. Recorded yields are given in Table 5.1 and Figure 5.5. It can be seen that first-year dry matter yields ranged from 0.6–2.7 t ha⁻¹ in Braunschweig. *M.* x *giganteus*, *M. sin.* Goliath and *M. sin.* Gr. Fontäne continuously reached the highest yields each year at all three locations. *M. sin.* Goliath had the highest mean dry matter yield (19.9 t ha⁻¹) over the six years, followed by *M.* x *giganteus* (19.3 t ha⁻¹) and *M. sin.* Gr. Fontäne (15.1 t ha⁻¹) at Braunschweig.

Table 5.1. Dry matter yield (t ha⁻¹) of Miscanthus *genotypes at Braunschweig from 1990 (first growing season) to 1995, and six years (3rd to 9th year) in Veitshöchheim. (Veits. + = high production site, Veits. − = low production site).*

	1990	1991	1992	Braunschweig 1993	1994	1995	mean	Veitshöchheim Veits. +	Veits. −
M. x giganteus	2.4	16.5	17.0	23.8	30.0	26.0	19.3	15–24	5–10
M. sin. Goliath	2.7	12.5	16.3	26.9	32.3	28.6	19.9	10–19	5–6
M. sin. Grosse Fontäne	1.4	13.1	11.0	20.0	22.9	22.3	15.1	10–15	3–4
M. sin. Silberturm	1.2	8.0	8.5	17.4	19.4	24.0	13.1		
M. sin. Malepartus	1.3	6.9	10.8	13.8	19.1	18.4	11.7		
M. sin. Undine	0.6	6.9	8.1	14.9	22.1	21.4	12.3		
M. sin. Wetterfahne	1.2	6.6	6.6	13.2	16.0	13.5	9.5		
Mean	1.5	10.1	11.2	18.6	23.1	22.0	14.4		

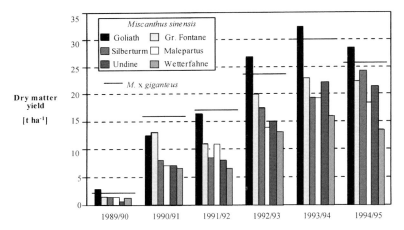

Figure 5.5. Dry matter yield (t ha⁻¹) of different Miscanthus *genotypes at Braunschweig, Germany, from 1990 (first growing season) to 1995.*

The trials were harvested in January or February. Dry matter content was found to range from 50.1 to 88.9% in all six harvests with *M.* x *giganteus* having the lowest dry matter content (Table 5.2). *M.* x *giganteus* is characterised by a significantly lower content of leaf material than the other genotypes: during winter the leaves completely dry out while the stem material remains moist. This may explain the lower dry matter content of *M.* x *giganteus*. In addition, it was observed that earlier flowering forms of *Miscanthus sinensis* have a higher dry matter content. *M.* x *giganteus* rarely flowers in northern European countries.

In the second trial three evaluation plots were again established at the same sites

Table 5.2. Dry matter content (%) of Miscanthus *genotypes at Braunschweig from 1990 to 1995 at the same harvest date in spring.*

	1990	1991	1992	1993	1994	1995	Mean
M. x *giganteus*	50.1	66.7	58.6	66.6	56.0	63.1	60.2
M. sin. Goliath	60.6	76.7	88.9	78.3	59.4	67.7	71.9
M. sin. Malepartus	72.6	72.9	86.4	77.0	68.4	69.8	74.5
M. sin. Silberturm	62.6	75.9	88.2	79.0	54.6	73.9	72.4
M. sin. Grosse Fontäne	65.6	67.6	72.5	75.2	60.7	65.4	67.8
M. sin. Undine	70.5	75.2	94.9	77.1	68.6	69.9	76.0
M. sin. Wetterfahne	70.6	76.0	90.8	75.1	52.0	75.2	73.3
Mean	64.6	73.0	82.9	75.5	60.0	69.3	70.9

Table 5.3. Dry matter yield (t ha $^{-1}$) of Miscanthus *genotypes at Braunschweig from 1992 (first growing season) to 1995, and six years (3rd to 9th year) in Veitshöchheim. (Veits. + = high production site, Veits. − = low production site).*

	Braunschweig					Veitshöchheim	
	1992	1993	1994	1995	mean	Veits.+	Veits.−
M. x *giganteus*	2.3	7.8	14.4	22.2	11.7	15–24	5–10
M. sin. Silberfeder	0.6	9.8	21.8	35.8	17.0	8–15	2–5
M. sin. Pünktchen	1.6	11.1	24.4	30.9	17.0		
M. sin. Poseidon	3.2	11.9	17.2	26.6	14.8		
M. sin. Silberspinne	1.7	12.1	19.6	22.9	14.1		
M. sin. Goliath	0.7	6.7	18.5	25.0	12.8		
M. sin. Grosse Fontäne	0.4	10.3	14.6	19.0	11.0		
M. sin. Kaskade	2.4	8.5	12.7	15.8	9.8		
M. sin. Roland	1.1	5.5	14.1	15.8	9.1		
M. sin. Wetterfahne	1.2	7.8	11.8	13.8	8.6		
M. sin. Gracillimus	0.5	6.0	13.6	13.7	8.4	6–17	2–2
M. sin. Spätgrün	1.4	2.6	5.5	7.4	4.2		
M. sin. Malepartus	0.4	5.3	9.4	13.5	7.2		
M. sin. Silberturm	0.9	6.5	8.3	11.4	6.8		
M. sin. Undine	0.5	4.8	1.1	13.7	5.0		
M. sin. Giraffe	1.0	3.3	3.5	6.00	3.4		
M. sin. Flammenmeer	0.1	0.2	1.5	2.2	1.0		
M. sin. Morninglight	0.4	1.2	0.6	0.7	0.8		
M. sin. China	0.1	0.2	0.5	0.8	0.4		
Mean	1.0	6.2	11.1	15.7	8.5		

and the planting density was again 1 plant per m^2. Some winter losses occurred in this trial with the highest losses being recorded in *M. sin.* var. 'Morninglight', 'Wetterfahne' and 'China'. The recorded yields are shown in Table 5.3.

As was observed in the first evaluation trial, *M.* x *giganteus* produced higher dry

Table 5.4. *Dry matter content (%) of* Miscanthus *genotypes at Braunschweig from 1992 (first growing season) to 1995.*

	1992	1993	1994	1995	Mean
M. x giganteus	75.7	61.6	60.7	60.2	64.6
M. sin. Silberfeder	67.1	66.4	78.1	76.1	72.9
M. sin. Pünktchen	72.3	64.6	68.8	64.8	67.6
M. sin. Poseidon	60.4	75.5	67.0	69.8	68.2
M. sin. Silberspinne	74.8	79.3	81.2	66.1	75.4
M. sin. Goliath	68.3	98.4	69.8	69.7	76.6
M. sin. Grosse Fontäne	59.6	75.1	76.7	68.8	70.0
M. sin. Kaskade	84.2	79.6	77.6	71.5	78.2
M. sin. Roland	63.5	81.5	71.8	76.4	73.3
M. sin. Wetterfahne	76.8	79.5	76.1	78.0	77.6
M. sin. Gracillimus	66.1	77.3	69.1	67.7	70.0
M. sin. Spätgrün	84.4	82.1	80.6	75.4	80.6
M. sin. Cornet	65.0	69.1	78.8	74.7	71.9
M. sin. Malepartus	66.9	78.8	75.0	72.8	73.4
M. sin. Silberturm	72.4	68.1	70.5	73.0	71.0
M. sin. Undine	69.8	71.7	72.3	70.6	71.1
M. sin. Giraffe	71.8	72.5	79.6	69.2	73.3
M. sin. Flammenmeer	86.2	90.2	85.4	71.0	83.2
M. sin. Morninglight	71.5	78.6	73.7	79.0	75.7
M. sin. China	86.4	92.3	76.6	78.6	83.5
Mean	72.2	77.1	74.5	71.2	73.8

matter yields than *M. sin.* 'Goliath' in the first two years of the trial. After the second growing season the dry matter yields of *M. sin.* 'Goliath' exceeded those of *M.* x *giganteus*. Four other *M. sin.* varieties had higher dry matter yields than *M.* x *giganteus* and *M. sin.* 'Goliath'. *M. sin.* 'Silberfeder' and 'Pünktchen' produced 17 t ha⁻¹ on average for four growing periods with maximum yields of 31 and 35.8 t ha⁻¹, respectively, in the fourth-year harvest. *M. sin.* 'Poseidon' and 'Silberspinne' also had higher yields compared with those of *M.* x *giganteus* and *M. sin.* 'Goliath'. The dry matter yields of *M. sin.* 'Morninglight', 'China', 'Giraffe' and 'Flammenmeer' were extremely low and indicate that these varieties are not suitable for biomass production, however their low productivity is partly due to plant losses during winter. The low productivity of some *Miscanthus* genotypes may also be attributed to flowering at the beginning of autumn which stops the plant's vegetative growth and leads to early maturation. Dry matter contents of the second trial were consistent with those recorded in the first trial, with *M.* x *giganteus* again exhibiting the lowest dry matter content compared to those of all other *Miscanthus* forms (Table 5.4). *M. sin.* 'Spätgrün', 'China' and 'Flammenmeer' reached a dry matter content higher than 80% on average in the four harvests.

FAL's genotype screening trials have highlighted that some *M. sinensis* varieties can produce the same and even higher biomass yields than *M.* x *giganteus*. *M. sin.* cultivars

'Goliath', 'Pünktchen', 'Silberfeder' and 'Silberspinne' produced higher average biomass yields in the fifth and sixth years than *M.* x *giganteus* at an annual nitrogen supply of 120 kg N ha^{-1}. The screening trials also highlighted the low dry matter content of *M.* x *giganteus* in comparison to *M. sinensis* varieties. This has been attributed to the higher leaf to stem ratio of *M. sinensis* and the higher winter loss of leaf material in *M.* x *giganteus* varieties. The ratio of leaf material in the harvested biomass will influence the suitability of the harvested material for particular end uses. Therefore, in summary, the choice of *Miscanthus* species or variety will be made according to the biomass yields and the proposed end use of the biomass.

Genotype Evaluations Carried Out in Germany by LWG

LWG evaluated the yield and plant development of *M.* x *giganteus* and a number of *M. sinensis* varieties over seven years. Each genotype was evaluated on good (silty loam, para brown earth) and poor (clayey loam, rendzina) soil near Veitshöchheim, Germany (Hotz *et al.*, 1996). The long-term annual rainfall at both sites was 606 mm with 290 mm between May and September.

Table 5.5 gives the height and yield (minimum and maximum) which was recorded in the evaluation trials while Figure 5.6 shows the influence of three different planting densities on yield development over the evaluation period.

A great variability in yield was observed. This is attributed to the amount of precipitation during the growing period and also the different soil types on which the trials were carried out. Highest yields were recorded for *M.* x *giganteus* which gave dry matter yields of 15–24 t ha^{-1} on good soils and 5–10 t ha^{-1} on poor soils. All genotypes other than *M.* x *giganteus* produced less than 20 t ha^{-1} with a spacing of 1 plant m^{-2}, but these yields increased when planting densities of two or three plants m^{-2} were used. Although *M.* x *giganteus* produced the highest dry matter yields, all tested *M. sinensis* varieties had higher survival rates during the first winter.

In the second trial carried out by LWG, 4000 plants obtained from *Miscanthus* seed-mixtures were planted in 1988 as a basis for selection purposes. Plants with a dry weight of more than 2 kg after the third year were selected and tested in field trials. 25 new genotypes which were selected in this way were grown in field trials from 1992

Table 5.5. *Height and dry matter yield of* Miscanthus *genotypes recorded during six years (3rd to 9th year; 1 plant m^{-2}) at Veitshöchheim.*

Miscanthus cultivar	Max. height (m)	Yield at high production sites t ha^{-1} dm (min – max)	Yield at low production sites t ha^{-1} dm (min – max)
M. x giganteus	4.15	15–24	5–10
M. sin. Goliath	3.10	10–19	5–6
M. sin. Gracillimus	2.90	6–17	2–2
M. sin. Grosse Fontane	3.00	10–15	3–4
M. sin. Silberfeder	3.00	8–15	2–5
M. sin. Ungarn	2.00	9–15	4–6

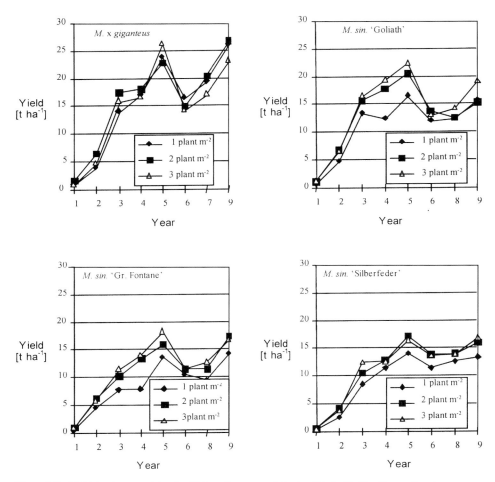

Figure 5.6. Yield development (t ha⁻¹) of M. *x* giganteus, M. sin. *'Goliath', 'Gr. Fontane' and 'Silberfeder' from 1988 to 1996 at different planting densities at Veitshöchheim.*

along with genotypes such as *M.* x *giganteus* and *M. sin.* 'Goliath' under good growing conditions. Several plant growth characters such as height, yield and flowering were assessed. The results of the trial are given in Table 5.6.

It can be seen from Table 5.6 that most of the genotypes showed a better survival rate after the first winter than *M.* x *giganteus*, which failed with losses of 98 to 100%. Eight of them had a better survival rate than *M. sin.* 'Goliath' which had winter losses of 32%. It was observed that all genotypes with high winter failures developed flowers very late in September or October or didn't flower at all.

Two genotypes (seedlings number 2 and 16, Table 5.6) showed very low winter losses of 3 and 7% respectively. In addition, the dry matter yields of these genotypes compared favourably with those of *M. sin.* 'Goliath' (13.26 and 14.49 t ha⁻¹ respectively after the fifth year of growth compared to 12.59 t ha⁻¹ for 'Goliath'). The risk of

Table 5.6. Screening of Miscanthus *genotypes from 1992 to 1997 at Veitshöchheim.*

Miscanthus genotypes		Mother plant weight (kg)	Winter loss (%) 1992–3	Height (m) Dec 1996	Yield (t ha⁻¹) Mar 1997	Flower formation
Miscanthus sin. Goliath			32	2.70	12.59	e
Miscanthus sin. Gracillimus			82	–	–	l
M. x giganteus (rhizome propagated)			98	2.00	5.54	n
M. x giganteus (*in vitro* propagated)			98	2.55	4.63	n
Danish cultivar			62	2.35	6.28	e
Seedling number	1	2.13	62	1.70	3.45	l
	2	2.16	3	2.30	13.26	m
	3	2.07	95	–	–	l
	4	1.97	67	–	–	l
	5	2.48	60	2.00	8.32	m
	6	2.35	80	–	–	l
	7	2.08	57	2.30	11.49	m
	8	1.91	25	2.25	14.53	m
	9	3.54	45	2.00	10.21	m
	10	2.07	52	2.25	11.52	m
	11	2.14	30	2.05	8.72	e
	12	2.29	45	2.50	10.38	m
	13	2.44	47	2.25	10.17	m
	14	1.94	90	–	–	l
	15	2.16	52	2.05	10.40	m
	16	1.92	7	2.00	14.49	m
	17	3.20	64	2.10	12.16	m
	18	1.95	69	2.25	5.60	e
	19	2.07	28	2.00	8.67	m
	20	2.66	58	2.30	8.83	m
	21	1.94	10	2.20	10.06	e
	22	2.12	72	2.25	8.48	m
	23	2.52	17	2.58	12.28	e
	24	1.92	60	2.00	10.29	m
	25	2.30	27	2.15	9.34	e

Flower formation
e   early (between late July and early August)
m   middle (between mid August and early September)
l   late (between mid and late September)
n   not flowering

naturalisation of these two genotypes is probably low because flower development occurs between mid-August and early September, while flower formation starts between late July and early August in 'Goliath'.

It was observed that all of the 25 new genotypes which were tested had a lower moisture content at harvest than *M. x giganteus* (between 20 and 30% for the genotypes in comparison to 44–50% for *M. x giganteus*). LWG is to test further some of the promising genotypes for a few more years. They will be assessed for growth and productivity-related characteristics as well as their quality for industrial use and their reproductive behaviour.

In June 1995 new trials were set up with 34 *Miscanthus* genotypes (21 new LWG selections, seven new genotypes from Denmark and six reference genotypes) at a good soil (silty loam, para brown earth) near Veitshöchheim. Thirty of these genotypes were planted at a comparable site in November 1995. Two *Miscanthus* x *sacchariflorus* hybrids and two other genotypes appear to have good winter survival and high growth rates. During the next five years further research will be carried out to determine the yield potential of the genotypes and identify the most suitable of them for use as an energy or industrial crop.

Genotype Evaluations Carried Out in Italy by A. Biotec

Trials were carried out in Italy by A. Biotec in order to investigate the genetic variability and the adaptability of different *Miscanthus* genotypes to local pedoclimatic conditions. Two trials were established in 1994: (A) a trial of 13 genotypes, with a small number of plants per genotype, and (B) a trial of four genotypes with a larger number of plants per genotype. The planting density was 2 plants m^{-2} in trial A and 4 plants m^{-2} in trial

Table 5.7. *Data from second year genotype trials performed by A. Biotec, Italy.*

Ref number	Genotype	Flowering date	Cycle length (days)	Fertility	Height (cm)
Trial A					
MS 18	*M. sin.* Goliath	05/08/95	117	sterile	260
MS 21	*M. sin.* Roland	09/08/95	121	fertile	240
MS 20	*M. sin.* Silberspinne	11/08/95	123	sterile	245
MS 17	*M. sin.* Poseidon	22/09/95	163	sterile	245
MS 10	*M.* x *giganteus* (Bock)	28/09/95	173	sterile	330
MS 10	*M.* x *giganteus* (Piccoplant)	02/10/95	175	sterile	320
MS 22	*M. sin.* Pünktchen	23/09/95	133	sterile	200
MS 12	*M. sin.* Zebrinus	11/09/95	157	sterile	230
MS 14	*M. sin.* Gracillimus	02/10/95	175	sterile	190
MS 06	*Miscanthus* sp. (Japan)	23/08/95	135	sterile	270
MS 08	*Miscanthus* sp. (Japan)	25/09/95	170	sterile	250
MS 09	*Miscanthus* sp. (Belgium)*	18/08/95	132	sterile	–
MS 11	*Miscanthus* sp. (France)	01/09/95	146	sterile	200
Trial B					
1	*M. sin.* Goliath	25/09/95	117	sterile	312
2	*M. sin.* Poseidon	05/08/95	168	sterile	230
3	*M.* x *giganteus*	27/09/95	170	sterile	238
4	*M. sin.* Grosse Fontane	16/08/95	128	sterile	252

* not harvested

Table 5.8. Productivity data from 2nd year genotype trials, by A. Biotec, Italy.

Genotype	Plants /m²	Culms /plant	Fresh weight yield		Dry matter yield	
			kg/plant t	ha⁻¹	%	t ha⁻¹
Trial A						
M. sin. Goliath	2.0	40	1.4	26.8	67.9	18.2
M. sin. Roland	1.9	46	1.0	19.0	67.9	12.9
M. sin. Silberspinne	1.9	54	1.2	22.6	67.2	15.2
M. sin. Poseidon	1.9	110	2.0	37.5	61.0	22.9
M. x giganteus (Bock)	1.9	57	2.9	54.0	62.2	33.6
M. x giganteus (Piccoplant)	1.8	51	2.1	38.0	62.3	23.6
M. sin. Pünktchen	1.9	106	1.9	34.9	61.6	21.5
M. sin. Zebrinus	2.0	55	1.7	33.7	58.1	19.6
M. sin. Gracillimus	2.0	127	2.1	41.9	63.3	26.5
MS 06	2.0	104	2.4	46.6	59.2	27.6
MS 08	1.9	113	3.7	71.2	59.8	42.6
MS 09 (*)	–	–	–	–	–	–
MS 11	2.0	28	1.4	28.0	56.6	15.9
Trial B						
M. sin. Goliath	3.9	39	0.8	33.1	64.5	21.4
M. sin. Poseidon	3.9	56	1.3	48.8	60.3	29.2
M. x giganteus	3.8	46	1.8	69.6	60.1	41.7
M. sin. Grosse Fontane	3.8	35	0.8	31.0	65.8	20.4

(*) not harvested

B. Weeding, irrigation and fertiliser applications were carried out as necessary to ensure successful establishment and growth of the plants, and the plants were harvested in January. The data recorded in the trials included emergence date, flowering date, fertility, height and biomass production. Tables 5.7 and 5.8 give the data recorded in the second year of the trial.

It was found that there was variability in cycle length, number of culms per plant, height and yield among the genotypes which were tested. *M.* x *giganteus*, *M. sin.* 'Gracillimus' and MS 08 had the longest cycles (all longer than 170 days). The number of culms per plant was found to vary from 28 to 127 according to genotype (*M. sin.* 'Gracillimus', MS 08, MS 06, *M. sin.* 'Pünktchen', and *M. sin.* 'Poseidon' all had more than 100 culms per plant). The genotype which achieved the greatest crop height was *M.* x *giganteus*. This was measured at 330 cm in the Bock accession and 320 cm in the Piccoplant accession.

The crop yield was calculated for each of the genotypes tested. It can be seen that in trial A, *M.* x *giganteus* was confirmed as one of the productive varieties with a dry matter yield of 33.6 t ha⁻¹ being recorded from the Bock accession and 23.6 t ha⁻¹ in the Piccoplant accession. In trial B, *M.* x *giganteus* was the most productive with a calculated dry matter yield of 41.7 t ha⁻¹. The higher yield in trial B may be attributed to the higher planting density (four plants m⁻² compared with two plants m⁻² in trial A). The genotype MS 08 which was obtained from a Botanic Garden in Japan

Table 5.9. Dry matter yield and mineral concentrations of M. x giganteus *and of* M. sinensis *(mean of 15 selections) for three years in Denmark. Source: Jørgensen, 1997.*

	Miscanthus species	1993	1994	1995	Mean 1993–5
Dry matter (t ha^{-1})	M x *giganteus*	4.6	8.9	9.5	7.7±0.6
	M. *sinensis*	6.2	9.6	11.0	8.9±0.3
N (% in dm)	M x *giganteus*	0.57	0.66	0.55	0.59±0.03
	M. *sinensis*	0.58	0.66	0.67	0.64±0.02
K (% in dm)	M x *giganteus*	0.81	0.60	1.03	0.81±0.05
	M. *sinensis*	0.39	0.31	0.48	0.39±0.02
Cl (% in dm)	M x *giganteus*	0.40	0.18	0.50	0.33±0.07
	M. *sinensis*	0.11	0.04	0.12	0.08±0.01

was considered to be particularly interesting with a dry matter yield of 42.6 t ha^{-1} in trial A. These trials need to be continued in order to confirm yield trends.

Genotype Evaluations Carried Out in Denmark by DIAS

In 1990 *M.* x *giganteus* and 15 selections of *M. sinensis* were planted on a loamy sand. This was done by field-planting plantlets at a density of four plants m^{-2}; the plantlets had been produced from rhizome pieces in the greenhouse. The 15 *M. sinensis* genotypes were selected for good winter survival and productivity in a Danish climate from seedlings from seeds collected on Honshu, Japan. The average dry matter yield over three years at spring harvest was calculated to be 8.9 t ha^{-1} for *M. sinensis* selections and 7.7 t ha^{-1} for *M.* x *giganteus*. The highest yields were recorded in 1995 (Table 5.9). The most productive selection of *M. sinensis* had a mean dry matter yield over the three years of about 12 t ha^{-1}. The yields recorded during the three years were low compared with earlier trials of *M.* x *giganteus* (Jørgensen, 1996). The decrease in yields was attributed to adverse climatic conditions.

It was observed that *M. sinensis* selections flowered and showed physiological senescence under Danish growing conditions, while *M.* x *giganteus* stayed in the vegetative stage until it was killed by the first frost of the winter.

The genotypic variation in dry matter percentage during the year was of the same order of magnitude as the variation observed between years within one genotype. One significant genotypic variation was the earlier drying in spring of *M. sinensis*. This offers opportunities for enlarging the harvest window of *Miscanthus* in northern Europe through the introduction of *M. sinensis* genotypes.

Significant differences between the two species was also shown for the contents of K and Cl at harvest in spring, which has a major influence on combustion quality. The percentage content in dry matter of K and Cl were 0.81 and 0.33 in *M.* x *giganteus* and

0.39 and 0.08 in *M. sinensis* as a mean of three years. However, there was a large variation within the selections of *M. sinensis*, which was related to their time of ripening in autumn. Genotype variation in the content of N was less pronounced.

6 | *Harvesting and Storage of* Miscanthus

by N. El Bassam and W. Huisman

6.1 Introduction

Miscanthus can be used as a raw material for energy production, building materials, geotextiles, paper and packing industries and as a plant substrate (Huisman *et al.*, 1996; El Bassam, 1998). Each end use has specific raw material requirements related to dry matter content, shape, size and particle consistency. Harvest, transport and storage methods are determined by the end use of the harvested biomass and the need for year-round availability.

For most applications of *Miscanthus* a year-round availability will be required. Consequently, the harvested material should be stored with minimum losses in quantity and quality. This means that conservation methods such as drying or ensiling should be applied.

Like most other crops, the costs of farm labour, machinery, storage and transport make up the highest proportion of the total cost of *Miscanthus* biomass production. The implementation of integrated chain management is required to ensure efficient and low-cost production and harvesting of *Miscanthus* biomass for its various end uses.

6.2 Harvesting

Basic elements of current harvesting techniques can be used for the harvest of *Miscanthus*. *Miscanthus* attains a height of 2.5–3.5 m and produces annual biomass yields of 20–25 t dm ha^{-1}. In addition, the stems are thicker and stronger than straw or grass. These characteristics of *Miscanthus* will necessitate the development of harvesters which are more robust and which are capable of harvesting tall stems of 3.5 m.

6.2.1 Harvest Dates

Harvesting of *Miscanthus* should be carried out after the crop has senesced, when the moisture content is lowest and before regrowth begins in the following spring. It is important that the crop has senesced so that translocation of assimilates has occurred; thus giving the plant enough rhizome reserves to survive the winter and support regrowth in the following spring. The moisture content at harvest is also important in ensuring a high quality biomass which will not have to be artificially dried. Harvesting should be carried out before the next year's growth begins in order to avoid sprout damage (sprouting begins when soil temperature is >10°C in spring). The harvesting time will also be dependent on whether the crop is grown in a northern or southern European region. Extensive research has been carried out by CRES (south European) and FAL (north European) on this subject.

In northern European regions the first frosts in autumn or winter signal the end of growth for the *Miscanthus* crop. At this time, crop senescence accelerates, nutrients are sequestered into the rhizomes and the plant begins to dry out. The moisture content of the crop at this time is 50–60%. In these areas, harvesting of *Miscanthus* will be carried out in early spring in order to obtain the lowest possible moisture content in the harvested material (the moisture content of the crop decreases during the winter months reaching typical levels of 25–40% in early spring). Spring harvesting should, however, be carried out before new shoot growth occurs. This normally starts at soil temperatures of 10°C. One of the disadvantages of leaving the crop in the field so late in the season is the risk of biomass yield loss (mostly tops and leaves) which occur as a result of unfavourable weather conditions during winter. However, the low moisture content of the harvested material in early spring is considered to compensate for the biomass losses which occur during the winter.

Figure 6.1 gives a schematic view of the timing of the harvesting of *Miscanthus*. The period between the point where the crop reaches the threshold moisture content (t_{begin}) and the point where maximum acceptable damage of the sprouts (t_{end}) occurs is called the 'harvest window'. Harvesting within this window allows minimisation of the total harvest costs. The timing of the actual harvest within the harvest window is dependent on the workability of the soil which is determined by the harvest method to be used

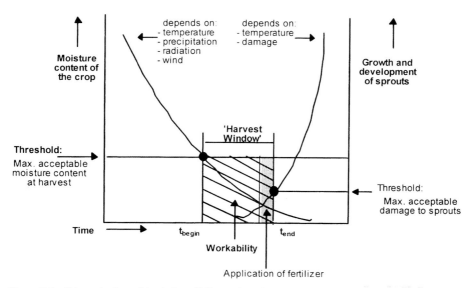

Figure 6.1. Schematic view of the timing of Miscanthus *harvesting. Source: Huisman, 1995.*

and the soil conditions. The harvest window will be shortened if a fertiliser application is required as this also needs to be carried out before the threshold for maximum acceptable damage to the new shoot growth.

In contrast to the situation in northern European countries, the growing period of *Miscanthus* grown in southern European countries ends at the end of August to middle of September when the inflorescence emerges. The emergence of the inflorescence is followed by the progressive drying out of the leaves and a simultaneous dying back of the stems. It has been found that the delay of harvesting in these areas until late winter to early spring (as is the case in northern Europe) causes additional dry matter losses of up to 50%. These high reductions are due to heavy losses of leaves and tops, which are accelerated by a succession of dry and humid weather conditions and strong winds at many sites. The moisture content of the crop ranges from 36–49% by late autumn, depending upon site and weather conditions. The low moisture content of the autumn-harvested plants in southern European countries combined with the weather conditions at that time of the year indicate that harvesting of the crop can be implemented in autumn instead of early spring thus avoiding biomass losses (tops and leaves) caused during winter.

In conclusion, it could be stated that in northern European regions, *Miscanthus* harvesting should be carried out in early spring when the moisture content of the harvested material is lowest. However, harvesting in southern European sites could be implemented in late autumn in order to avoid biomass losses caused by the adverse climatic conditions during winter. Further research is required to define the correct timing of autumn harvesting in order to achieve maximum yields without adversely affecting the ability of the crop to survive the winter and support shoot regrowth in the following spring. In addition, the soil conditions at the time of harvest must be assessed in order to minimise the damage caused by the weight of the harvesting machines on the soil structure.

6.2.2 Harvesting Techniques

Two systems were investigated by FAL for harvesting *Miscanthus*. These were:

- The Multi-Phase Procedure (several machines) which involves mowing followed by swathing and pick-up, compacting and baling.
- The Single-Phase Procedure (one machine) which involves mowing followed by a chopping, baling, bundling or pelleting line.

The observations of FAL with regard to the implementation of these systems for the harvest of *Miscanthus* are outlined below.

Multi-Phase Harvesting

No problems were encountered, using a conventional straw baler press, during the mowing, swathing and baling of *Miscanthus* grown in the establishment year. However, due to the increased plant height and stem hardness of *Miscanthus* in subsequent years, the harvest was more difficult. It was found that a rotary mower (Figure 6.2) did not work satisfactorily due to blunting and plugging of the mower unit by the hard

Figure 6.2. Rotary mower Krone 'AMT 323 C'.

Miscanthus stems. This indicated that mowing of *Miscanthus* would be better carried out with a double knife mower.

Miscanthus stems must be swathed before baling in order to allow the baler to pick up all of the material. If swathing is not included in the harvesting process, the bulk and length of *Miscanthus* stems will lead to obstruction of the pick-up unit of the baler. This prevents the baler from operating continuously over long periods of harvesting. Thus, swathing of *Miscanthus* is necessary for undisturbed pick-up of stems by the baling machine.

There are a number of baling machines which produce different bales (e.g. rectangular bales, round bales and compact rolls). The production of bales which have high dry matter densities is advantageous for further handling, transport and storage. It was observed that the Big-Round-Baler (Welger RP 200; Figure 6.3) and the Big-Rectangular-Baler (Welger D 4000) were capable of producing compact bales with dry matter densities of approximately 120 kg m^{-3}. The dry matter density of bales compacted by different big balers (Figure 6.4) was found to range between 120 and 160 kg m^{-3}. It was found that one of the disadvantages of the big baling machines is their low output (approximately one ha. per hour).

The newly developed compact roller baler enables higher bale compaction. The swath goes through pressing rollers which form the round bale and the bale is then cut by a partition unit after binding. The bales produced by the compact roller are approximately 0.40 m in diameter and 0.50–2.50 m in length and their dry matter density is about 350 kg m^{-3}. The high dry matter density minimises transport and

Figure 6.3. Big-Round-Baler (Welger RP 200).

Figure 6.4. Mower header and big baler (John Deere).

storage costs. Thus harvesting by a compact roller baler leads to higher harvesting and transportation efficiencies than other balers. The Compact-Round-Baler (Welger CRP 400; Figure 6.5) was tested by FAL at the Braunschweig *Miscanthus* trials. It was found that the baler had good pick-up and compaction characteristics but at times the partition unit had difficulty in separating the bales cleanly. The compact roller baler is still being developed and improved.

Figure 6.5. Compact-Round-Baler (Welger CRP 400).

Single-Phase Harvesting

The sections below outline the different single-phase procedures which can be implemented for harvesting *Miscanthus*.

Chopping Line

Two different systems can be used for a single-phase chopping line. The first option is the chopping system which is normally used for short rotation forestry. This consists of a mowing unit in front of a tractor in combination with a trailer (Figure 6.6). This system can be used in *Miscanthus* stands with or without a special row spacing, depending on the cutting unit.

The second option is the use of a forage harvester (normally used for maize harvesting) with an adapted mower. In most cases the use of a row-independent mowing attachment is necessary because the planted rows are not distinguishable as the age of the *Miscanthus* stand increases. A mower adapted to the forage harvester

Figure 6.6. Single-phase chopping, short rotation forestry system.

has been developed by the Claas company. This mower has two heavy mowing devices which enable cutting and chopping of the stems. The chopped stems are then transported by a pneumatic conveyer to a trailer. A disadvantage of this system is that strong wind can negatively influence the recovery of the biomass (Figure 6.7).

The dry matter density of the chopped biomass varies between 70 and 130 kg m^{-3} according to the length at which the stems are chopped. This low dry matter density of the chopped material necessitates a large transport and storage capacity.

Baling Line

The single-phase baling line is based on a machine developed by Claas (Figure 6.8). This machine (a *Miscanthus* harvester) is a self propelled big baler/harvester which enables mowing, pick-up, compaction and baling of *Miscanthus* in one drive. The product of the *Miscanthus* harvester is a square bale with a dry matter density of between 120 and 130 kg m^{-3}. The capacity of the *Miscanthus* harvester is approximately twice that of the multi-phase baler. The harvester combines the advantages of the single-phase procedure with the baling line and is characterised by very low biomass losses during the entire harvesting process.

Bundling Line

The single-phase bundling line requires a special machine and should be used only when a harvest of whole stems of *Miscanthus* is required for further processing. Such

Figure 6.7. Single-phase chopping, forage harvester with adapted mower.

Figure 6.8. Single-phase baling, Miscanthus *Harvester (Claas).*

harvesting method is based on that used for reed grass (reaper-binder). The harvesting machine developed by Agostini for the harvest of reed grass attaches to the three-point linkage of a tractor and consists of a mowing unit, binding equipment and a transport/deposit unit (Figure 6.9). The crop is cut with a cutterbar and transported via the binding unit to the side. The bundles which are produced have a diameter of 0.2 m, a weight of 9 kg and a dry matter density of 140 kg m^{-3}. The machine has a capacity of 0.35 ha h^{-1}.

Figure 6.9. Single-phase bundling, Reaper-Binder MLAG 140 (Agostini).

   Initial trials investigating the use of the reaper-binder for the harvest and bundling of *Miscanthus* have shown that the binding unit should be attached at a higher point for *Miscanthus* than for reed grass. The binding process takes place at the lower part of the stem in the Agostini machine, however, due to the *Miscanthus* plant height of up to 3.5 m and the loose binding, the bundles were not compact enough and began to fall apart. It was concluded from the trials that the machine needs modifications (e.g. a higher binding point) to enable the harvest of secure *Miscanthus* bundles. In addition, the development of loading and transportation technology for the bundles has to be completed.
   In The Netherlands, a self propelled reed bundling machine which makes small bundles was used for *Miscanthus* harvesting. The bundles were collected in a hopper, and when the hopper was full a big bundle (approx 1.5 m diameter) was made. Two people were required to operate the machine.

Pelleting line

The single-phase pelleting line is carried out using the newly developed 'Biotruck 2000' from the Haimer company (Figure 6.10). This machine allows mowing, chopping and pelleting in one phase in the field. The material is firstly mowed and chopped. It is then pre-dried by using the thermal energy of the engine and then it is compacted, pressed and pelleted without additional bonding agents. The end product of the process is a corrugated pellet with a length of 30 to 100 mm. The individual pellet density ranges from 850 to 1000 kg m^{-3} while the bulk density ranges from 300 to 500 kg m^{-3}. The Biotruck has a capacity of 3–8 t h^{-1}.

Figure 6.10. Single-phase pelleting, Biotruck 2000 (Haimer).

The single-phase pelleting method allows the reduction of the bulk density of harvested material which consequently leads to reductions in transportation and storage requirements. In addition, pellets are easier to handle than chopped material or bales and there is potential for the development of automatic handling systems for such pellets.

6.3 Drying

Drying involves the extraction of moisture from the product by natural ventilation and radiation or by artificial ventilation with ambient or heated air. The moisture content should decrease to a level which is in equilibrium with a relative air humidity of 70–80% depending on the storage temperature. If the moisture content is too high, microbiological activity will occur and will result in dry matter losses and fungal spore contamination (these can be damaging to human health).

6.3.1 Moisture Content

The moisture content of the biomass material determines its stability during storage. At high moisture contents (>50%), microbiological activity begins immediately and creates an increase in storage temperature (self heating). This can cause spontaneous combustion in hay but it is not known whether this would happen in *Miscanthus*. Table 6.1 gives the time required for *Miscanthus* to become visibly infected with fungal growth at two relative air humidities and three storage temperatures. Figure 6.11 shows the equilibrium moisture contents of *Miscanthus* for adsorption at various relative humidities (Huisman & Kortleve, 1994).

Table 6.1. Days until Miscanthus *showed visible mould in relation to the ambient temperature and relative air humidity (RAH).*

Temperature (°C)	Days until visible mould growth	
	RAH 90%	RAH 80%
30	10	75
20	45	300
10	90	>300

It can be concluded from Table 6.1 that the relative air humidity should be 80% or less for year-round storage of *Miscanthus* at a temperature of 10°C. When this information is combined with Figure 6.11 it can be seen that the equilibrium moisture content is about 15%, thus indicating that, for safe storage, the moisture content should be below 15%. For storage at 20°C the relative air humidity should be below 80%, and the moisture content of the material should be 12%.

Higher moisture contents can be used if some level of loss is accepted, however this increases the risk of the occurrence of fungal growth and self heating. Temperature rises may be minimised if natural ventilation is applied. Chopped *Miscanthus* with a moisture content of 66% was stored in a naturally ventilated pile in Denmark. After 187 days of storage the moisture content was 51% and storage loss was 5.4% (Kristensen, 1997). Also, when natural ventilation was applied to piles of wet whole stem bundles no self heating or fungal growth occurred. Jonkanski (1994) reported 12–15% dry matter loss for bales harvested in January at moisture contents of 45–50% and 7–10% dry matter loss for bales harvested in March at moisture contents of 25–30%. All bales were stored with natural ventilation. Dry matter losses of 4–9% were reported during storage (with natural ventilation) of chopped *Miscanthus* which was harvested in January and 2% for chopped *Miscanthus* harvested in March.

In summary, the maximum moisture content at storage will depend on the application of mechanical ventilation and the accepted level of loss. Although exact data are not yet available, it can be concluded that bundles of whole stems, loose bales

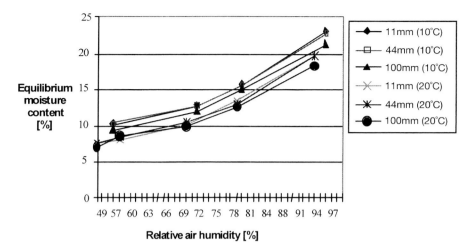

Figure 6.11. Adsorption isotherm of Miscanthus *for different temperatures and stem segment lengths. Source: Huisman & Kortleve, 1994.*

and chopped material can have higher moisture contents than high density bales of chopped material and/or bales of compact rolls.

6.3.2 Drying Methods

This section outlines the different methods which can be applied for the drying of *Miscanthus* to a moisture content which allows storage of the harvested biomass in a stable manner. The different methods which are described are:

• drying in the field
• drying in storage
• drying in industrial installations.

Drying in the Field

The most cost-effective way of drying *Miscanthus* is by using the ambient air and solar radiation to dry the material in the field. Drying of the standing crop starts in winter after the crop has died (from the first frosts in northern countries or when temperatures decrease or after a dry period in southern countries). Figure 6.12 shows the moisture content of a standing *Miscanthus* crop in various years in The Netherlands at Ter Apel (Kloosterveenweg, Meibos), Lunteren and Wageningen (Huisman, 1995).

It can be seen that there is a decrease in the moisture content of the standing crop from winter to spring with a large difference between years. It can be concluded from Figure 6.12 and from similar results at other sites that harvesting should take place during April and in good weather conditions if no additional drying process is planned. The moisture contents given in Figure 6.12 were measured in *Miscanthus* stands which

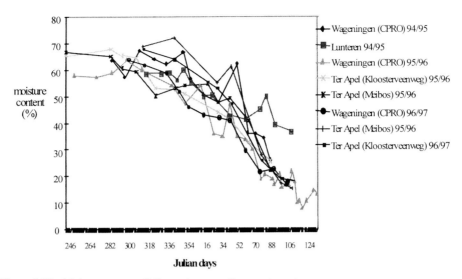

Figure 6.12. Moisture content of Miscanthus *standing crop in various years and at several locations in The Netherlands.*

had been grown in small plantations. However, it is expected that when plantations are very large, the air speed close to the soil is so low that moisture contents remain high at the lower part of the stems. In such cases mowing and drying in a swath could be used. Drying in a swath is advantageous in the sense that it will allow a more homogeneous drying of the biomass (including leaves which have fallen and are raked together in the swath). A disadvantage of this method is that more soil / stone material is taken up during collection which may cause problems in processing machinery and thus affect the costs of energy conversion.

Drying in Storage

The methods employed for drying in storage depend on the condition of the harvested biomass. When the moisture content of the harvested biomass is high, heated air is required to dry the biomass rapidly to a level where fungal growth will not occur. However, when moisture contents are close to 25%, unheated air is sufficient to dry the biomass. The form of the harvested biomass is also an important determinant of the drying method. Whole stems can be dried from high moisture contents without fungal growth in spring and summer time if they are stored in a well-ventilated situation (even natural ventilation). Mechanical ventilation is needed to ventilate air through high density bales (dry matter density of *c.* 150 kg m^{-3}). Drying of low density biomass like chopped material (dry matter density of 80–100 kg m^{-3}) and pellets is possible, with natural ventilation and low-pressure mechanical ventilation such as that employed in potato storage rooms. A number of experiments have been carried out at different locations to investigate drying in storage, and the main conclusions of these tests are outlined below.

Investigations were carried out in Denmark by Kristensen (1997) into the drying of chopped *Miscanthus* in a naturally ventilated pile. This pile was 1.5 m high, 3 m wide, covered in plastic and serviced by two ventilation ducts (one at the top and one at the base of the pile). It was found that during 187 days the moisture content of the chopped *Miscanthus* decreased from 63% to 51% while the recorded dry matter losses were 5.4%.

Another test was performed in Denmark to investigate the use of a platform dryer with unheated drying air for the drying of chopped *Miscanthus* material (Kristensen, 1997). In this test 2470 kg of chopped *Miscanthus* with a moisture content of 59% was ventilated with 21,500 m^3 air h^{-1}. It was found that the moisture content had decreased to 17.5% after 91 hours of ventilation. The energy consumption of the fan during this time was found to be 4 MJ kg^{-1} dry matter, equivalent to 3.2 MJ kg^{-1} evaporated water.

A small-scale test was carried out in The Netherlands to investigate the drying of *Miscanthus* in a potato storage facility. In this test 6 m^3 of *Miscanthus* at 33% moisture content was stored on a slatted floor of a potato storage facility which was ventilated with ambient air for 1–2 hours per day at daytime in April. After four weeks the moisture content of the biomass had decreased to 20% and after an additional one and a half weeks the moisture content had further decreased to 15%.

Extended research was carried out in Germany by Tack and Kirschbaum (1995) on drying in storage of baled and chopped *Miscanthus* at several high moisture contents. Firstly, 8500 kg of chopped *Miscanthus* biomass (50% moisture content) which had been harvested in January was stored. The temperature of this material increased to 60°C within 150 hours due to self-heating through microbiological activity (Figure 6.13). Drying by ventilation was then employed using the heat of the microbiological activity for drying. It was found possible to decrease the moisture content of the chopped *Miscanthus* from 48 to 36% by ventilating the pile four times after the temperature of the chopped material reached 60°C. However, this method of drying is not recommended because of:

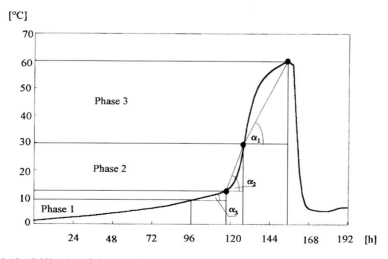

Figure 6.13. Self heating of chopped Miscanthus *(moisture content of 50%). Source: Tack & Kirschbaum, 1995.*

- the high risk of fire through self heating
- high dry matter losses
- the increase in moisture content in the top layer of the drying pile
- the high fungal growth
- the high condensation moisture which occurs in the storage / drying building.

It is recommended that drying with unheated air should be performed with biomass temperatures below 20°C. It was found that moisture contents drop to 15% in a few weeks in April with dry matter losses of 4–6%, while before April ventilation was required for cooling the biomass material.

The drying speed of small samples (400 g) of chopped *Miscanthus* was investigated by Zaussinger and Dissemond (1995). The research highlighted the fact that drying wet *Miscanthus* with unheated air can give rise to mould growth and concluded that the air speed used for drying should be at least 0.1 m s⁻¹. The results of the investigation were used to design a model of an on-farm store and drying room. The implementation of the model system would result in a drying time of three days for the reduction of the moisture content of a 4 m layer of chopped *Miscanthus* from 25% to 15% (wet base) with an air temperature of 20°C and air speed of 0.1 m s⁻¹.

The pressure drop of a *Miscanthus* layer was measured for different airspeeds (measured above the material) and layer heights. The data (Figure 6.14) were measured in a column (diameter 0.7 m) which was filled with chopped *Miscanthus* (28 mm length, 30% moisture content and density of 130 kg m⁻³). The pressure drop would be higher

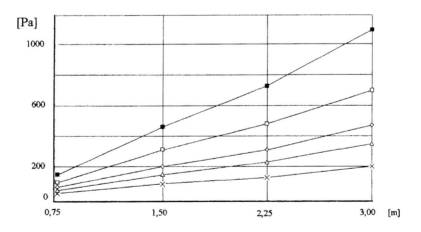

Air speeds

—×— 0,08 m/s
—△— 0,13 m/s
—◇— 0,2 m/s
—□— 0,25 m/s
—■— 0,33 m/s

Figure 6.14. Pressure drop of chopped Miscanthus *at different layer depths and airspeeds. Source: Tack &
Kirschbaum, 1995.*

if the moisture content of the material were higher and a longer storage period were used. It was concluded that when grain drying fans were applied, the maximum storage height should be about 5 m.

The cost of drying in storage when using ambient air is dependent on the drying potential of the ambient air and the moisture content at harvest. Heuvel (1995a) reported estimated costs of 8–25 ECU ton^{-1} dm for drying of forest residues. Jonkanski (1994) reports that the costs for drying chopped *Miscanthus* by mechanical ventilation decrease nearly linearly from 11 ECU ton^{-1} dm when harvested in January to 7 ECU t^{-1} dm when harvested in April, while the cost of drying bales by mechanical ventilation decreases from 15 ECU t^{-1} dm in January-harvested material to 6 ECU t^{-1} dm in April-harvested material.

Drying in Industrial Installations

A wide range of dryers are available for artificial drying in industrial applications. Some of these may be applicable for the drying of bulky materials like *Miscanthus.* These include rotary drum, band, pneumatic, steam, recompressive and fluidised bed dryers. These types of dryers could be of interest if waste heat were to be used as an energy source. This would improve the cost effectiveness and energy balance of *Miscanthus* to energy system (Heuvel, 1995a). If waste heat is used for drying *Miscanthus,* the type, capacity and energy input of the dryer will depend very much on the specific situation and process. No research has been carried out on this aspect of *Miscanthus* processing. Pierik and Curvers (1995) have outlined some of the technical and financial features of some commercially available rotary drum, fluidised bed, steam and recompressive dryers.

The energy consumption and costs of drying *Miscanthus* have been calculated using a theoretical calculation by Heuvel (1995a and 1995b). This calculation assumes a dryer efficiency of 85% and evaporation energy of the water of 2.260 MJ kg^{-1}. The calculated energy consumption and costs are given in Table 6.2.

Horvath (1997) carried out a theoretical calculation to determine the energy consumption and cost of drying chopped *Miscanthus* at 20°C from 26–15% moisture content using a rotary dryer with a capacity of 12 t h^{-1} and an inlet temperature of 230°C. The drying energy consumption was estimated to be 800 MJ while the cost of drying was estimated to be 24 ECU t^{-1}.

Table 6.2. Energy consumption and costs of drying as estimated by theoretical calculation. Source: Heuvel, 1995b.

Artificial drying[1] to 15% from MC of:	Energy consumption (% energy content of dried fuel)[2]	Cost (ECU t^{-1} dm)
20%	1.2	1.0
30%	4.2	3.7
40%	8.1	7.1
50%	13.5	12.0
60%	21.7	19.1
70%	35.4	31.2

[1] Drying by natural gas, at 85% drying efficiency
[2] Energy content of dried fuel (15% moisture content) is 15.87 kJ

A preliminary study was carried out to investigate the logistics of drying *Miscanthus* with the waste energy from a 1700 MW energy plant in the north of The Netherlands. It was concluded that sufficient waste energy was available when gasified *Miscanthus* was co-fired with natural gas (10% *Miscanthus*/90% natural gas) assuming a drying efficiency of 50% and drying of biomass from 60% to 8% moisture content. It was found that only 8% of the waste heat was used and the drying capacity was 3080 t dm day^{-1}. The costs of the drying process are not known yet.

6.4 Ensiling

When wet biomass is stored in anaerobic conditions (e.g. making a pile of *Miscanthus* air tight through sealing with plastic sheeting), the oxygen in the pile will be consumed and aerobic microbes will die. If sufficient sugars are available, the growth of lactic acid bacteria will result in the production of enough acid to kill most microbiological activity. The ensiled product is then in a stable condition and can be stored for a long period of time without biomass losses.

6.4.1 pH Requirements

The pH required to maintain ensiled *Miscanthus* in a stable condition depends on the moisture content of the stored material. It has been found that a pH of 4.2 is required for ensiling grass with a moisture content of 80%, whereas a pH of 5.2 is sufficient for grass with a moisture content of 50% and a pH of 7 is sufficient for moisture contents around 20% (the microbiological activity is negligible at this point). In general, it may be said that the lower the moisture content of the ensiled material, the higher the pH required for stable storage.

The important requirement of ensiling is that the storage remains anaerobic. As soon as oxygen enters the pile, aerobic microbial activity will begin and this will cause a temperature increase in the pile. A high protein content will give a high buffer capacity and more sugar should be available. It is possible to add sugars or acid to increase the rate of pH decrease.

6.4.2 Options for Ensiling Miscanthus

Ensiling *Miscanthus* is an option when moisture contents are too high for dry storage, especially if natural drying is impossible. The technology used for harvest and storage of ensiled maize can be applied to *Miscanthus*. The process used for maize involves harvesting using a forage harvester (chopper) with row-independent cutter, making flat silos, pressing as much as air as possible out of the pile by driving tractors over the pile and making the pile air tight by covering it with plastic at the end of the harvest day.

Ensiled *Miscanthus* can be used for paper pulp or energy production. However, if energy production is the end use, the moisture content of the material should be reduced by pressing in order to achieve higher energy conversion efficiencies. It was found that the moisture content of ensiled maize could be reduced from 77% to 40% by using a screw press (Stülpnagel, 1997). In addition, it was found that the content of all minerals except Si decreased. This would improve the quality of the biomass for energy conversion. The moisture remaining after ensiling and pressing will decrease the conversion efficiency, however this will not be a major disadvantage in applications which utilise lower value heat by flue gas condensation. The energy consumption of the screw press for decreasing the moisture content of the biomass material from 77% to 40% is only 1% of the energy content of the dry matter. If mechanical dehydration is performed at the farm before transport to the conversion plant, the quantity of biomass to be transported will be decreased while the liquid can be retained at the farm to be used as fertiliser.

6.4.3 *Research on Ensiling* Miscanthus

A small-scale test was carried out using *Miscanthus* in pots to investigate the pH decrease of ensiled *Miscanthus* (Huisman & Kortleve, 1994). It was observed that the glucose which was present in the harvested *Miscanthus* biomass (harvested on March 2) was rapidly converted to lactic acid. Figure 6.15 shows the decrease in pH of ensiled chopped *Miscanthus* at two moisture content levels and either inoculated with lactic acid bacteria or not.

It can be seen from Figure 6.15 that the material only contained enough sugars to decrease the pH value to 4. If the *Miscanthus* is harvested later than March the sugar content of the biomass will be lower and the pH values of the ensiled material will be higher, thus making the application of additives such as molasses necessary. After one year the pH of all variants was below 4.6, which is the required level for grass with a moisture content of 65% or lower. It was observed that inoculation doesn't seem to be necessary when harvesting is carried out in March. The dry matter loss during the ensiling of *Miscanthus* in the pots was only 0.4% in the first six months of storage.

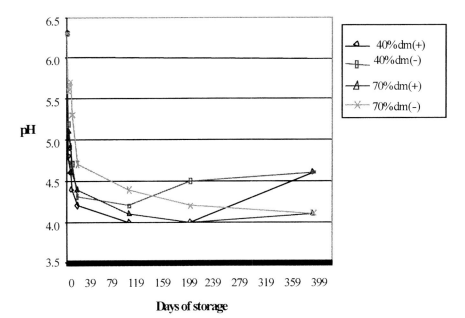

Figure 6.15. pH of chopped ensiled Miscanthus *(inoculated (+) with lactic acid bacteria or not(–)) at two moisture contents. Source: Huisman & Kortleve, 1994.*

6.5 Storage

This section outlines the storage of *Miscanthus* in terms of the requirements of the storage process and the different methods which may be employed.

6.5.1 Requirements of the Storage Process

The primary objective during the storage of *Miscanthus* is the maximisation of biomass quality while minimising costs and dry matter losses. Storage of *Miscanthus* at the farm is probably the easiest and most cost-effective method of storage. It avoids the coupling of the harvesting process with transport to the conversion plant and the requirement for large storage capacity at the conversion plant.

When the harvested *Miscanthus* biomass is relatively dry, no concrete floor is required for storage. However, if the biomass is wet and soil trafficability is poor, a concrete floor is recommended. In addition, easy access for loaders and trucks is required to allow quick and easy loading and unloading at the storage place. So concrete floors are required on soft soils or loading and unloading should only be carried out when soil conditions are good.

A large storage area will be required as the density of harvested *Miscanthus* biomass is low. It is estimated that 120 m^3 is required for the storage of every hectare of chopped *Miscanthus* biomass (assuming a dry matter yield of 12 t ha^{-1} and a dry matter density of 100 kg m^{-3}) while 80 m^3 is required for the storage of every hectare of baled *Miscanthus* biomass (assuming a dry matter density of 150 kg m^{-3}) (Huisman & Gigler, 1997).

6.5.2 Storage Methods

The methods used for storage of *Miscanthus* on the farm include:

- storage in the open air, without covering
- storage in the open air, covered with plastic sheeting
- storage in the open air, covered with organic materials
- storage in existing farm buildings
- storage in new farm buildings

These options are outlined in the sections below.

Storage in the Open Air, Without Covering

When bales, whole stems or chopped feedstock are stored in very large piles in the open without covering, rainfall will only moisten a relatively small amount of the total pile. Depending on the climate, the growth of fungi and algae will form a hardening layer in the top section of the pile.

Piles of bales may be covered with straw in order to fill the fissures between bales and thus prevent moisture progressing to the lower layers. In this case, only the top layer of bales gets wet. The bales in this layer might be reusable in a second year or they could be chopped and mixed with the rest of the bulk before being fed to the conversion plant. If this is not possible, only the decrease in value or removal costs must be compared with alternatives.

Tests carried out in The Netherlands on a small pile of chopped *Miscanthus* biomass which was stored in the open without cover during one summer and one winter revealed that the moist layer was about 500 mm in depth. Tests were also carried out on an uncovered pile (2.5 m height) of *Miscanthus* whole stems which was stored in the open throughout the summer and winter of 1996–7. In this test the moisture content of several layers of the pile at different heights were measured throughout the storage period. The results (Figure 6.16) indicate that the moisture penetrates to a depth of 500 mm–1 m from the top.

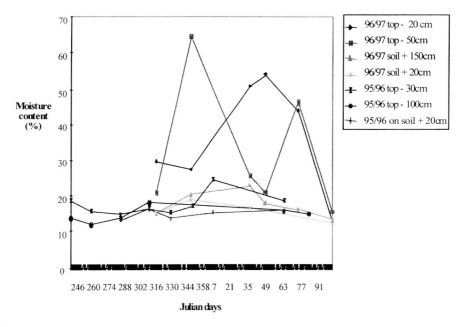

Figure 6.16. Moisture content in different layers of a pile of whole stems (height of 2.5 m) during the summer and winter of 1996–7.

In spring and summer, wet (70% moisture content) harvested whole stems, stored in bundles and piled not wider than the length of the stems, will dry out easily without fungal growth.

Storage in the Open Air, Covered with Plastic Sheeting

The covering of silage with plastic is very common in agricultural practice. It should also be possible to cover *Miscanthus* with this type of plastic. Piles of dry chopped *Miscanthus* could be completely covered by plastic while it is only necessary to cover the top of piles of bales (the sides can be left uncovered since rain will not penetrate deeply).

The covering of biomass piles with plastic sheeting may be labour-intensive, however this depends on the volume of biomass and the weather conditions. When the biomass piles are high there is a considerable risk of damage or removal of the plastic during high winds, however, when covering piles of bales, the bales can be used as a ballast for the plastic. The cost of storage, therefore, depends on the price of the labour and the anchoring measures taken.

When covering chopped material and bales, tunnel-like structures can be made to make natural ventilation through the piles possible. Also, piles of bales can be constructed so that some room is left between the bales in a horizontal direction. This facilitates drying by natural ventilation.

In order to calculate the costs of plastic sheeting, a distinction is made between coverage of bales, bundles and compact rolls under cloth and coverage of chopped biomass under plastic sheeting of 0.15 mm thickness. The latter is not suitable for covering of bales as the hard and sharp stem pieces will cut through the plastic. The cloth which is used for covering bales, bundles and compact rolls can be reused for up to five years while the plastic used for covering chopped biomass can only be used once. The costs of the covering material for the different forms of *Miscanthus* have been calculated by Venturi *et al.* (1996) as 8.4 ECU t^{-1} dm for bundles, 1.6 ECU t^{-1} dm for chopped biomass, 3.3 ECU t^{-1} dm for bales and 1.8 ECU t^{-1} dm for compact rolls.

Storage in the Open Air, Covered with Organic Materials

The covering of large piles of *Miscanthus* with waste or low-value organic matter is an option in order to avoid the contamination of the biomass material with plastic. This option has been used in Sweden where peat is stored under sawdust (R. Olsson, pers. comm.).

In The Netherlands an extended list of organic materials which could possibly be used to cover *Miscanthus* piles was made and four of these were selected for use in a small-scale test. The selected materials had to comply with four requirements:

• the costs should be low
• the materials should be available in large quantities in agricultural areas
• the materials' conversion to energy must be possible
• it should be possible to mechanise the materials' application by chopper-blower or liquid manure spreader.

The test involved covering a 1 t pile of chopped *Miscanthus* with one of four different kinds of materials. These were steamed potato peelings, chopped roadside hay, chopped straw and chicken manure. These piles were monitored during the summer and winter of 1995–96 in order to observe the behaviour of the covering materials. The following observations were made:

• When the steamed potato peelings were applied, the liquid component of the material immediately sank into the chips, thus indicating that it had been wasted. However, by the end of the season a crust layer had formed on the outside of the pile. This layer consisted of a mixture of *Miscanthus* chips, potato peels, mould and algae. The crust layer was about 300 mm thick and surrounded the pile. No moisture was found under the layer.

- The roadside hay also formed a wet layer which surrounded the pile, approximately 250 mm deep and developed into a closed crust layer.
- Straw did not form a closed cover/protective layer.
- The best covering layer was formed by the chicken manure. However, in The Netherlands, it is not permitted to expose large surfaces of manure open to the atmosphere in order to avoid ammonia emissions.

The costs of using organic covering were not found to be higher than plastic sheeting but they were largely dependent on availability and the transport distances from their source to the storage area.

Storage in Existing Farm Buildings

The use of existing farm buildings for storage of *Miscanthus* will probably be restricted to small amounts of *Miscanthus*. Potato storage rooms are highly suitable for storage and drying of *Miscanthus* but they will probably only be temporarily available as they will be used to store potatoes from September onwards (potatoes have a higher cash value than *Miscanthus* biomass and will therefore be given preference). Other farm storage buildings such as hay barns can also be used. These barns are generally used to give shelter and they are open at the sides. In addition the ground surfaces around them are often paved which makes handling easy.

Storage in New Farm Buildings

Another option for the storage of *Miscanthus* is the construction of specialised storage buildings on the farm. There is a German cheap storage building, System Weihenstephan, which can be built mainly by the farmer (Hartmann, 1995b). This roofed rough timber structure which is open at the sides costs 11 ECU t^{-1} dm or 12 ECU t^{-1} dm with a concrete floor (required for storage of chopped material). In The Netherlands the cheapest farm buildings are built of steel with a concrete floor, open at the sides and 3.85 m high at the sides (Venturi *et al.*, 1996). The costs for a storage building with a dry matter capacity of 72 t is 22.7 ECU t^{-1} dm for bundles, 17.6 ECU t^{-1} dm for chopped material, 14.3 ECU t^{-1} dm for bales and 8.1 ECU t^{-1} dm for compact rolls.

6.6 Optimisation of Harvesting, Drying and Storage Chain

The most appropriate harvesting, drying and storage systems are not only related to each other but also to the treatments after storage such as transport, chopping and pelleting. A model is being built that takes the whole chain into account (Huisman & Gigler, 1997). The model calculates the effects of different harvesting and drying options on costs and energy inputs of the whole process. However, since some of the inputs of the model are standard, such as weather data for many years, the model can also give information regarding harvest dates. Figure 6.17 gives an overview of the model, the main inputs of which are meteorological data, soil data and harvest methods. Standard meteorological data of the last 20–50 years are used while soil data for three different soil types (sand, clay and peat) are used. The model requires inputs

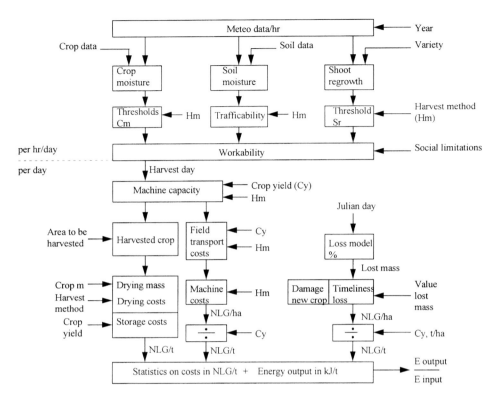

Figure 6.17. Optimisation model to calculate harvest time and total chain costs for various harvesting, drying and storage scenarios.

from a number of sub-models concerning crop moisture content, trafficability, shoot regrowth, workability, time loss, machine costs, drying in storage, soil damage and yield loss.

The model outputs are costs (NLG) and energy input of the whole chain. Various scenarios of different harvesting, drying and storage systems will be chosen and calculations will be made for all years so that the variation of the calculated costs and energy input can be examined and statistically described. The results should then give an insight into the costs and the variation in the costs that can be expected in the future for these scenarios (assuming no weather change in the future).

7 | *Utilisation of* Miscanthus

by P. Visser and V. Pignatelli

with contributions from U. Jørgensen and
J. F. Santos Oliveira

7.1 Introduction

Miscanthus was introduced into Europe in 1935 and has primarily been used as an ornamental plant since then (Jones *et al.*, 1994; Jørgensen, 1996). However, more recently, research results from several European countries have encouraged the development of a range of commercial uses for it.

Energy production and paper pulp production were the first end uses which were considered for *Miscanthus*, but the feasibility of other end uses is also being examined. These potential end uses include utilisation in building materials and also in the bioremediation of contaminated soil. This chapter outlines the different options for the utilisation of *Miscanthus*-harvested biomass.

7.2 Energy Production

One of the potential end uses of *Miscanthus* is as a fuel for energy production. The energy production alternatives which have been examined are co-combustion with coal, and combustion in farm heating plants. These two alternatives are outlined below.

7.2.1 *Chemical and Physical Characterisation*

If *Miscanthus* is to be used as a fuel for energy production, it is important to know the chemical composition of the biomass itself and its ashes. BTG has carried out an investigation as part of the *Miscanthus* Productivity Network to determine the physical and chemical characteristics of *Miscanthus*. The results of this research will be of use in determining the operating conditions of the conversion plant and the disposal of the ash.

BTG analysed a sample of *Miscanthus* (sample 1) in 1994 for its chemical and physical characteristics, another sample (sample 2) was analysed in 1995. Sample 2 had been used in droptube furnace experiments. Two further *Miscanthus* samples (samples 3 and 4) were analysed by MIDTKRAFT (A/S Midtkraft Energy Company, Skødstrup, Denmark) during large scale co-combustion tests in Denmark. In addition, data on the chemical and physical characteristics of *Miscanthus* have been found in the

Table 7.1. *Physical and chemical characteristics of* Miscanthus.

Parameter	Sample 1*	Sample 2*	Sample 3**	Sample 4**	Literature ***
Gross calorific value (MJ kg⁻¹)					
on dry basis	19.05	18.58			17.1
on wet basis	16.78	16.80			
Net calorific value (MJ kg⁻¹)					
on dry basis			17.77	17.63	15.8
on wet basis, as received	15.37	15.50	15.56	14.74	
Moisture content (%, wet basis)	11.9	9.6	11.9	16.4	
Fixed carbon (%)	11.2	17.8			27.7
Volatile content (%)	86.3	79.5			69.7
Ash content (%)	2.6	2.7	2.7	3.2	2.6
Chemical composition (%, dry basis)					
C	49.5	45.1			41.5
H	7.47	6.92			5.4
O	39.3	44.78			
S	0.17	< 0.01	0.19	0.10	0.11
N	0.61	0.41			0.5
CL	0.49	0.03		0.19	
Heavy metals (mg kg⁻¹, dry basis)					
Pb	3.9	0.9			
Cd	< 0.8	< 0.8			
Cu	2.1	3.0			
Hg	< 0.02	< 0.05			
Cr	2.1	< 1			
Zn	48	45			
Ni	2.0	0.8			
As	< 1	< 3			
Ash composition (% weight)					
SO_3	0.6	1.15	5.5	5.3	
P_2O_5	10.81	1.99	3.0	3.9	
SiO_2	37.88	75.73	45.3	48.1	
Fe_2O_3	2.03	1.82	1.6	1.7	
Al_2O_3	1.36	1.37	2.6	4.5	
CaO	14.43	2.35	9.8	7.2	
MgO	6.44	2.37	4.1	3.6	
Na_2O	0.66	0.77	0.72	1.2	
K_2O	23.38	6.49	22.4	20.5	
TiO_2	0.33	0.13	<0.1	0.16	
Mn_3O_4	0.87	0.13			
Ash melting temperatures (°C)					
softening point	935	900			1020
hemisphere point	1080	1270			1090
flux point	1120	1450			1120

*   Samples analysed for BTG, according to characterisation standards recommended by IEA.
**   Samples analysed by MIDTKRAFT Chemistry Department Laboratory.
*** Source: Kristensen, 1997.

literature. Table 7.1 gives the results of the analyses of samples 1 to 4 and also gives relevant data from the literature. It can be seen that the main characteristics of all the samples are almost identical. The lower heating value (net calorific value) of *Miscanthus* on a dry basis is around 17 MJ kg^{-1} with a 2.7% ash content. The average moisture content of the air dried samples was 16%, which brings the wet basis lower heating value (net calorific value) to approximately 15 MJ kg^{-1}.

The high chlorine content which was measured in the first sample (0.49%) was not observed in the other samples (0.03–0.19%). More research needs to be carried out to find the effects of site on chlorine contents. No other major differences were observed between samples except for the ash silicon content (75.73% compared with 37.88–48.1%) in sample 2. A possible explanation for this may be that different harvest methods would result in more or less soil being collected. However, if this was the case, the ash content should also have been higher than the value reported. Differences in soil types might also explain the high silicon content in sample 2 which also has an unusually low sulphur content (<0.01% compared with 0.1–0.19%).

7.2.2 *Co-combustion with Coal*

Co-combustion of biomass with coal has recently attracted wide interest as a means of reducing coal consumption without affecting power station outputs. Substitution of coal by biomass reduces the emissions of CO_2. Furthermore, biomass contains small amounts of fixed nitrogen and sulphur compared to coal on a weight basis which results in reduced NO_x and SO_x emissions during combustion.

At present, a number of types of combustion reactors are available for the conversion of the calorific value of coal into heat and combustion products. These include pulverised coal combustors, stoker combustors, atmospheric fluidised bed combustors and circulating fluidised bed combustors. Pulverised coal combustion is the most common reactor used in large-scale power generation operations (i.e. >500 MW$_{el}$). The factors which affect the conversion of pulverised coal inside a combustor can be interpreted and understood if the process is locally probed to measure relevant parameters such as temperature, velocity and local composition of the gas and solid phase.

The sections below describe the co-combustion of biomass with coal through the use of a droptube reactor and the implementation of large-scale co-combustion experiments.

Droptube Experiments on Co-combustion with Coal

Choosing a power station as an experimental set-up for research is difficult because of the scale of operation (>500 MW$_{el}$). In order to overcome this problem BTG designed and constructed a droptube reactor for carrying out well controlled biomass devolatilisation experiments with operational conditions that resemble those of a pulverised coal combustion reactor. A mathematical model was also developed to predict biomass decomposition in the droptube reactor. The goal of the model was to describe the processes which occur inside a pulverised coal combustion station and to determine if biomass contributes to the flame formation inside the combustion chamber.

The droptube reactor simulated the environment inside a pulverised coal combustion chamber. Default values for the experimental conditions such as temperature, particle residence time and gas phase composition were derived from pulverised coal combustion literature. The biomass particle diameter and type of biomass were independent variables defined during the experiments.

Operating Conditions of the Droptube Reactor

The reactor temperatures varied from 800–1400°C. A customised biomass belt feeder was designed to allow a continuous biomass feeding rate of 1 g h^{-1} (in order to study the thermal decomposition rate of single particles). Prior to each droptube reactor experiment the biomass particles were size-reduced using a hammermill, the material was then size-classified with a vibrating sieve stack where three biomass particle size classes were obtained. These were Class I (0.6–1.0 mm), Class II (1.0–2.0 mm), and Class III (2.0–2.8 mm). The experimental conditions employed in the reactor may be summarised as follows:

- temperature: 1000, 1200, 1300 or 1400 °C
- oxygen concentration: 20% vol
- particle size class: 0.5–1, 1–2, or 2–3 mm
- tube length: 0.4, 0.8, 1.2, or 1.6 m
- biomass type: willow, poplar, *Miscanthus* or reed

Each experiment started with the weighing of 0.5 g of a specific size class of biomass. The droptube was then operated for 30 minutes in a cyclical biomass feeding and gas flushing process and the solid product was collected continuously in a solid product collection vessel positioned downstream. Partially decomposed solid products were collected and their weight measured on a high precision balance. The mass conversion of biomass was defined as follows.

$$\text{mass conversion} = \frac{\text{initial biomass weight} - \text{solid products weight}}{\text{initial biomass weight}}$$

Modelling of the Biomass Decomposition Process

Visual inspection of the solid products which were formed during the high temperature biomass conversion process showed that the biomass particles decompose in two stages. Firstly, the biomass quickly devolatilises, with the resulting volatiles accounting for more than 80% of the calorific value of the original biomass and the remaining char accounting for approximately 10% of the original biomass weight. The second stage of the conversion process involves the slow combustion of the char. However, the BTG model only describes the devolatilisation stage of the conversion process, as this stage is of prime importance in the flame formation inside a pulverised coal combustor chamber. The mathematical model was used to simulate the thermal decomposition of willow particles. All necessary model parameter values are given in Table 7.2.

The model calculates mass conversion per particle per unit time (i.e. the reduction in wood content and formation of char inside a particle per unit time). As an example,

Table 7.2. Parameter values used in mathematical model for thermal decomposition of willow particles.

Parameter	Value	Unit of measurement
Willow particle shape	cylindrical	
Willow particle diameter (d_p)	1.3	mm
Willow particle length (L_p)	7.0	mm
Willow density	470	kg m^{-3}
Willow heat capacity	1335	J kg^{-1} K^{-1}
Willow heat conductivity	0.122	W m^{-1} K^{-1}
Heat of reaction	0.5	MJ kg^{-1} (wood)
Ultimate char mass fraction	0.1	
Gas phase medium	air	
Gas phase temperature	1573	K

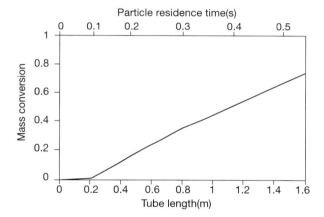

Figure 7.1. Mass conversion of a willow particle (cylindrical, 1.3 mm diameter and 7 mm long).

Figure 7.1 gives the mass conversion of a willow particle in the droptube. A mass conversion equal to 0 corresponds to the original wood particle and a mass conversion equal to 1 corresponds to a char particle.

The particle first falls a distance of 0.2 m down the droptube for 0.1 s without any conversion. This interval corresponds with the heating of the wood particle to the temperature of rapid pyrolysis (approximately 800 K). Conversion then begins and the particle continues to decompose until it leaves the 1.6 m long droptube. At the point of exit from the droptube, the particle consists of 30% wood and 7% char (% is on a weight basis).

Miscanthus Feedstock Analysis

Miscanthus stems were reduced by hammermill and sieved to produce particles of Class I (0.6–1 mm), Class II (1–2 mm) and Class III (2–2.8 mm). Visual inspection of the particles of each size class showed their shape to be nearly cylindrical. A random sample of 35 class II particles was studied in detail and it was found that more than 75% of the total particle volume was contained in the largest half of the particle sample. Therefore, the thermal conversion of a biomass size class is limited by these large particles. However, since hammermilling and sieving are realistic large-scale biomass pre-treatment operations, it was decided to numerically model the decomposition of a single cylindrical *Miscanthus* particle with a unique diameter and length. The thermal decomposition of real particle distribution can then be predicted by superposition of the outcomes of a numerical model run in series with the particle length-diameter co-ordinates as inputs.

Miscanthus Conversion and Model Validation

For calculation purposes the complex size distribution of the three size classes was simplified using the results of the sample analysis given in the previous section:

- Class I: 75%, d_p = 0.6 mm, L_p = 6 mm; 25%, d_p = 0.3 mm, L_p =3 mm.
- Class II: 75%, d_p = 1 mm, L_p = 10 mm; 25%, d_p = 0.5 mm, L_p = 5 mm.
- Class III: 75%, d_p = 1.6 mm, L_p = 16 mm, 25%, d_p = 8 mm, L_p = 0.8 mm.

All three size classes of hammermilled *Miscanthus* were fed into the droptube reactor. Figures 7.2, 7.3 and 7.4 give the measured mass conversion and corresponding droptube lengths.

It can be seen in Figure 7.2 that complete conversion of the Class I particles can be achieved for droptube lengths greater than 1 m. The model predictions deviate significantly from the measured data points; this may be attributed to the unknown thermal decomposition rate of *Miscanthus*. The measurement data indicate a mass conversion of 75% mass at a tube length of 0.4 m whereas the model predicts a similar conversion at approximately 0.2 m.

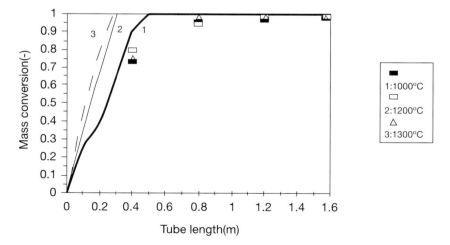

Figure 7.2. Mass conversion of Class I Miscanthus *particles as a function of the droptube length. The points correspond with measurements, while the solid curves correspond with the model predictions.*

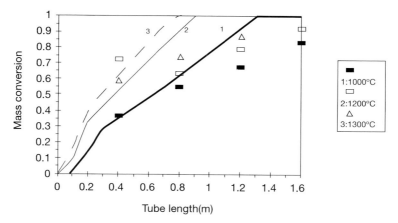

Figure 7.3. Mass conversion of Class II Miscanthus *particles as a function of the droptube length.*

Figure 7.3 gives results for mass conversion of the Class II particles. It can be seen that an almost complete conversion of biomass particles can be achieved at a droptube length of 1.6 m, particularly at a temperature of 1300°C which resembles the conditions inside the pulverised coal combustion chamber. The deviation between the model predictions given by the solid curves and the measured data are less than those observed for Class I particles (Figure 7.2).

Figure 7.4 gives the results obtained for the conversion of Class III particles. It can be seen that the model predictions and the measured data points correspond very well, thus suggesting that the model predictions for large particles are less dependent on the assumed *Miscanthus* reaction rate and the heat of reaction than the model predictions for smaller particles. However, further computer simulations and a sensitivity analysis should be made to establish this fact.

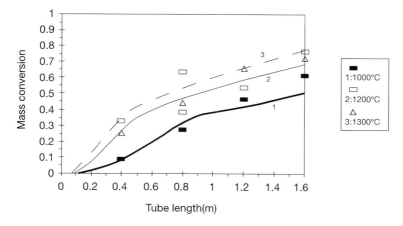

Figure 7.4. Mass conversion of Class III Miscanthus *particles as a function of the droptube length.*

Application of the Model to a Pulverised Coal Combustor

Goudey Power station is a pulverised coal combustor with many experimental facilities. The lower section of the furnace consists of a hopper in which ash is collected. No gas flows through the hopper, thus creating a zero convection environment in which the ash particles can sediment. Pulverised coal is fed into the windbox section (extending from 4 to 8 metres in the vertical direction) where a coal fire ball exists and coal volatiles are released. The thermal energy from the gas phase radiates into the furnace walls which are entirely made up of heat exchanger tubes in the radiant section (extending from 8 to 17 metres in the vertical direction). The temperature of the ash and slag particles drops below 1000°C in the radiant section, a threshold value below which the slag solidifies and does not stick to inserted heat exchanger tubes. The only particles which enter the heat exchanger section (situated above the radiant section at a height higher than 17 metres) are solid particles.

The numerical model, which was validated with the experimental results obtained in the droptube reactor tests, was used to predict the effect of feeding hammermilled *Miscanthus* of different sizes to the Goudey furnace. The model was used to predict the mass conversion of *Miscanthus* when co-fired with a fossil fuel. Single particle size classes were used in the simulations with all particles being fed together with coal particles into the windbox section at a height of 5 metres from the bottom of the furnace.

The lower biomass density of *Miscanthus* (300 kg m^{-3}) allows it to be well entrained (even for particle sizes up to diameters of 4 mm and lengths of 40 mm). However, these large particles devolatilise by 25% weight in the radiant section, leading to destabilisation of the coal flame, formation of hot spots in the radiant section and combustion of the volatiles which are released. This can also lead to reduced solidification of the molten slag particles in the radiant section which may lead to more extensive fouling of the heat exchangers which are positioned downstream. It was found that *Miscanthus* particles with a diameter of less than 3 mm (L_p/d_p = 10) can be co-fired well in a pulverised coal combustor, while the co-firing of larger *Miscanthus* particles was found to lead to a geometrical extension of the flame in the vertical direction.

Conclusions of Droptube Experiments on Co-combustion with Coal

Rapid screening of the combustion behaviour of energy crops can be successfully carried out in the droptube furnace which was designed, constructed and operated at the laboratory of BTG Biomass Technology Group B.V. The particle residence time in the hot zone of the reactor was a maximum of 1 second and the parameters which were varied for the droptube tests are as follows:

- the droptube temperature: 1000, 1200, 1300 and 1400 °C
- the heated droptube length: 0.4, 0.8, 1.2 and 1.6 m
- the particle size or sieve fraction: 0.6–1, 1–2 and 2–2.8 mm.

The results may be summarised as follows:

- visual inspection revealed that partially converted biomass particles have a charred envelope, implying that these particles underwent a rapid pyrolytic change with oxidation reactions only occurring outside the particle
- grass-like crops devolatilise faster than the wood-like crops
- particles of the smallest size class (0.6–1 mm) can be completely devolatilised in a 1.2 and 1.6 m long droptube, except at furnace temperatures of 1000°C
- the conversion rate of crops at reactor temperatures above 1200°C was over 90% at a tube length of 1.2 m or longer
- particles of the largest fraction (2–2.8 mm) of the grass-like crops completely devolatilised at 1400°C and droptube lengths of 1.6 m.

Apart from the experimental investigation, a numerical model was developed. Samples of willow, representing the wood-like crops, and *Miscanthus*, for the grass-like crops, were characterised in detail. These characteristics were used to validate the numerical model on the basis of the results from the droptube furnace. In this validation, no match-factors have been used. The numerical model was validated due to the correspondence of the numerical outputs of the model to the droptube experimental results.

The numerical model was applied to predict the biomass devolatisation behaviour in a pulverised coal power station. The model predicts full conversion of energy crop particles with a diameter smaller than 3 mm, given a maximum length-diameter ratio of 6. It was predicted that particles with a diameter larger than 4 mm are decoupled from the convective gas flow and cannot be fired in a pulverised coal station.

Large-Scale Co-combustion Experiments

Miscanthus was co-fired with coal in two large-scale experiments in two Danish installations which were designed for the co-firing of straw and coal. These experiments were carried out in collaboration with VEBA Oel of Germany and MIDTKRAFT Energy Company of Denmark. In the first experiment 10 tons of *Miscanthus* were co-fired with coal in a Circulating Fluidised Bed boiler in a 50 to 50% energy equivalent-based ratio. In the second experiment 100 tons of *Miscanthus* were fired in a conventional powdered coal burner in an 20% *Miscanthus* to 80% coal ratio. The main objective of the first experiment was to test if the pre-processing equipment for straw can also deal with baled *Miscanthus*. In both experiments the differences between the co-firing of straw and *Miscanthus* regarding boiler efficiency and emissions were assessed.

Co-combustion tests at CHP Grenaa – Circulating Fluidised Bed boiler
The Grenaa plant is a local plant providing electricity, district heating and industrial process steam from a single Circulating Fluidised Bed (CFB) boiler and steam turbine plant. The fuel used in the plant is a mix of coal and straw at an average energy content based ratio of 50–50%. The plant is the first commercial installation of its kind in northern Europe and became operational in 1992. The boiler capacity is 78 MW_{th} and the net electricity output is 17.8 MW_{el}. Straw handling equipment was developed to handle the large quantities of straw which are used to fuel the boiler. Hesston-type bales of straw (approximately 450 kg each) are delivered by trucks and unloaded by an automatic crane which handles 12 bales in each lift. The weight and moisture

content of the bales are recorded automatically during unloading. The main straw feed line diverts into four parallel lines with low energy consumption bale shredders, the processed straw is then pneumatically fed to the boiler.

The experiment carried out at the Grenaa plant involved co-firing 10 tons of *Miscanthus* with coal in the CFB boiler at a 50/50 energy based ratio and monitoring the fuel feeding system and the co-combustion process. The observations which were made during the tests at the Grenaa plant are summarised below.

The top and bottom layers of *Miscanthus* bales which had been stored outside were removed thus leaving only the dry bales for testing. The subsequent non-standard dimensions of the *Miscanthus* bales necessitated manual removal of the cords and stapling of the bales in two layers in order to cover the shredder inlet area and to minimise dust emissions. Of the four straw feeding lines, two were operated on the *Miscanthus*, the other two were idle.

The bales maintained a stable shape and the shredding and feeding to the boiler progressed as it would for straw. The only minor problem which was encountered was with the 'stone traps', caused by the relatively greater length and stiffness of the *Miscanthus* particles. The power consumption of the pre-processing plant was equal to that for straw.

No changes from the operational conditions during coal-straw co-combustion were observed except for a substantially higher dust emission due to the fact that the electrostatic precipitator (ESP) had not been specifically optimised for *Miscanthus*.

Fuel analysis showed that *Miscanthus* has a lower ash content and higher calorific value than straw. The potassium and chlorine content of the *Miscanthus* ash is significantly lower than that of straw resulting in lower fouling levels for *Miscanthus*.

The conclusions of the tests at the Grenaa plant are as follows:

• *Miscanthus* bales of similar quality (moisture content approximately 12%) as straw can be handled and pre-processed without significant problems by equipment of Grenaa standard.
• Hesston standard bales of *Miscanthus* may be pre-processed by Grenaa standard equipment without manual interference.
• Due to the significant reduction in the flux of K and Cl when replacing straw by *Miscanthus*, a substantial drop in the fouling potential may be expected.
• The lower concentrations of K and Cl in the *Miscanthus* ash may increase the options for utilisation of the fly ash when co-firing coal and *Miscanthus*.
• The low sulphur content of *Miscanthus* will lead to a reduction in SO_2 formation compared to coal combustion.

Co-combustion Tests at CHP Studstrup – Powdered Coal Burner
The Studstrup power plant is one of Denmark's largest and most advanced power stations. It generates heat and power from four separate production units of 160, 277, 375 and 375 MW_{th} respectively. The co-combustion tests were carried out at unit 1 (160 MW_{th}) of the plant. This unit had previously been converted for the co-combustion of coal and straw within the framework of a large experimental programme aimed at the use of straw as an energy source. The conversion included the installation of a straw handling and pre-treatment unit.

The straw plant consists of a storage and processing building situated approximately

450m from unit 1, the straw storage is divided into two sections each with a holding capacity of 576 Hesston bales. The straw is supplied to the power station by trucks carrying 20 or 24 Hesston bales. The trucks are unloaded by an overhead crane which unloads 10 or 12 straw bales at the same time; weight and moisture content of the bales are measured automatically by equipment on the crane. The location of the bales in the storage is controlled by a stock control system to make the straw retrievable when the overhead cranes are in automatic operation outside normal working hours. The bales are transported from the storage to the processing building by means of a chain conveyor system located at the end of each storage section.

In the straw processing building the straw bales are distributed to four parallel straw processing lines by means of chain conveyors with each line having a capacity of 5 t h^{-1} (i.e. total of 20 t h^{-1}). Each line contains chain conveyors where the bales are weighed and the binding strings are removed and the flow of straw is regulated by these conveyors. The straw is tipped from the conveyor into the straw shredder which consists of two cutter bars with slowly rotating knives. The straw is then transported to a pneumatic straw feeder which levels out the straw flow; from there, the straw is sucked into the hammermill passing on its way a stone trap where heavier solids are sorted out. The hammermill consists of a number of quickly rotating hammers which pulverise the straw; a screen determines the size and amount of straw to be pulverised. During the experiment a 30 mm screen was used. The pulverised straw is collected in a hopper under the hammermill from where it is transported to an air lock by a screw conveyor. The air lock feeds the straw to the pneumatic transport system which takes the straw over a distance of approximately 450 meters to the coal/straw burners in the boiler.

The boiler is a Babcock & Wilcox two pass boiler which has been in operation since 1968, normally fired with pulverised coal. The original firing system consists of three coal mills (Babcock 8.5E type) and 12 burners (axial swirl type) placed in three rows of four, each coal mill connected to all four burners in one row. The capacity of each of the coal burners is approximately 38 MW, the middle row of four burners has been rebuilt for co-firing straw and coal with the heat input from the straw and coal mixture being approximately 19 MW each at 100% load.

Two types of *Miscanthus* bales were used in the tests: Hesston bales and mini big bales. 25 tons of *Miscanthus* were delivered in Hesston bales, these ranged from 407–725 kg (average 535 kg bale^{-1}), they were all of good quality with regard to shape, humidity, and combustibility. The remaining 225 tons of *Miscanthus* was delivered as mini big bales. The main part of these bales measured 1200 × 700 mm (width x height) and the smaller part had dimensions of 800 × 700 mm. The length of the bales varied from 1200 to 2700 mm and the weight varied from 130 to 310 kg (this was mostly due to the variation in the length), the average weight per bale was 225 kg. Because the straw processing equipment was designed for Hesston bales with a minimum length of 2250 mm and a minimum weight of 400 kg it was not possible to achieve the desired *Miscanthus* load of 20 t h^{-1} with the *Miscanthus* mini big bales.

The Hesston bales had an average moisture content of 14% which was within the design limits of the plant while the moisture content of the mini big bales varied from 13% upwards. Mini big bales with extremely high water contents were frozen to 'ice blocks'. To avoid blockage of the hammer mills and/or the pneumatic transport system, the bales were selected in the storage room. Although the lowest quality

Miscanthus bales had been rejected it was not possible to avoid occasional stops of the processing lines in order to remove frozen bales from the chain conveyor before they reached the processing equipment where they would inevitably cause blockages.

It was planned that the test trials would be conducted with a load of 20 tons of *Miscanthus* per hour, however, this goal was not achieved. During the first test period of five hours a load of 9.74 t h^{-1} was achieved and during the second test period of five hours, the load was 13.3 t h^{-1}. The reasons for the decreased load were that many delays took place in the processing plant because of high water content of the bales (in spite of the selection procedure which had taken place in the storage room), and the mini big bales had an average weight of 225 kg per bale which was too low to achieve a straw load of 20 t h^{-1}.

It was concluded that the straw shredder design at the plant was not suited for *Miscanthus*. This was indicated by the presence of a high proportion of large stem parts (200–500 mm and longer). During the full test period 4000 kg of *Miscanthus* stems were removed in the stone trap despite the fact that generally the bales did not contain large amounts of solids.

For the test a total of 252.9 tons of *Miscanthus* were delivered to the power station but only 152 tons were burned due to the rejection of 101 tons of poor quality bales.

The emissions of SO_2, NO_x, HCl, CO, CO_2, O_2, and dust were monitored continuously, however, no reliable HCl emission data are available as the HCl analyser did not work properly. Coal samples were collected every five minutes during loading of the coal silo using the stationary equipment for coal sampling. *Miscanthus* samples were collected from the bales every 10 minutes using a specially designed drill for straw sampling. The samples were mixed, dried and shredded, the volume was then reduced providing average samples for each of the two test periods. Fly ash samples (approximately 200 g) were collected every 15 minutes, the fly ash was then volume-reduced thus providing representative fly ash samples for each test period. The dry bottom ash was collected simultaneously once every hour from three positions across the bottom of the boiler, the samples were mixed, crushed and volume-reduced to give average samples for each test period. The fuel and ash samples were analysed at the Midtkraft Chemistry Department Laboratory. Additional fuel analysis for C, H, and N were conducted at the Laboratory of Sønderjyllands Højspændingsværk. The main fuel properties and chemical composition of the fuel ashes are listed in Table 7.1.

The energy consumption for the processing of *Miscanthus* was calculated over a three-hour period. The calculations were based on average data logged every second minute. Table 7.3 compares the energy consumption which was measured during the processing of *Miscanthus* to the energy consumption for the processing of straw.

It is apparent from Table 7.3 that the total energy consumption for the pre-processing equipment was more than 50% higher when handling *Miscanthus* compared to straw. The main reasons for the higher energy consumption were the transport fans being operated at full power to avoid *Miscanthus* being sorted out in the separator, and the pneumatic transport system being operated at full power to get a low material/air ratio to minimise the risk of blockage when transporting *Miscanthus* with a high moisture content. It was found that the total energy consumption for the shredder and hammer mill was about 35% higher when processing *Miscanthus*. This energy

Table 7.3. Comparison of energy consumption of the processing equipment for straw and Miscanthus.

	Unit	*Miscanthus*	Straw
Load	kg h^{-1}	3.04	4.65
Test period	h	3.00	5.00
Shredder	kWh ton^{-1}	13.1	10.1
Hammer mill	kWh ton^{-1}	14.0	10.0
ID-fan	kWh ton^{-1}	14.9	7.2
Pneumatic transport	kWh ton^{-1}	15.1	9.8
Total	kWh ton^{-1}	57.1	37.1
Total (shredder and hammer mill)	kWh ton^{-1}	27.1	20.1

consumption does not include the air locks, bale transport system etc., all of which were practically independent of the biofuel.

The results of the analysis of the unburned particles contents in fly ash and bottom ash showed that the amount of unburned particles in fly ash varied between 3.2 and 4.6% (weight basis). In similar tests on co-firing straw and coal the unburned particle content varied between 2.4 and 7.8% while the share of unburned particles is normally about 4% in coal firing. The amount of unburned particles in bottom ash was found to vary between 20.8 to 28.8% (weight basis) which is much higher than that present after co-firing straw and coal (4.7–12.7%) or coal firing (approximately 5%).

The measurement of the O_2 and the CO_2 concentrations in the flue gas as functions of the gross production of electricity revealed that concentrations of O_2 decreased and CO_2 increased as the boiler load increased. The O_2 concentration ranged between 5.5 and 9%: this value is quite high and may promote NO_x emissions, and the high O_2 level may be explained by the age of the boiler. The CO concentration, apart from a few CO peaks exceeding 200 ppmv, remained well below 50 ppmv over the full range of operation (i.e. no major increase in CO emissions may be expected from co-combustion with *Miscanthus*).

The emissions of NO_x and SO_2 decreased with increasing boiler load, the drop in NO_x emissions was most likely related to the simultaneous decrease in O_2 concentration, however, the drop in SO_2 was a little less obvious. The emissions of NO_x followed the same trend whether co-combustion of *Miscanthus* was carried out or not. However, it appears that NO_x emissions were reduced during co-combustion of coal and *Miscanthus* compared to coal combustion. This reduction was not unexpected due to the lower N-content in *Miscanthus*. NO_x emissions seemed to be more sensitive to the boiler load during co-combustion of *Miscanthus* and coal than during coal combustion. The SO_2 emissions from the boiler during the 100% coal combustion test were not easily interpreted, and it was suspected that some kind of irregularity of the system occurred during the test. The lower sulphur content of *Miscanthus* led to reduced SO_2 emissions during co-combustion. However, because of the relatively low ratio of *Miscanthus* (11% and 14% on an energy basis) the dilution effect was limited. Nevertheless, the data indicates a reduction in the SO_2 emission with increasing boiler load as it was found during the co-combustion test.

It was concluded that co-combustion of *Miscanthus* and coal does not appear to affect the dust emission. Two mass balance closures each of five hours duration were conducted during the *Miscanthus* co-combustion test. The in- and out-going mass flows are summarised in Table 7.4.

Based on the mass flows listed in Table 7.4 and the chemical analysis of the fuels, the fly and bottom ash mass balance closures over the major components have been performed for the two periods. The results are presented in Tables 7.5 and 7.6.

Table 7.4. Mass flow during mass balance closures.

Mass flow		11^{00}–16^{00}	16^{00}–21^{00}
		tons	tons
IN	Coal	234	227
	Miscanthus	48.7	66.5
OUT	Bottom ash	1.85	1.82
	Fly ash	33.2	32.9
	Dust	0.3	0.3

Table 7.5. Fly and bottom ash mass balance closures during test 11^{00}–16^{00}.

		Si	Al	Ti	P	S	Fe (kg)	Ca	Mg	Na	K	Cl
IN	Coal	9662	3994	160	25	2036	2103	415	350	208	681	94
	Miscanthus	321	44	2	21	29	20	65	27	12	240	97
	Total	9983	4039	161	46	2065	2122	480	377	220	921	191
OUT	Bottom ash	318	102	4	1	1	49	18	12	5	20	2
	Fly ash	8749	3902	148	48	62	1636	418	322	171	3783	
	Flue gas	0	0	0	0	1720	0	0	0	0	0	?
	Total	9067	4004	152	49	1784	1685	436	334	176	398	5
Deviation		916	35	10	-3	281	437	44	43	44	523	186
%		9.2	0.9	5.9	-6.0	13.6	20.6	9.1	11.5	20.0	56.8	97.5

Table 7.6. Fly and bottom ash mass balance closures during test 16^{00}–21^{00}.

		Si	Al	Ti	P	S	Fe (kg)	Ca	Mg	Na	K	Cl
IN	Coal	9373	3875	155	25	1975	2040	403	340	202	660	91
	Miscanthus	417	31	2	37	53	20	108	46	18	321	106
	Total	9791	3906	157	62	2028	2060	511	386	220	981	197
OUT	Bottom ash	318	104	4	6	1	54	16	14	6	19	1
	Fly ash	8334	3766	153	54	61	1564	405	342	173	392	3
	Flue gas	0	0	0	0	1725	0	0	0	0	0	?
	Total	8652	3870	156	60	1787	1618	421	356	179	411	5
Deviation		1138	36	0	2	241	441	90	30	41	570	193
%		11.6	0.9	0.0	3.4	11.9	21.4	17.6	7.8	18.6	58.1	97.7

It appears that almost 95% of the ash (on a carbon-free basis) leaves the combustor in the form of fly ash, only 5% is found as bottom ash. During the *Miscanthus* co-firing tests the bottom ash was seen to contain large amounts of unburned *Miscanthus* stems which jammed the chain conveyers situated below the boiler and which are designed for bottom ash removal. With the exception of the potassium and chlorine mass balance closures there was a good correspondence between the in- and out-going flows of most components. The discrepancies for the chlorine and potassium data are explained below.

- **Chlorine:** The main reason for the discrepancy in chlorine mass balance closures was the missing HCl flue gas data; apparently less than 3% of the chlorine fed to the system was retained by the ash. Some chlorine may accumulate in the system, however, HCl emissions data from straw co-combustion revealed high HCl emission concentrations. It is therefore reasonable to assume that most chlorine (>95%) leaves the combustor (in the form of HCl) with the flue gas.
- **Potassium**: The mass balance closure showed that almost 60% of the in-going potassium could not be accounted for. As more than two thirds of the potassium originated from the coal, it is likely that less than 50% of the potassium fed to the combustor will be available as volatile. Most of the potassium in the coal will be chemically bound (probably as alumina-silicates or other non-volatile species) and therefore remains in the ash. Organically bound potassium and potassium in simple salts (i.e. KCl and K_2SO_4) may volatilise at high temperatures and either condense on the cooler superheater surfaces or form aerosols which are practically impossible to capture in the electrostatic precipitator. The discrepancy in potassium data could be explained by accumulation in the combustion system and/or by potassium-containing aerosols in the flue gas which pass the ESP (however, subsequent aerosol sampling conducted under co-firing of straw gave no indications of large quantities of water soluble aerosols in the flue gas).

Conclusions of Co-combustion Tests at CHP Studstrup

The observations from the co-combustion tests on *Miscanthus* which were conducted at the Studstrup power station can be summarised as follows:

- A mass input of 11% and 14% *Miscanthus* (on an energy basis) was achieved during the co-combustion tests; this was significantly less than the desired 20% mass input.
- If large amounts of *Miscanthus* are to be handled in the pre-processing plant the bales must be the same as straw bales with regard to size, quality and humidity.
- The total energy consumption of the pre-processing equipment was 35% higher for burning *Miscanthus* than the consumption for straw burning.
- The amount of unburned carbon in the fly ash for co-combustion was less or equal to that found during coal combustion (3.2–4.6% compared to 4%) while the amount of unburned carbon in the bottom ash was much higher than that found during coal combustion (20.8–28.8% compared to 5%).
- In order to lower the ratio of unburned carbon in the bottom ash it will be necessary to use hammermill screens with 15 mm holes or less, rather than the 30 mm holes which were used here.

- The shredders have to be rebuilt in order to avoid the large amount of discarded material in the separators.

The following conclusions were drawn from the chemical analyses:

- Co-combustion of coal and *Miscanthus* results in a reduction in NO_x emissions; the effects on SO_2 are less obvious.
- The reduction in NO_x emissions appears to exceed the dilution effect originating from the low N-content in the *Miscanthus*.
- Co-combustion of *Miscanthus* and coal will result in a reduced introduction of sulphur to the combustion system. However, the results show limited effects of co-combustion on the SO_2 emission levels.
- The emissions of NO_x, SO_2, O_2 and CO_2 are sensitive to boiler loads ranging between 80 and 100% load. It was found that increasing the load results in decreases in the emissions of NO_x, SO_2, and O_2 and increases in CO_2 emissions.
- NO_x emissions appear to be more sensitive to the boiler load during co-combustion than during 'pure' coal combustion.
- Except for a few peaks exceeding 200 ppmv the CO emissions never exceeded 50 ppmv (6% O_2, dry air) and the CO level stayed around 30 ppmv.
- Contrary to the observations at the CFB-plant in Grenaa, the dust emissions did not appear to be affected by the co-combustion of *Miscanthus* in the PF-fired boiler.
- As the HCl analyser was out of order during the *Miscanthus* test no emission data are available for HCl. However, the mass balance closure and subsequent trials with straw combustion indicate a substantial HCl emission (less than 3% of the chlorine was retained in the ash).
- The potential corrosion hazard from co-firing *Miscanthus* under the present conditions in a PF-boiler is believed to be negligible.
- When co-firing less than 40% *Miscanthus* on energy basis (with similar chemical composition) with coal in a pulverised fuel boiler, slagging and fouling should not become a problem due to the limited content of water-soluble alkali metals.

7.2.3 *Combustion in Farm Heating Plants*

Miscanthus may be used as a fuel for combustion in heating systems. Research has been carried out in Denmark to investigate *M. x giganteus* as a fuel for combustion in farm heating systems which are normally straw fired. This research involved characterising *Miscanthus* as a fuel for the farm heating plants, and carrying out combustion tests.

Investigation of Fuel Characteristics of **M. x** giganteus

A number of measurements (e.g. thermal value, ash content, etc.) were made on *M. x giganteus* samples which had been harvested using a number of different techniques; the results are given in Table 7.7.

The carbon and nitrogen content of the *M. x giganteus* was found to be 41.5 and 0.5 respectively. The thermal value of *M. x giganteus* (15.4–17.3 MJ kg^{-1}) was found to be similar to that of straw (14–17 MJ kg^{-1}). The high softening, hemispherical and flow temperatures which were measured are considered to be advantageous as high

Table 7.7. *Fuel characteristics of* M. x giganteus.

Harvesting method	1	2	2	3	4	5
Thermal value (upper), MJ kg^{-1}	16.8	16.7	17.3	16.8	17.2	17.1
Thermal value (effective), MJ kg^{-1}	15.5	15.4	16.0	15.5	15.9	15.8
% Moisture content	5.4	5.7	9.6	5.4	10.0	12.1
% Ash (dry basis)	1.9	2.6	2.5	2.0	2.0	2.6
% Volatile components (dry basis)	80.1	81.0	79.5	80.0	80.8	69.7
% Sulphur (dry basis)	0.11	0.09	0.10	0.10	0.10	0.11
% Fixed carbon (calculated)	18.5	17.5	16.3	18.5	15.5	16.0
% Hydrogen	5.3	5.3	5.4	5.3	5.4	5.4
Melting progress of ashes (°C)						
Softening temperature	–	–	980	–	1120	1020
Hemispherical temperature	–	–	1170	–	1210	1090
Flow temperature	–	–	1190	–	1230	1120

1 Forage chopper with conventional grass header.
2 Mowed, collected and baled with big baler.
3 Forage chopper with maize header independent of row intervals.
4 Sample consisting of straw containing no fragments of leaves.
5 Direct harvest with big baler fitted with chopper.
– No measurements taken.

temperatures will reduce the risk of ash melting and accumulation in the boiler. The highest ash melting temperatures were found in the *Miscanthus* samples which consisted of stems and no fragments of leaves. Previous studies on straw showed that the ash content varied from 2.0 to 8.6%, the sulphur content varied from 0.10 to 0.25%, the content of volatile ingredients varied from 60 to 80% and the hydrogen content varied from 4.4 to 5.4%. The softening temperature of the ashes from straw was found to vary from 880 to 1200°C and the flow temperature varied from 950 to 1500°C. The results in Table 7.7 show that the ash and sulphur contents are lower in *M.* x *giganteus* than in straw, but apart from this no considerable differences were found.

Combustion Tests on M. x giganteus

Two types of boilers were used for the combustion tests, these were the Pilevang batch stoker for big bales, type PM 330, and the Aunslev automatic stoker, type 6B-150, with fluffer, type 120.

Pilevang Batch Stoker for Big Bales, Type PM 330

Big bales (cross-section dimensions 1.22 × 1.29 m) of unchopped *M.* x *giganteus* were used in the big bale batch stoker. The boiler had a horizontal, cylindrical combustion chamber and an automatic fan was used to supply the combustion air which had been regulated in proportion to the smoke temperature.

An efficiency of about 80% was obtained during combustion of *Miscanthus* in the big bale batch stoker. This is about 5% more than the efficiency obtained during combustion of wheat straw in the same boiler. The average emission of solids was 240 mg m^{-3} of flue gas at an oxygen content of 10%, considerably lower than the average emission of solids measured during the combustion of wheat straw (550 mg m^{-3}). Figure 7.5 shows the progress of the combustion of a *Miscanthus* bale (weight 562 kg). The CO content of the smoke is also shown; this was found to be very low (around 0.1%). In general, a more regular and clean combustion was obtained than when straw was combusted, probably due to the fact that the *Miscanthus* bales were rather porous (despite the high specific weight) thus allowing the combustion air free access between the stems.

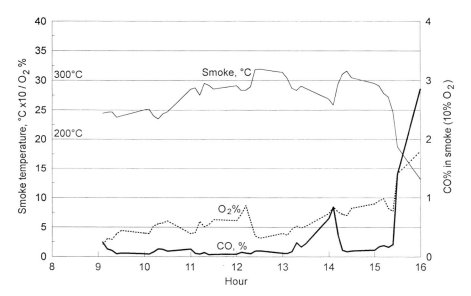

Figure 7.5. Temperature, CO and O_2 content of smoke produced during combustion of big M. *x* giganteus *bales in Pilevang batch stoker.*

Aunslev Automatic Stoker (6B-150), with Fluffer System (120)

The Aunslev stoker boiler equipped with fluffer system was used for combustion of big bales of both chopped and unchopped *M. x giganteus*, and loosely chopped *M. x giganteus*. In this system a straw conveyor belt was used to transport big bales towards the fluffer. This consisted of a rotating, horizontal fluffer drum which moved up and down alongside the bale end surface. The material was blown from the fluffer through a pipe and a cyclone into a stoker screw which then pushed the material into the combustion chamber for combustion under a ceramic plate. The combustion chamber was equipped with two nozzles, one on either side, to supply the combustion air. The results obtained for combustion of the three different forms of *Miscanthus* are outlined below.

Big Bales of Unchopped M. *x* giganteus
It was possible to tear the big bales of unchopped *Miscanthus* apart after adjusting the

forward speed and the rotation direction of the fluffer drum. However, many stoppages were encountered during the air transport of the material to the stoker screw due to clogging of the material in the fan and in the pipes. These blockages resulted in an uneven flow of material to the combustion chamber. An efficiency of 74% was obtained at an average stoking rate of 32 kg h^{-1} and the average emission of solids was 640 mg m^{-3} of flue gas at an oxygen content of 10%. These values are similar to those obtained for combustion of straw. The progress of the combustion is shown in Figure 7.6. It is evident from Figure 7.6 that the CO content in the smoke was highly variable.

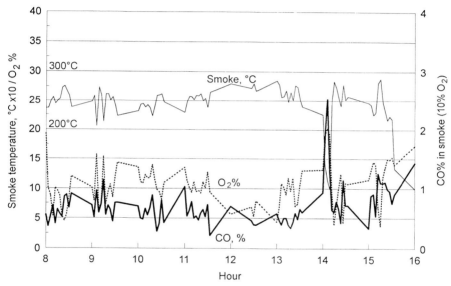

Figure 7.6. Temperature and CO and O$_2$ content of smoke produced during combustion of big bales of unchopped M. x gigauteus *in the Aunslev stoker boiler with fluffer system.*

Big Bales of Chopped M. x gigauteus
It was found that the fluffer could handle big bales of chopped *M.* x *gigauteus* more easily than big bales of unchopped *Miscanthus*, with only a few stoppages due to blockages in the conveyor pipe occurring. However, the flow of material was still uneven due to the loose structure of the bales, this resulted in large volumes of material periodically entering the fluffer. An efficiency of 73–78% was obtained at stoking levels of 34–39 kg hr^{-1} and the average emission of solids was 630 mg m^{-3} of flue gas at an oxygen content of 10%. Again these values are similar to those obtained for combustion of straw. The progress of the combustion is given in Figure 7.7, and it can be seen that the content of O$_2$ and CO in the smoke was highly variable due to the uneven flow of fuel into the boiler.

Loose Chopped M. x gigauteus
The final test concerned finely chopped *M.* x *gigauteus* which had been harvested with a forage chopper. The material was placed loosely on the big bale conveyor belt of the

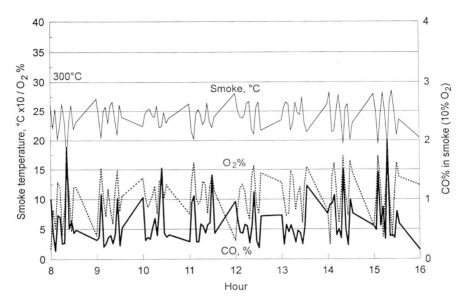

Figure 7.7. Temperature, CO and O₂ content of smoke produced during combustion of big bales of chopped M. *x* giganteus *in the Aunslev stoker boiler with fluffer system.*

combustion system which conveyed it at low speed towards the fluffer. No problems were encountered during the flow of material to the fluffer or during the transport of the material into the stoker screw and boiler. However, problems were encountered during the combustion process, because it was difficult for the combustion air to penetrate the comminuted and compact material. On some occasions an abundance of combustion air was supplied which resulted in emissions of partly combusted particles in the smoke, but this problem could be solved by improving the air supply through the installation of additional air nozzles. An average combustion efficiency of 73% was obtained which is similar to the efficiency of combustion of straw. The progress of the combustion is given in Figure 7.8.

For all of the combustion tests which involved *M.* x *giganteus* an approximately bottom ash content of 2.5% was found. This was somewhat lower than for combustion of straw. The ashes consisted of a fine, grey powder without hard clinkers.

7.3 Paper Pulp Production

In recent years interest has risen in the use of cellulose-rich herbaceous crops such as *Miscanthus* as a suitable raw material for the paper industry. The current European deficit in new cellulose fibre (about three million tons per year) indicates that there is considerable potential for the use of cellulose-rich herbaceous crops for paper pulp production.

At present, the use of fibres from non-woody crops for paper pulp production in Europe is below 1% of the total production. Paper pulp from non-woody crops is

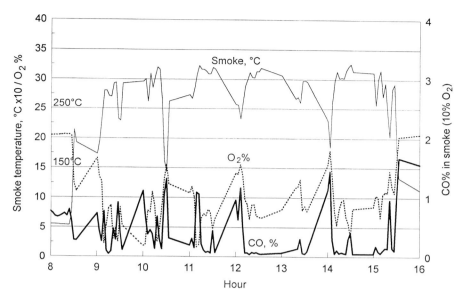

Figure 7.8. Temperature, CO and O$_2$ content of smoke produced during combustion of finely chopped **M. x** giganteus *in the Aunslev stoker boiler with fluffer system.*

mainly produced in developing countries and the raw materials which are most widely used are straw, bagasse and bamboo.

It has been established that the production of paper pulp from cellulose-rich herbaceous crops (as well as from some farming residues such as straw) is possible by several different chemical or thermomechanical processes. *Miscanthus* has been exploited for the production of paper pulp in China. In addition, a number of investigations have been carried out in different European countries on the production of paper pulp from *Miscanthus* using both conventional and innovative processes. The sections below outline the conclusions of this work.

7.3.1 Miscanthus *Utilisation for Paper Making in China*

Miscanthus sacchariflorus (Amur silver grass) is one of the main raw materials used for paper making in the Republic of China. This section outlines the methods used in the production of *M. sacchariflorus* paper pulp and the research which has been carried out in order to improve the process yield and the quality of the produced paper pulp.

Kraft Cooking Process Pulping Method

The pulping method most widely used by the Chinese paper industry is a chemical method called the Kraft cooking process. Such a process is based on the cooking of cellulosic raw material (both wood as well as straw or other non-woody biomass) at a medium-high temperature in an alkaline solution of sodium hydroxide and sodium

7 Utilisation of Miscanthus

sulphate (see Table 7.9) as an example of reaction conditions) in order to dissolve and remove the most of lignin fraction. *M. sacchariflorus* (Amur silver grass) is one of the main raw materials used for paper making in the Republic of China, due to its fast growing cycle, high biomass production, short cooking period and easy pulping. The chemical composition of *M. sacchariflorus* is reported in Table 7.8.

Table 7.8. Chemical composition (% dry matter) of M. sacchariflorus.

Biomass component	% (weight)		
	a	b	c
Ethanol/benzene extractables	1.81	4.47	5.01
Hot water extractables		8.41	12.67
1% NaOH extractables		39.01	42.65
Ash	2.22	2.78	
SiO$_2$	1.14		
Lignin	20.99 (*)	19.63	18.30
Holocellulose	78.63 (*)	74.56	69.78
Glucose	70.6		
Pentosan		23.15	19.76
Xylose	24.2		
Arabinose	5.3		

a   Yi-ming and Yu (1987)
b   Min and Hengzhong (1988)
c   Yuanlu and Zaizhong (1984)
(*) value corrected for ash

The effect of the Kraft cooking process on the content of the main components of *M. sacchariflorus* biomass is shown in Table 7.9 and Figure 7.9.

The delignification of *M. sacchariflorus* biomass during the Kraft cooking process has been extensively studied by Chinese researchers. The conclusions of this research are summarised below.

Table 7.9.   Decrease in the main components of M. sacchariflorus *during the Kraft cooking process (*).*

Cooking time (minutes)	0	30	60	80	100	125	145 (**)
Cooking temperature (°C)	room	65	100	125	150	165	165
Pulp yield %	100	80.70	64.68	59.78	57.74	54.49	54.15
Lignin content %	20.99	16.34	6.16	3.65	2.20	1.33	1.15
Lignin dissolved %	0	37.16	81.02	89.60	93.95	96.55	97.03
Carbohydrates content %	78.63	82.71	91.13	93.51	94.87	97.34	96.02
Carbohydrates dissolved %	0	15.11	25.04	28.91	30.33	32.54	33.46
Residue glucan %	100	89.46	80.17	77.84	77.76	75.39	74.36
Residue xylan %	100	77.17	65.36	59.93	57.29	55.47	54.72

(*)   cooking conditions: active alkali charge 15%, sulfidity 20%, liquid-solid ratio 4:1
(**)   including 20 min. at max. temperature

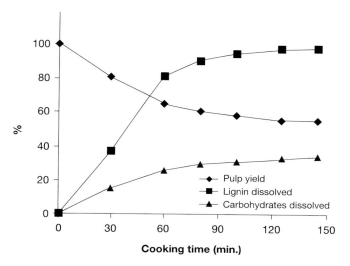

Figure 7.9. Change (%) in the main components of M. sacchariflorus *during the Kraft cooking process.*

- Kraft cooking of *M. sacchariflorus* is similar to that of wood, as it results in a high loss of carbohydrates during the initial cooking stage.
- The delignification process in *M. sacchariflorus* is completely different from that of wood. The percentage delignification of wood below 100°C is very low, while 81% delignification of *Miscanthus* can be achieved below 100°C.
- The Kraft cooking of *M. sacchariflorus* should be ended once the level of delignification meets the lignin content needs of pulp in order to avoid damage of cellulose fibres. It has been observed in laboratory tests that the fibre liberation point of *M. sacchariflorus* during the Kraft cooking is at 59.4% pulp yield. This yield fell between 125°C (gives 59.8% yield) and 150°C (gives 57.8% yield). Therefore, *Miscanthus* Kraft cooking should be ended between these two points in order to maximise both the pulp quality and yield.
- At the highest tested cooking temperature (165°C), the lignin content of the pulp was 1.33% and delignification reached 96.55%, thus meeting the requirement for unbleached Kraft pulp. When the cooking was continued for a further 20 minutes at this temperature, the lignin content came down to 1.15% and delignification was 97.03%. Therefore the extra 20 minutes cooking time only resulted in a 0.18% reduction in lignin content and a 0.48% increase in delignification. It was concluded that because of its negligible effect on lignin content the extra cooking time could be eliminated; this would also result in energy savings.

Optimisation of Pulp Quality and Paper Making Process

Miscanthus sacchariflorus Kraft pulp (BKP) is currently used, after bleaching, for paper-making in Chinese paper mills, together with a minor amount of pine pulp (mechanical and/or chemical). Problems such as sticking on press rolls and wet web breaks have been encountered when paper machines are run with material from non-wood fibres (e.g. *Miscanthus* BKP) and at paper sheet production speeds of over 200 m min⁻¹.

Wet web breaks seem to be related to the wet web strength value of the pulp, whereas the sticking on press rolls is probably due to the adhesive forces of the web on the wire and press roll surface. The wet web strength and adhesive force values are quite different depending on the kind of pulp and on the moisture content in the web (water retention value), which is in its turn dependent on the dewatering rate of the feedstock (drainage time) and on its beating degree, i.e. °SR (the beating degree, Schopper-Riegler, is a direct measure of the pulp refining). The effect of °SR on the water retention value and wet web strength of *Miscanthus* BKP produced in an industrial plant (Yueyang Paper Mill, Yueyang, Hunan) is shown in Table 7.10.

Table 7.10. The effect of beating degree (°SR) on water retention value and wet web strength of Miscanthus sacchariflorus *BKP.*

Beating degree (°SR)	Water retention value (%)	Web wet strength* (g 30 mm⁻¹)
33	83.0	224
25	82.0	174
21	79.5	157
14	74.9	25

* Measured on a Frank Tester with 30 mm web width at 80% moisture content.

It can be seen from Table 7.10 that water retention values drop significantly at low beating degrees. Although the wet web strength of *Miscanthus* BKP falls from 224 to 157 g 30 mm⁻¹ as the beating degree is decreased from 33 to 21 °SR, it is still higher than the wet web strength of a typical newsprint feedstock (125 g 30 mm⁻¹).

It has been established from laboratory tests and experience that a small amount of softwood pulp added to *Miscanthus* pulp improves the runability of the paper on the paper machine at higher speeds. Consequently, the Yueyang Paper Mill began the production of *Miscanthus* paper in 1969 and found that the paper machine ran satisfactorily at 360 m min⁻¹ when a pulp mixture consisting of 75–80% *Miscanthus sacchariflorus* BKP and 20–25% pine mechanical pulp was used. It has been found that if 15–18% long fibre pine kraft pulp was used to replace some of the *Miscanthus* pulp in the pulp mixture, the machine ran smoothly at over 400 m min⁻¹. In 1987, after the rebuilding of the Yueyang Paper Mill paper machine, the machine speed has reached up to 530 m min⁻¹. Since 1987, the Yueyang Paper Mill production of *M. sacchariflorus* BKP is approximately 120 t day⁻¹. The development of the paper-making process in terms of machine speed and pulp material used at Yueyang Paper Mill is given in Table 7.11.

It has been concluded that printing paper made using *Miscanthus* BKP as the major feedstock and pine mechanical and chemical pulp as the minor feedstock has good bulk, high opacity and good ink absorbency. It is deemed suitable for rotary letter press printing as well as off-set printing.

Table 7.11. Feedstock material used at Yueyang Paper Mill, China.

Year	Machine speed (m min^{-1})	*Miscanthus* BKP (%)	Pine mechanical pulp (%)	Pine chemical pulp (%)
1969–1973	280 – 320	80	20	–
1974–1976	340 – 360	75	25	–
1977–1986	380 – 420	60 – 55	25	15 – 20
1987 onwards	up to 530	60 – 58	20 – 25	20 – 22

Chemi-mechanical methods for pulp production

M. sacchariflorus has been tested at laboratory level in China for the production of high-yield pulp by chemi-mechanical processing (CMP). The high content of residual lignin in non-woody biomass such as *M. sacchariflorus* leads to the production of a high-yield pulp which has low strength and brightness. Studies carried out in China and other countries indicate that the key approach to increasing high-yield pulp strength is through:

- increasing fibre bonded area
- increasing fibre bonding strength per unit area

The fibre bonding area can be increased by the use of a chemical pre-treatment which softens the cell wall in order to improve fibre flexibility and consequently reduce pulp damages during refining. The bonding strength, which depends on the chemical characteristics of the fibre surface, can be increased by the use of substitution reactions which introduce polar or ionic functional groups on the cellulose chains.

Studies have shown that the use of a chemical pre-treatment under mild conditions followed by high consistency refining (e.g. rotating plates refiner) can considerably increase pulp strength. Experimental results indicate that chemi-mechanical processed pulp from *M. sacchariflorus* could be a suitable raw material for paper making when brightness of the commercial product is not required (e.g. corrugated paper, wrapping paper, cardboard etc.).

7.3.2 Miscanthus *Pulping by Innovative Chemical Processes*

At present, two-thirds of the world's paper pulp production is done through the use of sulphate (Kraft cooking process) and sulphite pulp production methods. However, the use of sulphurated chemicals for pulp production has serious environmental consequences due to the emission of sulphur compounds and the production of highly toxic organochloride compounds during bleaching with chloride derivatives.

Current research efforts on pulping systems are concentrated on avoiding or reducing the use of polluting chemicals, and searching for an almost selective separation of the main components of lignocellulosic biomass (cellulose, lignin and hemicellulose) in a low-degraded form, in order to obtain a range of products with a high added value. The main pulping methods which have been investigated are chemical and thermo-mechanical treatments. The most promising of the chemical methods which are being investigated are soda pulping, the use of organic catalysts, and treatment with organic solvents and dilute aqueous acids (organosolv processes). These methods are outlined in the sections below.

Soda Pulping

The use of NaOH solutions is an alternative method for producing chemical or semi-chemical pulp from non-woody biomass. There is a special interest in the application of the soda pulping process to straw-type materials because of their high solubility in dilute alkaline solutions. The chemical recovery is much simpler in the soda pulping process compared to Kraft pulping. It has been found in laboratory tests that the addition of Na_2CO_3 to the cooking liquor results in a decrease in the amount of NaOH required to obtain a pulp with the same strength properties.

Studies on the production of *Miscanthus* pulp by alkaline delignification at low temperatures were carried out by the University of Santiago de Compostella (USC) as part of the *Miscanthus* Productivity Network (Iglesias *et al.*, 1996). Several *M.* x *giganteus* samples were collected after the second year's harvest and analysed. The chemical analysis of the material is given in Table 7.12.

Table 7.12. *Chemical composition (% dry matter) of* M. *x* giganteus.

Biomass component	% (weight)
Cold water extractables	6.3
Hot water extractables	9.6
1% NaOH extractables	44.9
Toluene/ethanol extractables	3.2
Ash	5.7
Total sugars	65.9
Klason lignin	23.6

The *M.* x *giganteus* samples were processed in a HAATO multiple microdigester (Kraft process) in order to assess the potential for the production of chemical pulp for paper making from *Miscanthus*, and obtain samples of *Miscanthus* pulp by the Kraft process as a reference material. The HAATO microdigester is an experimental unit made of eight pressure cookers (each one of 0.22 litres capacity), with a revolving action that helps the contact between the milled material and the bleaching solution.

The operating conditions of the microdigester were fixed at the following levels:

- hydromodule 5/1
- sulfidity 25%
- active alkali 14–20% (e.g. Na_2O)
- cooking temperature 165°C
- rising time 90 min
- settling time 45 minutes.

The cooking was stopped by down-cooling the units in cold water. The pulp was then washed and filtered under vacuum pressure. The yield, kappa index and viscosity of the pulp for different levels of active alkali were determined; the results are given in Table 7.13.

Table 7.13. Characteristics of M. x giganteus *pulp from Kraft process at different levels of active alkali.*

	Active alkali (%)			
	14	16	18	20
Pulp yield (%)	48.8	46.5	46.4	44.0
Kappa index	9.1	8.7	8.4	7.6
Pulp viscosity (cm^3 g^{-1})	1234	1187	1180	1110

Fibre analysis was carried out on some samples in the KAJAANI FS-200, the results showing an average fibre length of 0.73 mm with a high fines content (38.7%). Some mechanical properties of the pulp were determined and are given in Table 7.14.

The results presented in Table 7.14 indicate that *Miscanthus* grown in Europe could be used as a substitute for hardwoods (e.g. *Eucalyptus globulus*) as raw materials in paper pulp production. Fibres from both sources have indeed the same properties when processed under similar conditions, particularly in the case of the Kraft process. Due to these promising results it was decided to investigate pulp production via alkaline delignification at low temperatures. The pulping tests involved treating *Miscanthus* with sodium hydroxide under the following range of conditions:

- NaOH concentration 1–2%
- solid/liquid ratio: 1/6, 1/8, 1/10
- temperature: 80 and 100°C
- time (minutes): 15, 30, 45, 60, 120, 180, 240.

Table 7.14. Mechanical properties of
M. *x* giganteus *pulp from the Kraft process*
(HAATO microdigester).

Beating degree (°SR)	18
Density (g cm^{-3})	0.63
Tear index (mN* m^2 g^{-1})	1.45
Burst index (Kpa*m^2 g^{-1})	32.5
Stretch (%)	1.8

Table 7.15 shows the influence of changing the solid/liquid ratio on the pulp yield and the amount of dissolved lignin for *Miscanthus* samples treated with 2% NaOH at 100°C.

No appreciable change in the selectivity of the system was observed in the range of the study. Table 7.16 indicates that the relationship between dissolved lignin and

Table 7.15. Effect of changing solid liquid ratio on pulp yield and dissolved lignin in soda pulping tests of M. *x* giganteus.

Time (minutes)	Solid/liquid ratio					
	1/6		1/8		1/10	
	Yield (%)	Dissolved lignin (%)	Yield (%)	Dissolved lignin (%)	Yield (%)	Dissolved lignin (%)
15	70.3	57.8	65.6	62.3	65.1	60.2
30	66.0	65.7	62.5	69.6	61.9	68.4
45	64.7	66.7	61.5	72.1	59.1	73.2
60	61.5	72.8	59.7	72.5	57.4	78.5
120	62.4	72.2	59.0	75.5	57.1	77.6
180	61.2	71.6	56.2	77.5	54.7	80.0
240	60.0	73.7	56.7	77.7	54.3	82.7

Table 7.16. Kinetic variations of the ratio dissolved lignin : weight losses during soda pulping tests of M. *x* giganteus.

Time (minutes)	Dissolved lignin : weight losses			
	80°C 1% NaOH	100°C 1% NaOH	80°C 2% NaOH	100°C 2% NaOH
15		0.43	0.40	0.41
30	0.42	0.43	0.40	0.42
60	0.44	0.44	0.40	0.42
90	0.45	0.43	0.41	0.41
120	0.48	0.45	0.40	0.41
180	0.46	0.45	0.41	0.41
240	0.46	0.49	0.41	0.41

weight loss is practically constant. This relationship is useful as it facilitates accurate estimation of the amount of residual lignin in pulps by only knowing the yield.

It was concluded that the use of NaOH as a delignification agent allows the production of *Miscanthus* pulp at moderate temperatures with good yield (about 60%) and acceptable values of residual lignin (less than 10%, corresponding to a lignin solubilisation close to 80%).

Organic Catalysts

Extensive research on *Miscanthus* pulping based on the addition of an organic catalyst to enhance the effect of the delignification agent were carried out in Germany in the early 1990s. Interesting results were obtained in the use of anthraquinone in both Kraft and soda cooking (Kordsachia *et al.*, 1992). Anthraquinone is known as a powerful redox catalyst in such processes especially when non-woody raw material is cooked. However, because it is expensive and cannot be recovered, the addition of even the smallest quantity of anthraquinone can only be accepted if it dramatically improves the yield or the quality of the pulp produced. The effects of anthraquinone on the Kraft and soda cooking of *Miscanthus* are shown in Table 7.17.

Table 7.17. Effect of anthraquinone addition on Kraft and soda cooking of Miscanthus. *Source: Kordsachia et al., 1992.*

Cooking process	Anthraquinone concentration (%)	Pulping yield (%)	Kappa number	Brightness (% ISO)	Pulp viscosity ($cm^3 g^{-1}$)
Kraft cooking	0	56.5	16.0	50.4	1110
Kraft cooking	0.05	57.2	10.9	47.3	1270
Soda cooking	0	54.6	27.2	26.6	1080
Soda cooking	0.05	53.2	16.9	31.3	1010

It was observed that the addition of 0.05% anthraquinone substantially enhanced delignification in both processes without affecting the pulping yield. In both cases, the application of anthraquinone may be justified by the remarkable reduction of the kappa number which makes a chlorine-free bleaching to high brightness values feasible.

Preliminary investigations of *Miscanthus* pulping using both an alkaline agent and an organic solvent were also carried out according to the general features of the ASAM process. The ASAM process is an industrial process used for pulping poplar and other hardwood, based on alkaline sulphite cooking with the addition of anthraquinone and methanol. The results of these investigations are reported in Table 7.18.

Table 7.18. Effect of methanol addition on Miscanthus *pulping (Kraft cooking + 0.05% anthraquinone). Source: Kordsachia et al., 1992.*

Methanol (% v/v)	Pulping yield (%)	Kappa number	Brightness (% ISO)	Pulp viscosity (cm^3/g)
10	58.3	9.0	46.6	1340
0	57.2	10.9	47.3	1270
Populus (ASAM process)	56.5	13.6	60.2	1182

It can be seen that the Kraft pulping process with anthraquinone is further improved by the addition of methanol. This effect, however, is much smaller than that observed in hardwood pulping. It was consequently concluded that the use of methanol does not seem to be necessary for the industrial exploitation of *Miscanthus* as a substitute for poplar wood.

Organosolv Processes

Research was carried out on organosolv treatment of *Miscanthus* by the University of Santiago de Compostella (USC) in the framework of the *Miscanthus* Productivity Network. The advantage of organosolv processes compared to traditional methods of pulp production is that an extensive and speedy delignification of lignocellulosic material is achieved with lower pressures and temperatures than those used in commercial processes. Moreover, the three main polymeric fractions (cellulose, hemicellulose and lignin) of the biomass can be separated in different phases or steps and are recovered more easily. Two different organosolv processes were examined, the Battelle and the Acetosolv methods.

The Battelle Method

The Battelle method is an organosolv treatment where lignocellulosic materials are fractioned by the action of a liquor which contains phenol and dilute aqueous HCl. The hydrochloric acid partially degrades the lignin structure, thus making it more soluble in phenol, and, at the same time, hydrolyses hemicelluloses to obtain a mixture of monosaccharides in solution. Water and phenol are miscible at the reaction temperature (100°C), but after the reaction, a phenolic and aqueous phase are obtained as the temperature decreases. The system operates at atmospheric pressure.

The Battelle fractioning of *Miscanthus* was modelled by describing the influence of process variables around an experimental region where the selectivity (ratio of pulp yield / residual lignin) in the pulp is a maximum. A multivariable regression method was used for this purpose.

The plants used for the tests were collected from a two-year old experimental plantation of *M.* x *giganteus* located at Santa Comba (La Coruña, Spain), relatively near the sea and about 30 km from Santiago de Compostella. The material which was collected was stored until its moisture content dropped to 12%. At this point the *Miscanthus* was hammermilled, sieved and the fraction with particles sized between 0.1 and 1 mm was separated for use in all of the experiments.

The experimental tests involved boiling the samples in a 500 cm^3 round bottom flask, operating at total reflux and with the liquid/solid ratio fixed at a value of 15. Reactions were stopped by adding cold distilled water to the reaction flask and by stopping the heating. The pulps were filtered through medium pore size filtering crucibles, washed with water until neutral, and a fraction of them dried in an oven to determine the pulp yield. Liquids were subsequently transferred to a decantation funnel to separate the two liquid phases. After neutralising with CaCO$_3$, an analysis of the reducing sugars in the aqueous phase according to the Somogyi-Nelson method was carried out in order to determine the efficiency of the pre-hydrolysis process. Once the pulp yield was determined, a portion of the pulp was submitted to quantitative hydrolysis in order to determine the contents of residual Klason lignin (RKL) and total polysaccharides of the pulp.

A factorial design was used to evaluate the influence of three independent variables on the selectivity of the process, the variables examined were time (0.37–2.35 hours), phenol concentration (41.6–58.4% weight), and HCl concentration (0.0098–0.0602 g HCl per g dry *Miscanthus*). The steepest ascent method was then used to evaluate the selectivity (SEL) up to the maximum value observed. It was found that the maximum value corresponded to: time: 1 hour 15 minutes; phenol concentration: 51% weight in the liquid phase; and HCl concentration: 0.045 g HCl per g dry solids.

A new design was then constructed in order to quantify the effects of the above mentioned independent variables on five dependent variables (pulp yield, RKL, reducing sugars, total polysaccharides and selectivity). This new design corresponds to a rotatable second order central composite design. Experimental results for the five variables studied were fitted to second order linear models by means of a multiple regression method. The expressions obtained showed R^2 values varying between 0.80 and 0.99, thus indicating fittings from acceptable to good depending on each case.

The results of this work indicated that when the Battelle process is applied to *Miscanthus* the effect of phenol concentration on pulp yield is less than the effect of the acid on pulp yield. The acid concentration was also found to be the most influential factor on the content of residual lignin in the pulp, although time and phenol concentration are more influential than in the case of pulp yield. The minimum RKL value predicted by the model is a little below 9%, which implies a delignification yield of approximately 82%. The content of reducing sugars was found to be influenced by HCl concentration and time. The model predicts a maximum value of 22.7% (within the range of independent variables which were studied), i.e. almost a quarter of the dry mass of *Miscanthus* could be separated as reducing sugars in aqueous solution. All of the independent variables studied were found to have a similar influence on the content of polysaccharides in the pulp with maximum pulp polysaccharide values corresponding to the maximum independent variable values. The highest value of pulp polysaccharides predicted by the model is 94.7%. Finally, the parameters corresponding to selectivity show a behaviour which is difficult to explain, because the phenol concentration is the only variable which shows a significant influence.

The Acetosolv Method

The Acetosolv method is based on the use of acetic acid and dilute HCl for the fractioning of biomass. Figure 7.10 shows a simplified schematic representation of the process.

The effects of the main process variables (temperature, operation time, acetic acid concentration and hydrochloric acid concentration) on the Acetosolv fractionating of *Miscanthus* were studied at Santiago University. The work was planned through an experimental design (face-centred composite design) which considerably reduced the workload. In addition, a function was found which related each independent variable with the response function, and the degree of significance of each variable was established.

The fractionation process was followed by measuring the different polymeric fractions present, and taking account of two dependent variables, the pulp yield (expressed as % oven-dried *Miscanthus*) and the residual lignin content in the pulp (expressed as % oven-dried pulp).

The solid/liquid ratio used in the tests was 1:10 while the operating conditions for each test were selected according to the experimental design. The selected variable values which were used were:

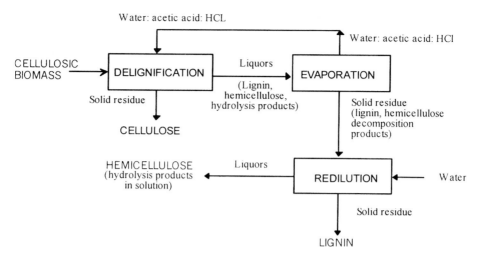

Figure 7.10. Schematic representation of the Acetosolv process.

- temperature: 110, 135 or 160°C
- time: 1, 2.5 or 4 hours
- acetic acid concentration: 70, 82.5 or 95% (acetic acid weight/100 g solution)
- hydrochloric acid concentration: 0.16, 0.84 or 1% (HCl weight/100 g oven-dried *Miscanthus*).

When the cooking process was complete, the resulting pulp was filtered out and washed with acetic acid and water. The residual klason lignin (RKL) content was determined through hydrolysis of the pulp. The results obtained are reported in Table 7.19.

A statistical study of the non linear regression maximising R^2 concluded that the most important variable in the Acetosolv fractionating of *Miscanthus* was temperature. It was found that increasing temperature (within the investigated range) increases the process. It was also found that the process is favoured by increasing the HCl concentration and reaction time, while the acetic acid concentration has very little influence on yield and delignification.

7.3.3 *Steam Explosion of* Miscanthus

In recent years, there has been increasing interest in the use of steam explosion for the production of pulp from herbaceous crops (e.g. kenaf) and lignocellulosic residues (e.g. bagasse, wood industry wastes etc.). Steam explosion tests were carried out at ENEA on samples of *Miscanthus* obtained from field trials using a small pilot reactor (Pignatelli, Nanna *et al.*, 1995; Pignatelli, Viggiano *et al.*, 1995; Pignatelli *et al.*, 1996).

The steam explosion process involves molecular fragmentation of the polymeric components of biomass (hemicelluloses, cellulose and lignin) by means of a hydrothermic treatment with saturated steam under high pressure and temperature conditions, followed by a chemical separation of the products. The main advantage of steam explosion over other pre-treatments is the ability to determine and vary the

Table 7.19. Acetosolv fractionating of M. *x* giganteus.

Temperature (°C)	Time (hours)	Acetic acid concentration (%)	HCl concentration (%)	Pulp yield (%)	Residual lignin in pulp (%)
110	4	95	1	79.2	18.1
110	4	70	0.16	90.7	18.5
110	1	70	0.16	97.6	20.2
110	1	70	1	93.8	19.2
160	1	70	0.16	79.8	17.7
160	1	95	1	62.1	18.6
160	4	95	0.16	58.2	13.4
160	4	70	1	48.6	14.1
160	4	95	1	50.0	13.1
160	4	70	0.16	50.8	13.2
160	1	70	1	75.3	16.5
160	1	95	0.16	89.4	19.1
110	4	70	1	82.3	18.3
110	4	95	0.16	93.2	17.8
110	1	95	1	93.2	20.2
110	1	95	0.16	93.7	20.0
110	2.5	82.5	0.84	90.7	21.1
160	2.5	82.5	0.84	56.5	13.9
135	1	82.5	0.84	89.9	17.7
135	4	82.5	0.84	60.5	14.6
135	2.5	70	0.16	65.6	17.0
135	2.5	95	1	69.2	16.9
135	2.5	82.5	0.84	73.1	17.2
135	2.5	82.5	0.84	56.0	16.5
135	2.5	82.5	0.84	66.0	15.0
135	2.5	82.5	0.84	65.5	16.6
135	2.5	82.5	0.84	66.4	16.8
135	2.5	82.5	0.84	70.0	15.6

vital characteristics (e.g. degree of polymerisation, purity, etc.) of the end product material by varying the process conditions. Steam explosion also has environmental benefits in that the pulping process which is used after steam explosion requires less chemicals than pulping after other traditional processes.

The ENEA steam explosion pilot plant (STAKETECH, see Figure 7.11) is an independent unit which is particularly suitable for research activities. It is completely encased in a steel body. The reactor is a pressure vessel made of stainless steel, which has a capacity of 10 litres, the highest working pressure is 3 MPa. The reactor is surrounded by a steam jacket, in order to ensure that the internal and the external temperature are the same and to minimise vapour condensation.

The pilot plant was specifically designed for batch processes. Biomass is introduced into the reactor through a pneumatic loading valve (3 inches diameter) and then soaked with saturated steam. After some minutes, a blow valve is opened, pressure decreases dramatically in a very short time and exploded biomass is discharged into a storage

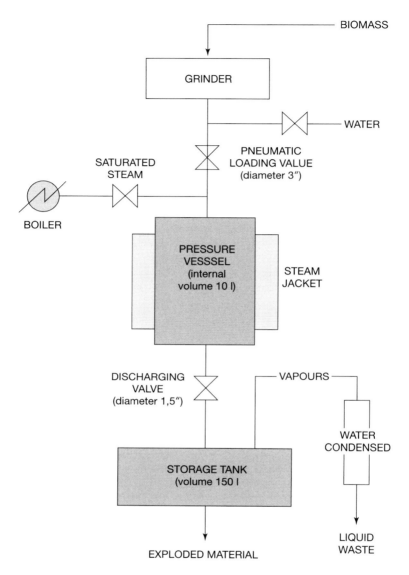

Figure 7.11. Flow diagram of the STAKETECH batch pilot plant.

tank (150 litres volume). This tank has a fast-opening hatchway which allows quick removal of the treated material. A water condenser is connected with the storage tank in order to recover and remove the vapour charged with volatile organic compounds which is produced during the process in the form of a liquid waste.

Miscanthus stalks from a second-year crop were supplied by A. Biotec-Cervia and were used as raw material for the steam explosion tests. The samples were composed of 52% basal section, 33% centre section and 15% top. The stalks were cut into pieces (approximately 10–20 mm length and 2 mm diameter), these were mixed in order to obtain a homogeneous sample, and wetted to reach a sample humidity of 40%. The chemical composition of the sample material is given in Table 7.20.

Table 7.20. Chemical composition of Miscanthus *samples used for steam explosion tests.*

Biomass component	% (weight)
Ethanol extractables	2.24
Dichloromethane extractables	0.78
Toluene/ethanol extractables	0.04
Total extractables	3.06
Ash	2.98
Xylose	24.32
Arabinose	2.28
Total pentoses	26.60
Galactose	0.60
Glucose	38.77
Total hexoses	39.37
Total sugars	65.97
Klason lignin	23.64
Acid soluble lignin	1.55
Total lignin	25.19

Miscanthus samples (600 g at a time) were treated in the STAKETECH pilot plant under different temperature, pressure and reaction times. The different experimental conditions used in the pilot plant are given in Table 7.21.

The exploded material for each log R_0 (see Table 7.21 for explanation) value was divided into two portions (4 kg each). The first portion was put into linen bags, extracted in a washing machine with 6 litres of NaOH (1%) at 90°C for 15 minutes,

Table 7.21. Operating conditions of STAKETECH pilot plant.

log R_0	T (°C)	p (MPa)	t (minutes)
4.12	219	2.3	4
4.06	219	2.3	3.5
3.99	219	2.3	3
3.82	219	2.3	2
3.42	199	1.5	3
3.24	194	1.4	3
3.07	188	1.2	3

R_0 is the 'severity factor', defined by the following equation:

$$R_0 = t.exp\,[(T-100)/14.75]$$

where: t = reaction time (mins) and
T = temperature of saturated steam (°C).

washed twice with 8 litres of cold water and then centrifuged. The other portion was put into bags and some drops of formaldehyde were added in order to avoid fungal colonisation. Table 7.22 shows the effect of steam explosion and washing on the lignin and sugar content of the *Miscanthus* sample.

Table 7.22. Lignin and sugar content (% weight) of steam-exploded Miscanthus *samples.*

	Starting material	Exploded log R_0=3.82	Exploded log R_0=3.82 washed	Exploded log R_0=3.42 washed	Exploded log R_0=3.07 washed
Klason lignin	23.37	26.86	4.5	6.9	9.4
Ac. sol. lignin	1.6	2.19	0.4	0.5	0.9
Extr. lignin (*)			15.7	10.7	8.9
Total lignin	**24.97**	**29.05**	**20.6**	**18.1**	**19.2**
Arabinose	2.28	0.91	0.09	0.38	0.9
Xylose	24.32	16	2.8	7.44	13.87
Galactose	0.60	0.44	0.037	0.079	0.15
Glucose	38.77	42.83	55.9	50.7	50.5
Total sugars	**66**	**60.2**	**58.8**	**58.6**	**65.4**

(*) Lignin extractable with NaOH 1.5%

A comparison of the results of the washed and unwashed samples exploded at log R_0=3.82 reveals that treatment with NaOH (1%) in a washing machine only removed 29% of the lignin. This is considerably lower than the theoretical value of 59% which was observed in repeated laboratory extractions. It was concluded that the severity factor (R_0) did not seem to significantly influence the effectiveness of extraction. An examination of the mass balances and an analysis of the material recovered by washing solution suggests that glucose, and, consequently, cellulose, were not degraded by steam explosion treatment (within the investigated range of log R_0) nor solubilised by washing with water and NaOH 1%.

Four samples of the exploded *Miscanthus* (log R_0 = 3.82 unwashed and 3.82, 3.42, 3.07 washed) were selected for pulp and paper production in the SIVA S.p.A. Technical and Industrial Centre for Pulp and Paper laboratories in Rome. Here, the samples were further refined with a BAUER refiner and the purified material was subsequently screened with the WEVERK sorter (0.16 mm plate). Samples were refined at three different drainage levels (Shopper Riegel, °SR) and the resulting pulps were used to make standard handsheets (80 g m^{-2}). The handsheets were analysed and characterised in order to evaluate the potential for the utilisation of *Miscanthus* pulp after steam explosion for paper making. The main results of this work are summarised below.

Polymerisation Degree of Cellulose

The degree of cellulose polymerisation is an important parameter for a general evaluation of the final product quality. It was found that the degree of cellulose polymerisation decreased as the severity factor used in the steam explosion treatment

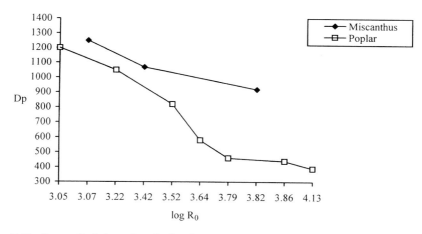

Figure 7.12. Degree of cellulose polymerisation (Dp) vs severity factor (log R_0) in steam exploded Miscanthus *and poplar wood.*

increased (Figure 7.12). This trend has been observed by several researchers and is due to the hydrolysis of the glycosidic bonds of the cellulose chain. It is of interest to note that the decrease in the degree of cellulose polymerisation is much lower than the decrease observed in poplar wood samples which are subjected to the same treatment. This would indicate that the *Miscanthus* fibre has a higher strength than poplar fibre.

Mechanical Characteristics

It was found that as the severity factor used in the steam explosion process was decreased, the tensile index, tear index and burst index of the exploded material increased significantly (Table 7.23). The sample log R_0 = 3.07, °SR 32 deserves special mention as it showed remarkably high tensile, tear and burst indexes. The experimental results compare well with published results for *Miscanthus* pulp produced by conventional processes as well as for hardwood pulps (e.g. poplar, eucalyptus etc.).

Brightness and Opacity

The brightness (%) of the handsheet samples was examined and it was found that brightness increased significantly with the decrease of the severity factor used in the steam explosion process. It was found that this decrease in severity factor and consequent increase in brightness did not compromise the opacity of the paper (Table 7.24).

It was concluded from the tests carried out at SIVA S.p.A. that pulp obtained from steam-exploded *Miscanthus* samples has positive physical, mechanical and optical characteristics. This indicates that *Miscanthus* paper would be suitable both for printing and office uses as well as for wrapping and food packaging. It was found that the paper prepared from *Miscanthus* which had been exploded at log R_0 = 3.07 showed the best

Table 7.23. Mechanical characteristics of pulp from steam-exploded Miscanthus.

$\log R_0$	°SR	Tensile index $(N^*m\ g^{-1})$	Tear index $(mN^*m^2\ g^{-1})$	Burst index $(Kpa^*m^2\ g^{-1})$	Notes
3.82	19	19.1	2.5	0.62	–
3.82	29	15.4	2.9	0.88	–
3.82	20	25.6	3.4	0.96	w
3.82	31	32.3	3.6	1.26	w
3.82	20	30.4	4.3	1.23	w b
3.82	21	29.9	4.8	1.10	w c
3.42	19	26.3	4.0	1.02	w
3.42	28	31.0	4.9	1.30	w
3.42	40	41.3	4.5	1.70	w
3.42	31	33.9	4.5	1.50	w b
3.07	19	27.8	4.7	1.10	w
3.07	**32**	**51.8**	**6.4**	**2.10**	**w**
3.07	42	41.5	4.6	1.80	w
Miscanthus		32.5			s
Eucalyptus		30.5			s
CMP Poplar	58	30.4	3.0		c
CMP Kenaf	66	33.8	3.3		k

w: washed with NaOH 1%
b: bleaching with standard peroxide process
s: chemical pulp from sulphate process (Bao *et al.*, 1992)
c: chemi-mechanical pulp
k: chemi-mechanical pulp 60% kenaf

Table 7.24. Brightness and opacity of paper from steam-exploded Miscanthus.

$\log R_0$	°SR	Brightness (%)	Opacity (%)	notes
3.82	19	13	100	–
3.82	29	14	99	–
3.82	20	15	99.5	w
3.82	31	15	100	w
3.82	20	23	99.5	w b
3.82	**21**	**52**	**91.5**	**w e**
3.42	19	24	98.5	w
3.42	28	23.5	99.5	w
3.42	40	23.5	99.5	w
3.42	31	36	87.5	w b
3.07	19	25.5	96.5	w
3.07	**32**	**26**	**98**	**w**
3.07	42	26.5	99.5	w

w: washed with NaOH 1%
b: bleaching with standard peroxide process
e: cold extraction with H_2O_2/NaOH

characteristics, suggesting that the best steam explosion conditions may be at an even lower log R_0 value.

Future work should investigate the possibility of eliminating the alkaline leaching stage of the process as it was found (see Table 7.22) that alkali leaching was not a very efficient means of lignin removal. The elimination of the alkali leaching stage of the process would result in the development of a much less complicated, more cost-effective and more environmentally friendly process.

7.4 Other Uses of *Miscanthus*

7.4.1 Construction / Building material

Miscanthus has been a subject of interest as a source of fibre to be used in building materials. In order to aid the development of this area of research, the European Union supported a demonstration project in 1992 which investigated the use of *Miscanthus* for the production of building materials, namely panel boards and building blocks (Mangan, 1994; von Wüllerstorff, 1994). In addition, research has been carried in order to achieve new and better solutions for the industrial and commercial use of *Miscanthus* in building materials.

Chip Board and Medium Density Fibre Board (MDF)

Harvey & Hutchens (1995) reported that the *Miscanthus* fibre structure is particularly suitable for the production of medium density fibre board (MDF). They have also found that sample MDF boards made from *Miscanthus* were comparable with those made from wood chips.

Light Natural Sandwich Materials (LNS)

Light Natural Sandwich materials (LNS) are light building materials used for plane and mould structural parts with high form stability at low weight, used for a broad range of applications. LNS can substitute sandwich materials made from plastics or light metals which are regarded as 'high-tech-products' as well as wood-based materials (fibre board, particle boards, etc.) or insulating materials (plastic foams, multicellular glass, mineral wool, etc.).

A LNS material with wood-based top layers and a core of plant stalks is currently being developed in the Wilhelm-Klauditz-Institute at Braunschweig (Germany). Figure 7.13 gives a schematic drawing of the LNS.

The LNS consists of wooden upper and lower outer layers and a core of evenly oriented hollow plant stalks which are bonded with a natural adhesive (e.g. gluten foam). The manufacture of the LNS starts with the arrangement of the stems in blocks during harvest, the stem blocks are then embedded in a foam matrix and cut into slices onto which the outer wood layers (plywood) are glued. The low specific weight, favourable strength characteristics and bonding qualities makes plywood a perfect material for the top and bottom wood layers. The use of high strength stalks in the core of the honeycomb-like structure ensures the production of a high quality product. The core material can be made up of stalks from a number of different plant species

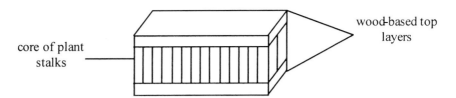

core of plant stalks

wood-based top layers

Figure 7.13. Schematic drawing of a LNS developed at the Wilhelm-Klauditz-Institute at Braunschweig, Germany.

each with differences in stem characteristics which influence the stability, flexibility and the weight of the final product (Table 7.25).

Table 7.25. Characteristics of LNS using different sandwich materials. Source: Moller & Schwarz, 1996.

Type of board	Thickness	Top layer	Core	Density (kg m^{-3})	Bending strength (N mm^{-2})	Bending module (N mm^{-2})	Transverse compres-sion (N mm^{-2})	Transverse tension (N mm^{-2})
Light rye natural sandwich	19 mm	birch plywood (1.5 mm)	rye stems	205	18	4000	3.3	1.5
Light *Miscanthus* natural sandwich	30 mm	birch plywood (2.5 mm)	*Miscanthus* stems	295	33	5000	15.0	2.5
Synthetic fibreglass sandwich	20 mm	fibreglass	PVC	230	35	3800	1.2	2.2

The benefits of using whole stems for the core material can be summarised as follows:

- The stalks are an environmentally benign, renewable raw material which can be grown in large quantities.
- There is no need for splitting or other preparation of stems.
- Whole stems have a very low density because of the internal hollow spaces.
- The strength values and E-moduli are high along the stem axis.
- Stalks are a raw material which do not require much energy for production and processing.

The use of *Miscanthus* as the core material for LNS can be advantageous as *Miscanthus* develops longer and stronger stalks than most other plants, and the strength of the stalks reduces the risk of damage during harvesting and manufacture. However, despite the superior quality of *Miscanthus* stems, there are still problems regarding the stem quality of *Miscanthus* for LNS production. Future research is required for the development of cultivation methods and selection of new varieties in order to increase whole stem quality to make it more suitable for LNS production. The use of *Miscanthus* for LNS production may also be economically favourable. LNS which contains *Miscanthus* stems as the core material is more stable than LNS which contains stems of other plant species as the core material. This increased stability provides a better opportunity for *Miscanthus*-based LNS to replace the more expensive sandwich materials which are made from plastics or light metals. LNS produced on a commercial scale using *Miscanthus* stalks as the core material will cost between 175 and 350 ECU m^{-3}. This is considerably lower than plywood prices (500–850 ECU m^{-3}) and the price of LNS made from plastics (from 1500 ECU m^{-3}).

A new project on LNS funded by the EC (FAIR) has recently been set up, coordinated by Kai-Uwe Schwarz, DIAS. The project will provide a basis for scaling up the production of high performance LNS through the development of the whole chain from primary production to the processing of the product. The project will allow assessment of the factors which determine optimum stem quality and optimisation of the harvesting process in order to allow the harvest of bundles of leafless stems.

Thatching

Miscanthus has been used as a thatching material in Japan for centuries. In Denmark, reed is used for thatching but local thatchers have shown interest in the use of *Miscanthus* as the quality seems very similar to that of reed. *Miscanthus sinensis* is considered to be most suitable for thatching, as the stems *of M.* x *giganteus* are too thick. Selected clones of *Miscanthus sinensis* have been grown in small plots for local Danish thatchers, and the stems have been used for thatching small huts. The oldest *Miscanthus* thatch is eight years old at present, and appears very similar to conventional reed thatch and it seems to have a durability as good or better than the reed thatch.

A pilot project entitled 'Thatching: use of *Miscanthus*' was conducted during 1995–6 in Denmark, aimed at scaling up production and investigating possible commercialisation of the utilisation of *Miscanthus* for thatching. One hectare of *Miscanthus* was established in the spring of 1995, a preliminary market survey was made, yields were measured, the quality of straw for thatching was evaluated, preliminary tests on harvest machinery were carried out and experience was exchanged with Japanese thatchers on a study tour to Japan.

The observations and outcomes of the project are listed below:

- The experience from Japan is difficult to transfer directly to Danish conditions because a different style of thatching is used in Japan.
- The stability of *Miscanthus* is thought to be the same as for reed.
- *M. sinensis and M. tinctorius* are both used for thatching in Japan. Seed and rhizomes from both species were brought to Denmark, and are now planted at Research Centre Foulum (DIAS-Danish Institute of Agricultural Sciences, Denmark).
- In the spring of 1997 another hectare of *Miscanthus* was planted and it is planned to thatch a house with this when enough material is harvested.
- Further steps may be carried out; these include carrying out a test on the durability of the thatch at DTI (Danish Technological Institute, Denmark), development of

machinery for establishment and harvesting, and plant breeding to produce optimal clones.

- The market survey showed that it is difficult to get an overview of the Danish thatching business. It is estimated that there are 200–225 thatchers in Denmark. Between 1990 and 1994, approximately 0.5–1 million bundles of reed for thatching were imported annually, in addition, approximately 2.5 million bundles per year are produced in Denmark. The total consumption of reed for thatching in Denmark is therefore in the region of three million bundles per year. During the market survey, a number of thatchers were visited and shown a bundle of *Miscanthus*, the general reaction was one of surprise at the high quality of the *Miscanthus*.
- The harvesting tests which were carried out showed that it is possible to harvest *Miscanthus* for thatching by using existing machines, however some modifications are needed in order to optimise machine performance. The economics of using *Miscanthus* for thatching is significantly influenced by the costs of harvesting and grading of the straw. In contrast to reed, opportunities exist for the reduction of the costs of harvesting and grading *Miscanthus* as it grows on dry land and therefore cheaper machines may be used. It was calculated that the cost of *Miscanthus* harvesting will be at least 50% lower than reed harvesting costs. The planting of larger fields and the optimisation of logistics will also minimise the costs.

7.4.2 *Bioremediation*

The pressures exerted on soils have increased since the end of last century due to intensive agriculture, industrialisation, the expansion of urban areas and other factors. The result of these factors is that land in many areas is contaminated, damaged or destroyed, e.g. in Europe, extremely degraded areas account for 1.4 % of the total land surface area (Lehmann *et al.*, 1996). It is argued that this contaminated land should be taken out of food production and used for production of non-food crops such as energy crops. The establishment of crops on this contaminated land can be beneficial for the reduction of aerial dispersion and runoff, the improvement of visual impacts, the supply of wildlife cover, and possibly, the production of an economically viable product (Wilkins & Abrutat, 1995).

M. x *giganteus* is being assessed for its ability to grow in west Cornwall, UK, on land which is polluted by heavy metals as a result of the intense tin mining activity of previous centuries. The growth and heavy metal uptake of *Miscanthus* grown on soils and mine waste polluted by copper, zinc and arsenic was studied over a two-year period by CSM Associates. The aim of this study was to acquire information on the uptake of pollutants by *Miscanthus* and the environmental implications of the combustion of material grown for energy production in polluted areas. Table 7.26 gives the heavy metal content of the above-ground biomass of *M.* x *giganteus* which was grown on different soils.

The results obtained showed that the copper, arsenic and zinc content in above-ground biomass was slightly lower in *Miscanthus* grown on unpolluted soil than on polluted soil. However, *Miscanthus* grown on mine waste did not show enhanced metal uptake, although biomass production was lower than on unpolluted soils. Heavy metal concentrations were seen to decrease in late winter of the first year at harvest but this decrease was not repeated in the second year. The conclusions of the study were that

Table 7.26. *Heavy metal uptake of* Miscanthus *($\mu g \ g^{-1}$). Source: Wilkins & Redstone, 1996.*

Soil		1st year (1993–4)				2nd year (1994–5)				
	Aug	Oct	Jan	Feb	May	July	Oct	Dece	Jan
Unpolluted soil									
Cu 17	11	17	18	15	15	20	30	22	24
Zn 108	8	16	20	17	12	25	24	40	24
As 35	19	18	24	18	10	15	21	23	24
Polluted Soil									
Cu 188	13	10	21	15	8	12	20	27	23
Zn 292	93	35	51	36	22	25	22	20	24
As 309	58	45	56	40	31	36	28	26	30
Mine Waste									
Cu 924	12	15	20	10	12	26	29	34	29
Zn 165	41	56	50	18	10	18	27	32	30
As 2339	18	22	20	8	7	28	32	24	22

copper, arsenic and zinc uptake by *Miscanthus* from various substrates was not completely related to total soil concentrations (Bullard *et al.*, 1996). Also it was shown that ash from the combusted material is likely to have elevated metal concentrations (e.g. zinc in polluted soils) which could compromise the utilisation of the crop for energy production.

A study is being performed in Monte de Caparica (Portugal) to investigate the use of sewage sludge as a fertiliser for *Miscanthus*. This involves monitoring heavy metal uptake in the above-ground and below-ground biomass; the results are given in Table 7.27.

It was observed in this experiment that the high content of heavy metals in the soil negatively affected the growth and productivity of the *Miscanthus* crop (Fernando *et al.*, 1996). The results obtained showed that at harvest, the underground fraction of the plants (roots and rhizomes) contained a significant accumulation of the heavy metals content of the contaminated sewage sludge. It was observed that there were no significant differences in the heavy metal content of the above-ground biomass between plants grown on polluted and unpolluted soils. This observation agrees with the previously mentioned conclusions of Bullard *et al.* (1996) that heavy metal uptake by the aerial fraction of *Miscanthus* is not related to total soil concentrations. The low heavy metal content of the above-ground biomass may allow the use of this material for energy production, however, further research is required on the full environmental risks of growing and using such plants.

7.4.3 Composting

Miscanthus is currently being investigated for its use as a component of farm-produced composts and mulches and as a plant growth substrate (Harvey & Hutchens, 1995; Molenaar *et al.*, 1996). There are two different composting options; the first is composting *Miscanthus* with clean raw materials to produce inputs (organic fertilisers,

Table 7.27. Heavy metals uptake (mg kg⁻¹ dry matter) of Miscanthus. *Source: Fernando et al., 1996.*

Plant fraction	Heavy metal type	Heavy metal content (mg kg⁻¹ d.m.)		
		Unpolluted soil	Polluted soil 5.5 kg sludge m⁻²	Polluted soil 11 kg sludge m⁻²
Aerial	Cu	26.37	78.10	65.87
	Zn	218.50	192.3	389.6
	Ni	6.07	28.36	16.07
	Cd	nd	nd	nd
	Cr	19.09	98.92	39.39
	Pb	nd	nd	nd
Rhizome	Cu	52.30	62.91	64.23
	Zn	67.34	119.3	114.7
	Ni	0.96	3.44	2.82
	Cd	nd	0.05	0.18
	Cr	2.39	5.57	5.78
	Pb	nd	0.17	1.60
Roots	Cu	190.8	239.6	294.7
	Zn	181.8	400.5	742.9
	Ni	2.75	10.83	13.82
	Cd	nd	2.79	6.05
	Cr	5.05	38.06	53.37
	Pb	nd	10.05	14.74

nd: not detectable
dm: dry matter

plant growth and landscaping media) for the horticultural, home and amenity markets. The second is composting *Miscanthus* for the biological consolidation of wet organic wastes separated from municipal solid waste, sewage sludge or animal slurries. Table 7.28 shows the characteristics of a compost obtained from the co-composting of *Miscanthus* material with sewage sludge (N source) and paper pulp effluent (source of microbes which degrade lignocellulose) at the start of composting and after six months.

It can be seen from Table 7.28 that an effective decrease of organic matter (due to cellulose degradation) occurred in the compost after six months. This compost had good characteristics as fertiliser or as an organic soil corrector, with a final C:N ratio of 17 and a humus content of 9% (dry weight). It was concluded that the most significant problem with the final compost was the high cadmium and chromium contents.

Generally, the compost obtained from this sort of composting process can pose problems in terms of quality, contamination, environmental pollution and disease transmission. There is a clear need for further research and development in order to improve final compost quality and thus raise its market value.

7.4.4 Fermentable Products

Due to its high cellulose and lignin content, *Miscanthus* has been evaluated as a raw material for the production of fermentable pentose sugar solution. Papatheofanous *et*

Table 7.28. Compost (based on Miscanthus, *sewage sludge and paper pulp effluent) characteristics at start (T0) and after six months (T6). Source: Rodrigues* et al., *1996.*

Characterisation of the Biomass	T0	T6	Metal content (mg kg^{-1} d.m.)	T0	T6
Moisture (%)	35	65			
Organic matter (% dm)	89	78	Ca	32907	94494
Nitrogen (% dm)	1.8	2.6	Mg	2479	3248
C:N	27	17	Na	6460	2526
Cellulose (% dm)	41	33	K	4937	3723
Phosphorous (% dm)	0.61	1.4	Fe	1276	3119
pH	8.6	6.7	Mn	37.68	123.6
Humus (% dm)	6.1	9.2	Cu	57.24	145.9
			Zn	242.5	466.5
Microbiological analysis (MPN g^{-1}wm)			Ni	10.70	19.58
			Pb	nd	1.03
Total coliforms	1×10^6	2×10^4	Cr	76.12	201.9
Faecal coliforms	< 1	7×10^3	Cd	7.24	46.18
Total *Streptococci*	2×10^9	2×10^6			
Faecal *Streptococci*	9×10^7	1×10^4			
Clostridium	5×10^7	1×10^5			

nd: not detectable
d.m.: dry matter
w.m.: wet matter
MPN: most probable number

al. (1996) reported that 86% (w/w) of the original pentosans are hydrolysed to a fermentable sugar solution after a two-stage chemical treatment (hydrogen peroxide digestion followed by H_3PO_4 treatment). Table 7.29 gives the chemical composition of *Miscanthus* and the fermentable sugar yields after a number of different treatments.

It appears from Table 7.29 that the hydrogen peroxide process is very effective with respect to lignin removal (88% w/w of the original lignin was removed). The total hydrolytic de-polymerisation of pentosans reached 77 to 86% (w/w) of the original component after the H_3PO_4 and NaOH treatments respectively. The solid residue obtained was enriched in cellulose and had a very low lignin content (85–88% and 2.5–5.7% w/w, dry product basis, respectively).

7.4.5 *Other Possible Uses of* Miscanthus

The increasing number of publications, communications, reports and meetings regarding *Miscanthus* in past years has brought about an interest in the investigation and development of commercial end uses for the crop. Some of the uses which have not already been mentioned in this section but which are being considered are the use of *Miscanthus* fibre material in packaging materials or geotextiles (Molenaar *et al.*, 1996), its use as canes to support ornamental pot plants (Harvey & Hutchens, 1995) and the use of *Miscanthus* ash arising from combustion processes as a fertiliser.

7 *Utilisation of* Miscanthus

Table 7.29. Chemical composition of Miscanthus, *fermentable sugar yields and solid residue composition after* $H_2O_2{}^a$ *and* $H_3PO_4{}^b$ *or* $NaOH^c$ *treatments. Source: Papatheofanous et al., 1996.*

| | Whole crop | pre-treated H_2O_2 | | | pre-treated H_2O_2 and | | | |
| | | | | | H_3PO_4 – treated | | NaOH – treated | |
		solid residue	liquid phase	solid residue	liquid phase	solid residue	liquid phase
Yield[d]		61.3	49.4	41.8	31.0	44.2	26.8
Cellulose[d]	43.1	63.7		57.8	4.4	63.5	1.7
Hemicellulose[d]	26.7						
Pentosans[d]		30.4	15.4	4.3	24.2	6.2	22.4
Lignin[d]	22.1	4.3	21.1	3.9	0.2	1.8	2.1
Ash[d]	3.9	0.6	3.7	0.5	0.1	0.1	0.3

a: H_2O_2 solution: 24h at room temperature, pH = 11.5, solid to liquid ratio = 1:25 w/v;

b: 2% w/v ortho-phosphoric acid, 2h at 138¡C, solid to liquid ratio = 1:10 w/v;

c: 10% w/v NaOH, 24h at room temperature;

d: % w/w on dry raw material.

8   *Economics of* Miscanthus *Production*
by M. Bullard

8.1 Introduction

This chapter presents 1997 production costs for *Miscanthus*, expressed as both break-even costs and theoretical gross margins, against a context of the range of potential market prices for the crop. For each potential market an analysis of the viability of *Miscanthus* is given. Where appropriate markets are identified, an assessment of the potential value of the market in terms of market substitution, import substitution and feed stock value is given.

It should be noted that the markets for *Miscanthus* continue to develop, and judicious political intervention may re-position *Miscanthus* with respect to the cost effectiveness of certain markets.

8.2 Economics of *Miscanthus* Production

The economics of *Miscanthus* production are analysed below by calculating the costs associated with each step of the production process and thus determining the break-even costs of production. The opportunities for the reduction of production costs are also outlined.

8.2.1 Analytical Methods

The 'farm gate' production costs of *Miscanthus* are presented both in terms of break-even price per tonne (assuming a twenty-year yielding profile) and also hypothetical gross margins. Both are set in context against the equivalent figures for cereals and break crops grown on arable land. The break-even price was calculated as follows:

$$P = \frac{\sum\limits_{t=1}^{T} \dfrac{C}{(1+d)^t}}{\sum\limits_{t=1}^{T} \dfrac{Y}{(1+d)^t}}$$

where:
- P = break-even price (per tonne)
- T = duration of productive crop
- t = sequential year of crop
- Y = yield
- d = discounted rate (5% p.a.)
- C = costs (fixed and variable).

The fixed costs used for the break-even price calculations were average figures obtained from *The Agricultural Situation in the European Union* (CEC, 1996a). These average fixed cost values use the 'mean' agricultural holding size for each country (Table 8.1); the actual holding size has been reported to have dramatic impacts upon the economics of *Miscanthus* production (Bullard, 1997).

Table 8.1. *Fixed costs of production on an 'average' size cereal farm in each EU member state. Source: CEC, 1996a.*

Country	Fixed cost per hectare farmed (ECU ha^{-1})
Belgium	1,259
Denmark	872
Germany	1,362
Greece	867
Spain	303
France	834
Ireland	680
Italy	883
Netherlands	1,955
Portugal	471
UK	758

8.2.2 *Costs of* Miscanthus *Husbandry*

The costings of production are based on 1997 'best practice guidelines' which are detailed below. A number of different scenarios are considered in order to demonstrate the flexibility in the costing system and the degree to which it could be used to respond to a changing set of socio-political market forces.

Site Preparation

The provision of a good quality 'seed bed' is very important and will improve establishment (and consequently yield) by improving soil–plant contact and consequent moisture and nutrient supply. Site preparation will not deviate from the methodology employed for the establishment of any spring-sown annual, although more provision may be needed to ensure good subsoil structure before the crop is planted. Subsoiling, ploughing, discing and harrowing are all conducted as general farm overhead practices, and as such no specialist contractor costs are factored into the break-even cost model.

Propagule and Establishment Costs

Current experiments involve the establishment of *Miscanthus* at planting densities of between 10,000 and 40,000 plants per hectare. The most appropriate density for each soil type has not yet been established, but it is expected on current evidence to be nearer to 10,000 plants per hectare. The most cost-effective method of crop propagation would probably be through sowing of seed, however, currently assessed 'varieties' do not set viable seed. Two alternatives, establishment from micro-propagation or rhizomes, are currently used. Establishment of micro-propagated material (small plantlets produced via tissue culture) has proven to be very expensive, as has establishment of small-scale trials using hand-lifted rhizome sections. However, the use of rhizome cuttings from fields of mature *Miscanthus* (see Chapter 3) for establishment can allow a low-cost propagule production system. Rhizome cuttings are produced by rotovating or power harrowing an established crop in March/April, and then harvesting the rhizome sections with a bulb harvester. It is possible to produce enough rhizome cuttings to plant 30 ha. from 1 ha. of 'mother crop' in this way. This can reduce the cost of planting propagule to as little as 0.03 ECU (Huisman & Kortleve, 1994).

The calculations used here consider that a unit price of 0.03 ECU per rhizome piece is unobtainable. This is because the price of 0.03 ECU assumes that the potential grower is actually the owner of the mature *Miscanthus* crop and, consequently, no provision is made for producer profit, transport costs or contractor costs associated with specialist machinery. A unit price of 0.075 ECU is considered to be a more realistic price in the immediate future. The effect of this reduction on establishment costs is still dramatic, with the propagule cost of 750 ECU ha^{-1} amortised across the 20 year lifetime of the crop.

The development of rapid, accurate mechanical planting methods for *Miscanthus* is a challenge due to the lack of uniformity of rhizome cuttings in terms of shape and size. The most cost-effective method of planting at present is to use a potato ridger to open up shallow 150 mm ridges into which the rhizome pieces are placed by hand. The ridges are then back-filled mechanically and the site is rolled. Alternatively, a semi-mechanical potato planter can be used. It is not anticipated that planting would be carried out by specialist contractor and the planting costs are categorised as general fixed overhead costs. However, if specialist contractors are used, this 1 in 20 year operation is compensated by lower fixed costs in the subsequent 19 years. Further research is required in order to assess existing planting machinery and the modifications which are required in order to achieve a more uniform planting depth and seed bed conditions.

Costs of *Miscanthus* production could be further reduced if a proportion of the crop is used as a 'mother crop' for the production of rhizome cuttings during the middle of the 20 year production cycle. The reduction in yield which occurs due to this operation will be compensated by the revenue obtained from the sale of the rhizome cuttings. This scenario is considered in a later section and is dependent on the continual increase in a market for *Miscanthus* products.

Crop Longevity

As *Miscanthus* is a perennial crop, all establishment costs can be amortised over the productive life of the crop. As the potential lifetime of a *Miscanthus* crop is uncertain, a default value of 20 years has been used in the costings in this chapter. Costs are amortised at a constant rate of 5% depreciation per year.

Fertilisation

Research has provided basic information on the nutrient requirements of *Miscanthus*. Evidence suggests that for optimum growth (crop canopy development) a nitrogen input of not more than 130 kg ha^{-1} is required, in most cases a significant proportion of this will be provided by the soil. Offtake figures of 7 kg t^{-1} N, 10 kg t^{-1} K and negligible offtake of P have been reported (Bullard *et al.*, 1996). The economic model used in this chapter does not relate predicted yield with fertiliser requirements. Instead, a hypothetical (average) value is used which assumes an annual post-establishment application of 80 kg N, 10 kg P and 60 kg K ha^{-1}; however, it may transpire that these levels are higher than actually required. Clearly there will be great site to site variation in the fertiliser regime required. Additional application of micro-nutrients and lime are not included as *Miscanthus* does not appear susceptible to any particular micro-nutrient deficiency. It is presumed that any field deficiencies would be corrected during general farm management and can therefore be considered a fixed cost.

Weed Control

The importance of effective weed control during the establishment of *Miscanthus* is well known (see Chapter 3). Specific herbicide requirements (or mechanical methods) will vary tremendously from site to site in the establishment year. However, subsequent weed control could be achieved with annual March applications of translocated herbicide. The economic model presumes one annual pre-emergence application of glyphosate, with an additional broad spectrum tank mix during the establishment year.

Irrigation

While there is an increasing awareness that *Miscanthus* has a high water demand despite a relatively high water use efficiency, it is unlikely to be economically (or environmentally) feasible to consider irrigation a viable tool for increasing yield, regardless of the end market, in any EU region. Therefore, no allowance for irrigation is included in this model.

Harvesting

The economic model considers two different harvesting techniques, the choice of which depends on the end use of the crop. If the crop is to be used for energy production it is presumed that it will be baled. This will be done either by using existing farm machinery (e.g. hay cutter with mower conditioner followed by Hesston baler as a two-phase operation), or in one operation using specially modified combine harvesters (e.g. the Claas single phase baling harvester, see Chapter 6). As the hay cutter system is likely to cause less trafficking damage than the heavier Claas harvester, the economic model only considers the former option (operation is considered as a fixed cost).

The economic model considers that the *Miscanthus* biomass should be supplied in the form of 2–5 mm chips for alternative markets. These can be consistently produced (internal screens can produce a 2–14 mm range of chip size) using self-propelled forage harvesters (see Chapter 6). A contractor's cost is used to determine break-even cost and gross margin where specialist machinery is required.

Storage

It is assumed that field storage time is minimal for the range of end uses which are considered by the model. Storage is not considered in the break-even production costs This decision was made on the following basis:

- If the *Miscanthus* is to be supplied to the energy industry it will be dried in windrows prior to baling, it will therefore be of a sufficiently low moisture content for direct transport.
- The most economically effective way to dry *Miscanthus* before combustion is to utilise waste heat at the site of energy generation (Nellist, 1997). Current biomass boilers produce electricity at 30% efficiency. The surplus heat is used to dry the biomass rather than attempt to dry in-field or in storage sheds. Appropriate modifications to the model are computed where markets require a different approach. Transporting fresh weight material will increase transportation costs by approximately 50–100% depending on moisture content.
- The conversion facility considered by the economic model runs on a seasonal mixture of coppice (supplied from December onwards), *Miscanthus* (supplied from March onwards), and cereal straw (supplied from July onwards). This will result in the minimisation of storage times (both on-field and in factory) and dry matter losses.
- If storage is necessary, it will be carried out on field margins, thus minimising the disruption to the subsequent season's growth.
- If the *Miscanthus* is to be supplied to the fibre product industry the harvested material will be required to be harvested fresh and transported fresh-cut to the processor. An increased harvesting window from November to March is afforded in this system, again reducing the need for field storage.

Subsequent sections deal with these issues in detail. It is recognised that this is perhaps over-simplistic and that a degree of prolonged field storage and drying (with an associated cost) may be required. Prolonged field storage is likely to increase production costs by 10–20% (Allen *et al.*, 1997).

Subsidies

The break-even economic model assumes no planting grants, tax credits or area payments, and therefore represents the worst-case scenario, where EU policy does not recognise environmental benefits of renewables, and will expect all crops to 'stand alone' commercially. However, it is likely that some form of subsidy, even with the proposed modifications to CAP, should be available in the immediate future. Additional grant 'aid' in the future may come from tax credits, additional tax on fossil fuels or planting grants. Hypothetical gross margins which are considered in later sections of this report compare likely 1997 margins, and do so by including 1997 area aid payments for set-aside.

Yield and Crop Value

The revenue generated by a *Miscanthus* crop will be determined by yield and crop value. EU *Miscanthus* and national programmes are assimilating valuable data on the yields that can be expected throughout Europe. At present, however, insufficient data is available to accurately predict yields as there are likely to be regional and seasonal variations in yield, and, as mentioned earlier, the productive life-span of the crop is still unclear. It is anticipated that mean dry matter yields of 15–20 t ha^{-1} should be achievable under appropriate conditions and for the purposes of this analysis, a productivity band between 12–24 t ha^{-1} with increments of 3 t ha^{-1} is used. Crop value is dependent on the end product and is also considered below.

Transport

Transport costs for *Miscanthus* will be slightly lower than for cereal straw (*Miscanthus* has a slightly higher bulk density of 125–60 kg m^{-3}), but they are not considered in this study. This is principally because transportation costs for any end market will depend on the proximity of the factory to the field and no information exists on the likely frequency of power stations or processing plants. Therefore any estimation of transport distances may distort the production costs.

8.2.3 Break-even Costs of Production

Standard Production

Table 8.2 gives the break-even costs which were calculated by the economic model for the production of *Miscanthus* on cereal farms in different member states with varying yields and fixed costs. The assumptions used in the calculation of these break-even costs are listed below:

- Average Farm Fixed Costs are used (Table 8.1); farm type is 'mainly arable with combinable break crops'.
- Existing large-scale plantations are used as 'mother crops' to provide rhizome cuttings for planting new plantations. This is both realistic and essential if we are to avoid distortions caused by studying the 'first of its kind' scenario. The next section examines the effect on production economics if 50% or 100% of the crop is rotovated after 10 years to provide propagules for sale. The re-sale price is set at 60% of the original purchase price of 0.075 ECU, and this is projected in 10 years time. There may be significant scope for higher re-sale prices to be obtained.
- A productive lifetime of 20 years is assumed.

Table 8.2. Break-even costs for Miscanthus *on cereal farms in different member states according to yield and fixed costs*.*

| | Break-even cost assuming predicted annual yield (ECU t^{-1}) | | | | |
	12 t ha^{-1}	15 t ha^{-1}	18 t ha^{-1}	21 t ha^{-1}	24 t ha^{-1}
Belgium	125.11	101.70	85.67	74.00	65.14
Denmark	90.21	73.33	61.78	53.37	46.97
Germany	134.39	109.25	92.03	79.50	69.98
Greece	89.76	72.97	61.47	53.10	46.74
Spain	38.90	31.63	26.64	23.01	20.26
France	86.78	70.55	59.43	51.34	45.19
Ireland	72.90	59.26	49.92	43.12	37.96
Italy	91.20	74.14	62.46	53.95	47.49
Netherlands	187.86	152.72	128.65	111.13	97.82
Portugal	54.05	43.94	37.02	31.97	28.14
UK	79.93	64.98	54.74	47.28	41.61
Mean	105.11	85.45	71.98	62.18	54.70

* Whole Farm Fixed Costs (1993–4) based on CEC (1996a)

- One annual application of glyphosate is used with no fungicides or insecticides.
- Application of fertiliser is minimal. Substitution with sewage sludge may reduce fertiliser costs, although the cost of sewage sludge and its application may be equivalent to the costs of inorganic fertiliser.
- Depreciation is calculated at 5% p.a.

Break-Even Costs using Existing Crop as Nursery

This section outlines the break-even costs when the existing plantation is used as a 'mother crop' to produce rhizome cuttings which are sold in year 10, the crop is then re-planted. Table 8.3 gives the break-even costs (at different yields and fixed costs) of a *Miscanthus* crop where 100% of the crop was used as a 'mother crop' while Table 8.4 gives the break-even costs where 50% of the crop was used as a 'mother crop'. The assumptions made in the calculation of these break-even costs are listed below.

- Average Farm Fixed Costs are used (Table 8.1), farm type is mainly arable with combinable break crops.
- Existing large-scale plantations are used as 'mother crops' to provide the propagules for planting of new crops.
- 50% or 100% of the crop is rotovated after 10 years to provide propagules for sale at a price of 0.045 ECU, and the crop is re-planted. It is assumed that 30 rhizomes are obtained from each 'mother' plant (an extremely conservative estimate).
- Crop division in year 10 is arbitrary, division can occur from year 4 onwards.
- A productive lifetime of 20 years is used.
- One annual application of glyphosate is used with no fungicides or insecticides.
- Application of fertiliser is minimal. Substitution with sewage sludge may reduce fertiliser costs.
- Depreciation is calculated at 5% p.a.

Table 8.3. Break-even costs when 100% of the crop is used to provide propagules for sale in year 10*.

	Break-even cost assuming predicted annual yield (ECU t^{-1})				
	12 t ha^{-1}	15 t ha^{-1}	18 t ha^{-1}	21 t ha^{-1}	24 t ha^{-1}
Belgium	80.24	65.23	54.95	51.25	45.31
Denmark	47.75	39.26	33.33	28.96	25.60
Germany	94.28	77.52	65.81	57.18	50.55
Greece	47.28	38.87	33.00	28.67	25.35
Spain	–	–	–	–	–
France	44.14	36.30	30.82	26.77	23.67
Ireland	29.52	24.27	20.61	17.91	15.83
Italy	48.80	40.12	34.06	29.60	26.16
Netherlands	154.38	126.93	107.77	93.63	82.78
Portugal	9.68	7.96	6.76	5.87	5.19
UK	36.93	30.36	25.78	22.40	19.80
Mean	65.23	53.55	45.42	39.84	35.23

* Whole Farm Fixed Costs (1993–4) based on CEC (1996a)

Table 8.4. Break-even costs when 50% of the crop is used to provide propagules for sale in year 10*.

	Break-even cost assuming predicted annual yield (ECU t^{-1})				
	12 t ha^{-1}	15 t ha^{-1}	18 t ha^{-1}	21 t ha^{-1}	24 t ha^{-1}
Belgium	100.77	82.37	69.65	60.26	53.22
Denmark	64.97	53.11	44.91	38.85	34.31
Germany	110.30	90.16	76.24	65.96	58.25
Greece	64.51	52.73	44.59	38.58	34.07
Spain	12.34	10.09	8.53	7.38	6.52
France	61.46	50.24	42.48	36.75	32.46
Ireland	47.21	38.59	32.63	28.23	24.93
Italy	65.99	53.94	45.61	39.46	34.85
Netherlands	165.15	134.99	114.15	100.97	89.17
Portugal	27.88	22.79	19.27	16.67	14.72
UK	54.43	44.49	37.62	32.55	28.74
Mean	77.50	63.35	53.57	46.57	41.12

* Whole Farm Fixed Costs (1993–4) based on CEC (1996a)

8.2.4 *Opportunities for Reducing Production Costs*

Use of Landfill and Derelict Land

The production of *Miscanthus* on good quality soils should give reliable yields in excess of 18 t ha^{-1} yr^{-1}. However, it is probable that most sites and soils which are conducive to very high *Miscanthus* yields are more likely to be cropped with higher value crops.

It may be appropriate to use reclamation land, particularly areas of municipal landfill, for the production of *Miscanthus*, especially if it is being grown for the energy generation market. These areas require a period of bioremediation and soil stabilisation, which might form a suitable niche for a perennial crop such as *Miscanthus*. Lower overheads and rental prices on these lands should reduce the associated production costs, however, further research is required to determine whether the yield reductions which occur on such sites are compensated by the associated savings in fixed costs.

Disposal of Wastes on the Crop

Application of sewage and other liquid wastes (e.g effluents from the brewing and glass-making industries) may have the double benefit of providing nutrients and additional moisture to the crop while at the same time generating a small income to the farmer for the regular disposal of these wastes. Research is currently underway to establish the long-term effects of sewage sludge on *Miscanthus* (Chapter 9). These methods of cost reduction might only be feasible if the crop is being grown in areas adjacent to the producer of the waste and, as such, special cases are not integrated into the break-even cost analysis.

Opportunities for the production of *Miscanthus* on long-term sewage disposal land owned by water utilities should not be overlooked, particularly in view of the increasing demand for the disposal of sewage on land rather than at sea. While this area of land is not likely to be sufficient for energy markets, it may be appropriate for smaller niche markets.

8.3 Assessment of *Miscanthus* Markets

This section assesses the energy and fibre markets which exist for *Miscanthus*.

8.3.1 Energy

Fuel in Large-Scale National Grid or CHP Stations

A market for large- or medium-scale bioenergy already exists in the EU but is heavily supported by the exchequer. In order for biomass to compete with fossil fuels, a revised approach is required for the comparison of production costs of fossil fuel sources and non-fossil fuel sources such as biomass (which is not financially supported). Various reports suggest that 7–18% of EU energy production should be from renewables by 2020, with energy crops and wind power dominating the contribution to this figure (CEC, 1996b). The EU has recently set a target of 12% of energy generation from renewables, this may necessitate the use of up to 10% of the EU's total agricultural land area for energy crop production. The current level of energy generation in the EU from renewables is 5.4%, as much as half of this is produced from biomass systems which use agricultural and forestry wastes and crops grown specifically for energy production.

It is not possible to speculate about the likelihood of carbon taxation or tax breaks on renewables, but the 'internalisation of externalities' will enhance the economic viability of crops that can probably already compete under certain conditions. A full review of the effect of market distortions caused by non-inclusion of environmental costs in pricing fossil fuel energy is provided by Hall (1997). EU primary energy generation in 1994 was 2,160 Mtoe (UN, 1996), therefore 259.2 Mtoe of energy generation from renewables will be required in order to meet the EU's target of 12% energy generation from renewables by 2020 (assuming primary energy consumption does not increase). It is likely that biomass will be one of the major contributors to this target. Assuming 25% of this target will be met from biomass (including agricultural residues) it is further reasonable to assume that *Miscanthus* will occupy a significant niche in certain areas. If we assume 10% of biomass energy generation is from *Miscanthus*, this would equate to 6.48 Mtoe. At annual yield levels of 18 t ha^{-1} yr^{-1}, this would equate to 900,000 ha. of EU agricultural land given over to the production of *Miscanthus* (sufficient to provide annual fuel for eighty 30 MW boilers). GIS-based prediction systems for locating suitable areas of land are being developed to facilitate location of power stations, but the final viability of the system will relate to the ability to accurately predict *Miscanthus* yield.

While cereal straw is sometimes plentiful (*c.* 12 Mt annually in the UK alone), demand and value is sporadic and consequently the value of this 'waste material' can fluctuate between 10–100 ECU t^{-1}. The volatility of this market, together with the restrictions which are associated with security of supply contracts indicate that cereal straw will not be the strong competitor which was once anticipated. Much of the straw available after harvest is immediately chopped and incorporated into the soil. Approximately half of the available harvested straw is used for animal bedding, while much of the remainder is so geographically dispersed that it could not contribute to an economically run power station of any significant size. With straw yields of 3–5 t ha^{-1}, the area required to produce sufficient fuel for a large power station is very large and consequently straw-powered stations would only be viable in the most intensive cereal areas. Consequently, the value of *Miscanthus* will not be tied to straw prices.

It is more realistic to tie biomass fuel prices in with crude oil prices on an oil equivalency basis. The 1997 price for Brent Blend, which could be taken as a benchmark, was US $18.92 per barrel at the oil field (c.f. 'farm gate'). During 1997 the price of a US barrel fluctuated between $17–25 per barrel. Prices are generally higher in the winter and traditionally it is a very volatile world market with prices increasing rapidly if there are problems in the Middle East. For the purpose of this comparative study an oil field price of $23 is assumed. Assuming that one tonne of oven-dry biomass has an energetic value equivalent to 400 kg of crude oil, and that a barrel of oil currently sells for a pre-delivery price of 20 ECU ($23), we can estimate that on a purely substitutional basis *Miscanthus* (or coppice) would have a market value of 56 ECU t^{-1}.

The high capital cost involved in commissioning a biomass burner / gasifier indicates that the market price for the biomass may initially have to be significantly less. This report assumes that significant policy measures stimulate the demand for *Miscanthus* to be grown commercially and that therefore a market price of 49 ECU can be obtained.

The low product value of *Miscanthus* for fuel renders most unsupported farm-based production uneconomic in all countries except Spain and Portugal (Table 8.2). At a price of 49 ECU t^{-1} *Miscanthus* production for large-scale energy generation will not break even under the current model unless produced on very large farms and at high yields (>18 t ha^{-1}; see Table 8.2). However, under scenarios where a proportion of the crop is used as a 'mother crop' it can be seen that many more crops fall within a zone where crop value (49 ECU t^{-1}) exceeds break-even costs (Tables 8.3 and 8.4).

If the current level of area payments are factored into the model then *Miscanthus* production becomes extremely economic for any site where yields are at least 15 t. Thus, under the present farming framework *Miscanthus* can be an economic energy crop.

Gross Margins on Agricultural Land

Table 8.5 compares a hypothetical '1997' gross margin of a mature *Miscanthus* crop with gross margins of crops of winter wheat, winter oilseed rape and a mature crop of SRC-willow in the UK: a spot comparison which allows the relative value of the crop to be considered. It can be seen that the low variable input costs of *Miscanthus*,

Table 8.5. Gross margins for Miscanthus, *winter wheat and oilseed rape[1] sold as fuel for National Grid (under Non Fossil Fuel Obligation) production in the UK. Values in ECU.*

	Miscanthus[2]	winter wheat[3]	winter oilseed rape[4]	short rotation coppice[5]
Variables				
Rhizomes/seed[6]	56	70	53	–
Sprays	35	175	144	–
Fertiliser	42	85	126	–
TOTAL VARIABLES	133	330	323	235[7]
yield (t)	18	7.5	3	12
price per tonne (£)[8]	49	150	245	49
CROP VALUE	882	1,125	735	588
Area Payment	455	360	637	455
GROSS MARGIN ha^{-1}	1,337	1,485	1,372	1,043

1: 1996 variable costs of production are used (Nix, 1997).
2: Assumes identical variable costs to those in section 8.2.3.
3: Average wheat yields of 7.25 t ha^{-1}. Price per tonne from Nix (1997) does not reflect the current volatility of the grain market induced by the strong position of sterling during July 1997.
4: Average yields of 3.0 t ha^{-1}.
5: Assumes a productive lifetime of 8 harvests.
6: Annualised rhizome cost: 10,000 plants, 0.075 ECU each (£500), amortised (5%) over 20 years or similar for coppice.
7: Mean hypothetical gross margin calculated by Ryan & Buckland (1997), includes price of propagules, sprays, fertilisers and specialist contractors for planting and harvesting operations.
8: *Miscanthus* – hypothetical to farm gate price.
   Wheat – mean July 1997 spot price.
   Oilseed rape – mean July spot price.
   Short rotation coppice – hypothetical to farm gate price.

coupled with high yield and set aside payment, render the crops' gross margin higher than any alternative and significantly higher than coppice.

The gross margin data used in Table 8.5 for short rotation coppice are derived from Ryan and Buckland (1997). While this provides economic information based upon the most 'comprehensive' field studies, the report acknowledges that the two main limitations to evaluating the true performance of coppice are the lack of viable yield data and the lack of information on likely crop value.

In conclusion, unless grown on a very large scale and at high yields it is unlikely that *Miscanthus* can produce an economic return as an energy crop in an unsupported fashion (Table 8.2). However, the use of at least some of the established area as a 'mother crop' for production of rhizome cuttings for re-sale will significantly improve the economics of production (Tables 8.3 and 8.4). A real opportunity for *Miscanthus* cropping for energy production would arise if the crop received a carbon-neutral tax credit. It was concluded that most crops yielding 15 t ha^{-1} would return a strong profit at a sale price of 49 ECU t^{-1} and the receipt of area payments.

8.3.2 *Fibre Production*

Amended Break-Even Costs of Production

The break-even costs of *Miscanthus* production for the fibre market will differ from the break-even costs of production for the energy market. The expected variations in break-even costs are outlined below.

Harvesting

As stated in an earlier section, the break-even costs of production for the fibre market will differ from the break-even costs of production for the energy market because of the need to use a single phase harvester on contract. The break-even cost model is amended to include 62 ECU ha^{-1} (average contractors cost for the use of a self propelled forage maize harvester). The break-even costs of production for a *Miscanthus* crop which is harvested by means of a single-phase specialised harvester are given in Table 8.6. With a wider harvest window of December–April, immediate transportation to the appropriate processing site is assumed.

Transport Costs

Although not directly considered in the economic model, it is necessary to mention that the processors of fibre products are more dispersed than is likely to be the case with the energy market, and therefore transportation costs are likely to add more than the 10–20% on to total costs suggested for energy supply market. This needs to be considered when assessing the likely value of the raw material against likely product values.

Markets for Miscanthus Fibre

There is an annual 50 million tonne trade deficit of plant fibre materials for pulp, timber and panels/packaging industrial uses in the EU (CEC, 1996a). This figure

Table 8.6. Break-even costs for Miscanthus *where annual self propelled chipper harvesters are used on cereal (with combinable crop) farms.*

	Break-even cost assuming predicted annual yield (ECU t^{-1})				
	12 t ha^{-1}	15 t ha^{-1}	18 t ha^{-1}	21 t ha^{-1}	24 t ha^{-1}
Belgium	130.27	105.90	89.21	77.06	67.83
Denmark	95.37	77.53	65.31	56.42	49.66
Germany	139.56	113.45	95.57	82.56	72.66
Greece	94.92	77.16	65.00	56.15	49.42
Spain	44.07	35.82	30.18	26.07	22.95
France	91.95	74.75	62.97	54.66	47.87
Ireland	78.06	63.46	53.46	46.18	40.64
Italy	96.37	78.34	65.99	57.01	50.18
Netherlands	193.03	156.91	132.18	114.19	100.50
Portugal	59.22	48.14	40.55	35.03	30.83
UK	85.10	69.17	58.27	50.34	44.31

excludes agricultural feeds, agricultural bedding and textiles. The cost of this imported material is approximately ECU 21 billion. Consequently there is a large import substitution market for crops with appropriate properties that can be produced economically in the EU.

The industrial potential of fibre products from *Miscanthus* has been investigated in EU and national research programmes. The potential of *Miscanthus* as a fibre crop has been summarised by Hague (1997) and the generic potential of fibre crops has been discussed by Bolton (1995). Potential markets can be split into three main areas:

- woven and non-woven textiles and geotextiles
- pulp for paper and packaging
- composite materials including particle board, chip board, wafer board, plyboard and MDF

Woven and Non-Woven Textiles, Geotextiles

The relatively short fibres of *Miscanthus* (*c.* 2 mm) are not suited to woven textile or geotextile production and research indicates that no viable markets exist in this area. In addition, the textile industry consumes a small proportion of the total tonnage of plant fibres used (cotton, jute and flax constitute only 1.2% of the total fibre production). While textile fibres command the highest prices of all plant fibres (cotton at *c.* 2100 ECU t^{-1}), the total land area involved in the production of textile fibres is small when seen in the global context.

Pulp for Paper and Packaging

On a worldwide scale less than 10% of paper products are made from non-wood fibres. However, it has been demonstrated that *Miscanthus* has qualities that render it to be a high potential non-wood alternative (Hague, 1997). Indeed chemically pulped *Miscanthus* produces high quality paper with similar properties to spruce- and eucalyptus-derived pulp. While *Miscanthus* can be used as a blending component in lower grade pulp products (from semi-chemical and mechanical pulping) it is very unlikely that the low price that the raw material would command would make production economic. Table 8.7 shows the proportion of pulp products currently produced using waste (i.e. recycled) pulp in the UK.

Table 8.7. Use of waste pulp (percentage of total) by sector (1996). Source: UK Paper Federation (pers. comm.).

Sector	Percentage recycled pulp used in manufacture
Newsprint	90
Wrapping paper, etc.	65
Graphics/high quality paper	10
Case materials	100
Sanitary (tissues, etc.)	85
Folding boxboard	75
Others	65

It is highly unlikely that *Miscanthus* could compete on a cost basis with any product market where recycled fibre is acceptable (e.g. newspapers, sanitary products, boxboards and case materials). However, the recently introduced EU Producer Responsibility Obligation (Packaging Waste) regulations (PRO) create recovery and recycling targets for all companies within the packaging chain. Recovery includes waste to energy and recycling of cardboard and plastics. It is possible that the inclusion of a renewable fibre source such as *Miscanthus* as a minor constituent to some of the products will enable companies to realise their recycling targets more readily. More information is required in this area.

High-quality writing/printing paper would seem to be the most suitable sector to target with *Miscanthus* fibre as this is the largest individual market. There is some potential to market paper products from *Miscanthus* at an environmental premium by assigning an 'eco-friendly' label to the product. However, the necessity for chemical pulping mills and the negative environmental implications of their use constitute a major barrier to the feasibility of using *Miscanthus* as a fibre source for the high-quality paper pulp market. The use of combined *Miscanthus*/straw mills might be a possibility, but this would demand a high level of investment which is unlikely, given the socio-politically volatile nature of international pulp markets. Table 8.8 compares the gross margin for *Miscanthus*, winter wheat and winter oilseed rape which are produced as a feedstock for the pulp products market.

Table 8.8. Gross margins for Miscanthus *(ECU ha⁻¹), winter wheat and oilseed rape[1] sold as feedstock to the pulp products market.*

	Miscanthus[2]	winter wheat[3]	winter oilseed rape[4]
Rhizomes/seed[5]	56	70	53
Sprays	35	175	144
Fertiliser	42	119	126
Contract harvesting	62	0	0
TOTAL VARIABLES	195	364	323[6]
yield (t)	18	7.5	3
price per tonne (£)[7]	56	150	245
CROP VALUE	1008	1,125	735
Area payment	455	360	637
GROSS MARGIN ha⁻¹	1,268	1,121	1,049

1: 1996 variable costs of production are used (Nix, 1997).
2: Assumes identical variable costs to those in section 8.2.3.
3: Average wheat yields of 7.25 t ha⁻¹. Price per tonne from Nix (1997) does not reflect the current volatility of the grain market induced by the strong position of sterling during July 1997.
4: Average yields of 3.0 t ha⁻¹.
5: Annualised rhizome cost: 10,000 plants, 0.05 ECU each (£500), amortised (5%) over 20 years or similar for coppice.
6: Mean hypothetical gross margin calculated by Ryan and Buckland (1997), includes price of propagules, sprays, fertilisers and specialist contractors for planting and harvesting operations.
7: *Miscanthus* – hypothetical to farm gate price.
   Wheat – mean July 1997 spot price.
   Oilseed rape – mean July spot price.

Medium-Density Fibre Board

Research conducted on behalf of MAFF (UK Ministry of Agriculture, Fisheries and Food) has identified MDF as the wood-based product which is most suited to substitution by *Miscanthus* (Hague, 1997). FAO statistics suggest that the global demand for wood-based products will double by the year 2010, this will require an increase in wafer board, particle board and MDF manufacture which must be met with a corresponding increase in raw material production.

The relationship between supply and demand is fragile. During recent years many MDF plants have been established in south-east Asia but this development was so rapid that demand could not keep up with the supply and a reduction in sales prices has been the result (e.g. US $200–220 m⁻³ compared to predicted price of *c.* US $340 m⁻³). This situation will not change the near future, although in the long term an increased demand for wood panel products and a commensurate increase in sale prices can be anticipated. There may be a niche market for the production of MDF from

Miscanthus at a raw product purchase cost of 42–84 ECU odt⁻¹ (the equivalent soft wood supply cost). It is anticipated that 20% substitution of *Miscanthus* in MDF production systems might be attained (J. Hague, pers. comm.). Table 8.9 indicates that the gross margin which can be attained for *Miscanthus* destined for the MDF market is 1,772 ECU ha⁻¹, significantly higher than the gross margin of 1,268 ECU ha⁻¹ which is obtained for *Miscanthus* destined for the pulp products market (Table 8.8). Technology transfer is required to enable MDF producers to fully utilise this potential renewable source of fibre.

Table 8.9. Gross margins for Miscanthus, *winter wheat and oilseed rape[1] (ECU ha⁻¹) (*Miscanthus *is for sale to the wood-based products industry).*

	Miscanthus[2]	winter wheat[3]	winter oilseed rape[4]
Rhizomes/seed[5]	56	70	53
Sprays	35	175	144
Fertiliser	42	119	126
Contract harvesting	62	0	0
TOTAL VARIABLES	195	364	323[6]
yield (t)	18	7.5	3
price per tonne (£)[7]	84	150	245
CROP VALUE	1,512	1,125	735
Area payment	455	360	637
GROSS MARGIN ha⁻¹	1,772	1,121	1,049

1: 1996 variable costs of production are used (Nix, 1997).

2: Assumes identical variable costs to those in section 8.2.3.

3: Average wheat yields of 7.25 t ha⁻¹. Price per tonne from Nix (1997) does not reflect the current volatility of the grain market induced by the strong position of sterling during July 1997.

4: Average yields of 3.0 t ha⁻¹.

5: Annualised rhizome cost: 10,000 plants, 0.075 ECU each (ECU 750), amortised (5%) over 20 years or similar for coppice.

6: Mean hypothetical gross margin calculated by Ryan and Buckland (1997), includes price of propagules, sprays, fertilisers and specialist contractors for planting and harvesting operations.

7: *Miscanthus* – hypothetical to farm gate price.
   Wheat – mean July 1997 spot price.
   Oilseed rape – mean July spot price.

8.4 Conclusions

The conclusions of the investigations on the economics of *Miscanthus* production and use are as follows:

• Market opportunities have been identified for *Miscanthus* as a fuel and as a constituent of medium density fibre board.

- *Miscanthus* is a viable feedstock for chemical pulp mills for the production of speciality paper.
- Break-even costs of production vary to a degree of four- or five-fold between the most expensive countries (The Netherlands, Belgium and Germany) and the least expensive (Spain and Portugal).
- *Miscanthus* is not a viable feedstock for woven and non-woven textiles or geotextiles.
- The production of *Miscanthus* as a fuel for energy may be economically viable without grant support if high crop yields of greater than 18 t ha^{-1} are obtained on large farms (i.e. relatively low fixed costs per hectare).
- Moderate *Miscanthus* yields of 15 t ha^{-1} will only be economically viable as a fuel for energy if the crop is supported by some form of tax credit/subsidy which reflects the positive environmental nature of a renewable fuel source.
- There is an opportunity to reduce production costs by treating existing plantations as a nursery bed 'mother crop' for multiplication and resale of rhizomes.
- The realistic basis for assessing the viability of *Miscanthus* must be that the first large-scale crop is established as a loss leader. Subsequent establishment costs will be sufficiently reduced to enable low-cost production.
- It is clear that annual husbandry costs will be low.
- Existing farm machinery can be used to harvest and bale *Miscanthus*.
- High crop moisture content is a positive benefit for *Miscanthus* in the MDF market. Forage harvesters chipping at 50% moisture content followed by immediate transportation to the processing plant is therefore an inexpensive viable option.
- Opportunities for minimising costs of production exist by growing *Miscanthus* on landfill sites and disposing of liquid wastes on the crop during growth.
- The inclusion of environmental considerations in the price of renewable biomass fuels is urged, so that the true costs of production from renewables and fossil fuels can be seen.

9 | *Environmental Aspects of* Miscanthus *Production*

by J. F. Santos Oliveira

with contributions from P. Duarte, D. G. Christian, A. Eppel-Hotz and A. L. Fernando

9.1 Introduction

Relationships between the environment and energy crops are varied and complex. It is generally considered that biomass crops have more beneficial than harmful effects on the environment. However, this is not always the case, and specific guidelines have to be respected in order to achieve this balance (Gosse, 1995; Mitchell, 1995).

This section addresses the environmental aspects of *Miscanthus* production and utilisation in Europe.

9.2 Replacement / Conservation of Fossil Energy Sources

The use of *Miscanthus* for energy production allows the conservation of primary energy sources such as oil and coal, e.g. 20 t of *Miscanthus* is equivalent (on an energy basis) to 12 t of hard coal (Lewandowski *et al.*, 1995) while 30 t is equivalent to 12,000 litres of oil (El-Bassam, 1996). Table 9.1 shows the avoided fossil fuel-derived energy when *Miscanthus* is used as an energy source. The quantification of avoided fossil fuel-derived energy depends on several factors such as the cultivation method, biomass yield, biomass water content, biomass losses in storage and the electricity generating technology (Bijl, 1996; Kaltschmitt *et al.*, 1996).

Table 9.1. Net avoided fossil fuel energy (GJ ha^{-1}) when Miscanthus *is used for energy production.*

Net avoided fossil energy (GJ ha^{-1})	Conversion route	Reference
153	gasification/CHP	Bijl (1996)
134	gasification	Bijl (1996)
99	co-firing	Bijl (1996)
240	not known	Hartmann (1995a)
102	not known	Jørgensen and Jørgensen (1996)
160	not known	Kaltschmitt et al. (1996)

The amount of net avoided fossil energy in GJ ha^{-1} is equivalent to the net energy balance of the crop, calculated by subtracting the energy input of the crop from the energy output of the crop. The energy input (in GJ ha^{-1}) was calculated for each of the constituent phases of the process chain, (i.e. from production through transportation, storage and treatment to utilisation). The energy output (in GJ ha^{-1}) was the total energy output during combustion. According to several authors (Hartmann, 1995a; Jørgensen & Jørgensen, 1996; Lewandowski *et al.*, 1995) the energy input corresponds to *c.* 5–6 % of the total energy output with transportation and harvesting being the first and second most energy-intensive phases of the production process (Jørgensen & Jørgensen, 1996). *Miscanthus* is reported to have a high net energy balance compared with other energy crops (Kaltschmitt *et al.*, 1996).

9.3 Emission of Greenhouse Gases

The greenhouse effect is mainly due to emissions created by the combustion of fossil fuels. One way of reducing greenhouse gas emissions is through the use of carbon dioxide (CO_2) neutral fuels (e.g. biomass) for energy production. Biomass such as *Miscanthus* is considered to be CO_2 neutral as its combustion does not result in a net increase in atmospheric carbon dioxide (this is due to the absorption of CO_2 by the crop during photosynthesis).

The climatic effects of CO_2, N_2O and methane (CH_4) can be quantified in terms of CO_2 equivalents or, alternatively, in terms of the so-called Global Warming Potential (GWP). The quantity of avoided greenhouse gas emissions arising when fossil fuels are replaced by biomass for energy production is equivalent to the sum of the greenhouse gas emissions which would be produced if the substituted fossil fuel were used for energy production. In the case of *Miscanthus*, the avoided greenhouse gas emissions can be calculated by adding the avoided CO_2 and N_2O emissions as the CH_4 emissions are considered to be negligible (Kaltschmitt *et al.*, 1996). Table 9.2 shows the avoided greenhouse gas emissions (expressed as tonnes CO_2 equivalent per hectare) which arise when *Miscanthus* replaces fossil fuels for energy production purposes.

The quantity of avoided greenhouse gas emissions depends mostly on the methods used for biomass production, the type of fossil fuel which was substituted and the conversion technology used. The quantity of avoided greenhouse gas emissions

Table 9.2. Net avoided greenhouse gas emissions (t CO_2 equivalent ha^{-1}.) when Miscanthus *is used as a fuel for energy production.*

Net CO$_2$ equivalent reduction (t ha^{-1})	Conversion route	Reference
10.7	gasification/CHP	Bijl (1996)
10.3	gasification	Bijl (1996)
7.8	co-firing	Bijl (1996)
17.2	not known	Hartmann (1995a)
8.8	not known	Jørgensen and Jørgensen (1996)
11.5	not known	Kaltschmitt *et al.* (1996)

increases from substitution of natural gas to light heating oil through to hard coal substitution (Kaltschmitt *et al.*, 1996). It has been reported that substitution of coal combustion with *Miscanthus* combustion results in up to 94% reduction in CO_2 emissions (Lewandowski *et al.*, 1995). It has also been reported that thermochemical conversion routes (i.e. combustion and gasification processes) for electricity production have the highest potential for reducing CO_2 emissions (Heuvel, 1995c; McCarthy & Mooney, 1995).

As indicated above, the substitution of fossil fuels in energy production systems with *Miscanthus* results in significant avoided greenhouse gas emissions. However, the quantity of avoided emissions is reduced by the production of CO_2 through the application of nitrogen fertiliser (N-fertiliser production is energy demanding), harvesting and the production of N_2O emissions (Jørgensen & Jørgensen, 1996; Lewandowski, *et al.*, 1995). N_2O emissions are produced during the combustion process and are emitted into the soil or water through denitrification processes. *Miscanthus* produces low N_2O emissions compared to other biomass crops (1 Kg N_2O ha^{-1} year^{-1}: Jørgensen & Jørgensen, 1996; Kaltschmitt *et al.*, 1996) and according to Jørgensen & Jørgensen (1996), N_2O emissions only reduce the avoided greenhouse gas emissions by about 6%. Therefore, N_2O emissions do not appear to be a serious threat to the use of *Miscanthus* as a low CO_2 fuel. However, as N_2O is an ozone-depleting gas, its emission will always have to be considered as a negative aspect.

9.4 Emission of Acidifying Gases

The emission of acidifying gases produces acid rainfall and is a negative aspect of fossil fuel combustion. The acidification potential of a fuel is calculated by adding up the airborne acidifying pollutants which are produced during its combustion. These pollutants are sulphur dioxide (SO_2), nitrogen oxides (NO_x), hydrogen chloride (HCl) and ammonia (NH_3). The acidification potential of a fuel is measured in SO_2 equivalents.

When *Miscanthus* is used as an energy source, acidification potential is essentially determined by the NO_x and SO_2 emissions released during the combustion of the biomass material (Kaltschmitt, *et al.*, 1996). The reduction in acidification potential through the substitution of fossil fuels with biomass for energy production depends on the conversion technology, the method of biomass cultivation and the fossil fuel which is substituted (Kaltschmitt, *et al.*, 1996).

SO_2 emissions form a smaller proportion of the total acidification potential of *Miscanthus* biofuel than NO_x emissions (Hartmann, 1995a). This is partly due to the low sulphur content of *Miscanthus* compared to fossil fuels, which results in a reduction in the formation of SO_2. It has been reported that when coal and *Miscanthus* are co-combusted, the SO_2 emissions decrease as the proportion of *Miscanthus* increases. This is not only attributed to the dilution of the high sulphur containing coal with the low sulphur containing biomass, but also to the increased capture of SO_2 by calcium oxide which is present in the biomass ash (Kicherer *et al.*, 1995).

9.5 Effects on the Quality of Soil and Water

The production of biomass is relatively land-intensive and therefore presents a risk of soil and groundwater pollution with nitrates, phosphates, potassium and pesticides. *Miscanthus* seems to have a low susceptibility to pests and diseases (McCarthy & Mooney, 1995) and thus has low pesticide requirements, reducing the risk of groundwater contamination and consequent risks to water and soil organisms.

Preliminary results reveal low levels of nitrate leaching in *Miscanthus* crops compared with other crops, making it a favourable crop in terms of protection of surface and groundwater quality. The level of nitrate leaching appears to be affected by the level of fertilisation and age of the plantation in addition to other factors such as climate and type of soil. Research has shown that the nitrate concentrations were generally below the EU limit for drinking water except in treatments fertilised with 185 Kg N ha^{-1} or more, this implies that N-fertilisation must only slightly exceed the nitrogen removed by the harvested crops in order to prevent leaching (Jørgensen & Mortensen, 1997). A higher leaching effect in the establishment year was also observed, most probably because the root system was not yet fully developed and the biomass production was limited.

Research by Christian *et al.* (1997b) has shown that the losses of nitrate from *Miscanthus* are similar to those reported from unfertilised grass and has concluded that these levels of nitrate losses are unlikely to lead to contamination of groundwater (Table 9.3).

Table 9.3. Nitrate losses (Kg N ha^{-1}) on unfertilised and fertilised Miscanthus *plots. Source: Christian* et al., *1997b.*

Year	Leaching losses (Kg N ha^{-1})		
	Nitrogen fertiliser rates(Kg ha^{-1} yr^{-1})		
	0	60	120
1993–4	154	187	228
1994–5	8	24	87
1995–6	3	11	20

It can be seen that leaching losses in 1993–4 (the establishment year) were significantly higher than other years, even in the unfertilised plots. These higher losses may be a result of the mineralisation of residues from the previous crop (winter beans) and the fertiliser which was applied to the newly planted *Miscanthus*. In the second year (1994–95) losses on the unfertilised plots and those which received 60 kg of nitrogen fertiliser in the spring had declined to very low levels. By the third year, losses were small on all treatments but there was a trend to greater losses on plots receiving highest fertiliser applications. In order to avoid nutrient leaching there is a need for careful nitrogen management if the environment, especially groundwater, is to be protected.

9.6 Use of Resources

Miscanthus has shown good potential as a low input alternative agricultural crop. In contrast to annual plants, the fertiliser requirements of *Miscanthus* are low (Schwarz & Liebhard, 1995). This is mainly due to the translocation of nutrients from the aerial to underground parts in autumn, these reserves being demobilised in spring for regrowth (Jodl *et al.*, 1996).

On the other hand, the specific water requirements of *Miscanthus* could be a limiting factor which might contribute to groundwater depletion (Hartmann, 1995a). This could be particularly important in southern Europe, where in summer the soil water content is less than the specific water requirements of the crop.

Uptake of heavy metals from polluted soils by energy crops is of concern where subsequent combustion of the crop may give rise to the production of ash which contains unacceptable levels of heavy metals. A study which investigated the uptake of copper, zinc and arsenic was carried out by a subcontractor, CSM Associates (Chapter 7). The results of this study suggest that *Miscanthus* may be a potentially valuable crop for growing on contaminated soils as it does not show the elevated uptake of heavy metals that had been noted in some grasses growing on metalliferous mine waste (Wilkins & Redstone, 1996).

9.7 Soil Erosion

According to El-Bassam (1996), perennial C_3 and C_4 species have a lower Soil Erosion-Index than annual crops with the best results being recorded in perennial C_4 species (Table 9.4).

Table 9.4. Soil erosion rates (t ha^{-1} year^{-1}) for different cropping systems. Source: El-Bassam, 1996.

Annual crops		Perennial energy crops	
Corn	Soybeans	Herbaceous	Short rotation woods
21.8[a]	40.9[a]	0.2	2.0

[a] based on early 1980s data. New tillage practices used today may lower these values.

9.8 Biodiversity

Energy crops appear to have a beneficial impact on wildlife and biodiversity in comparison to the agricultural crops which they replace. The increase in numbers of insects in the canopy leads to increased numbers of insect-eating birds. A comparative study between the fauna occurring in plots of *Miscanthus* and plots of the annual cereal, rye (*Secale cereale*) was performed at IACR, at Rothamstead, UK (Christian, Bullard and Wilkins 1997). The results obtained show that more beetles were found in the rye than in the *Miscanthus* but there was a greater species diversity in *Miscanthus*. However, in both crops the beetle population decreased during the sampling period. The spider population was three times greater in *Miscanthus* than in rye and there were also more spider species present in the *Miscanthus*. The spider population did not fluctuate during the sampling period. Web-spinning spiders like *Erigone* were not found in the *Miscanthus* plots but there was a greater presence of *Lycosa* species (hunting spiders). In both crops there were more beetles found than spiders, however the total populations were not untypical of those found on arable land in the autumn.

Christian, Bullard and Wilkins (1997) also assessed the presence of earthworms in *Miscanthus*. Earthworms of the *tanylobus* type are of the species *Lumbricus*, deep-burrowing species. They feed on litter and are important for mixing of organic matter between topsoil and subsoil; the holes and channels which they make can help drainage and aeration of the soil. *Epilobus* types can be both burrowing and soil-living species and generally inhabit shallower depths of the soil. In the study it was reported that between October 1993 and December 1995, the total number of earthworms increased by 123%. The number of *tanylobus* and *epilobus* types increased by 50% and 11% respectively. Immature earthworms of both types had increased but no mature *tanylobus* types were found and mature *epilobus* types had increased by 412%. The increase in the number of earthworms between 1993 and 1995 suggests that *Miscanthus* had not adversely affected earthworm populations. The summer of 1995 was very dry and this may have influenced both the number of earthworms found and their stage of maturity. In addition, earthworms may have been living below the roots and rhizomes and may not have been affected by the formaldehyde solution used for sampling.

In another study, where the fauna occurring in German plantations of *Miscanthus*, corn and reed were compared in order to determine the ecological value of the three plantations (Eppel-Hotz & Jodl, 1997), the occurrence of insects, especially beetles, spiders and small mammals was monitored using various trapping systems. The occurrence of bigger mammals and birds was recorded according to sound, tracking and watching.

It was found that for a variety of species like roe deer (*Capreolus capreolus*), European hare (*Lepus europaeus*), quail (*Coturnix coturnix*) or partridge (*Perdix perdix*) the *Miscanthus* plantation functioned as a substitute for hedges and copses. This was especially obvious in agricultural areas and open fields that had been cleared. *Miscanthus* was found to function as a retreat in the winter months because, in contrast to the other crops, it is not harvested before March. The *Miscanthus* plants, which can grow up to four metres in height, provided shelter and protection from predators as well as from climatic influences. The presence of a nest of reed warblers (*Acrocephalus scirpaceus*) and the successful breeding of linnets (*Acanthis cannabina*) indicated the use of *Miscanthus* plantations as a breeding habitat for birds. A total of seven species of birds were recorded in the *Miscanthus* plantation, compared to three in the cornfield and just one in the reeds. The fact that the *Miscanthus* plantation was so attractive to birds is probably due to the presence of insects and larvae as well as wild herbs in the more open zones of the plantation (these provide a food supply for quails and partridges). The *Miscanthus* plantations were also found to be attractive to beetles and spiders with a total of 104 species being registered compared to 94 in the reeds and 82 in the cornfield (Table 9.5).

The results of the German study indicate the higher number of 'ecological niches" which exist in a *Miscanthus* plantation compared to corn and reed plantations. The plant grows like a thicket, yet leaves free spaces between individual plants during the early years of growth. These spaces and the ground layer of leaf litter contribute to the higher number and variety of ecological niches in the *Miscanthus* plantations. In

Table 9.5. *Number of species recorded in* Miscanthus, *corn and reed plantations in Germany. Source: Eppel-Hotz & Jodl, 1997.*

		Number of species		
	Mammals	Birds	Beetles (df)	Spiders (df)
Miscanthus	7	7	62 (24)	42 (21)
Corn	2	3	62 (19)	20 (5)
Reed	3	1	55 (21)	39 (22)

df – 'differential species' = species only occurring on one expanse

contrast to the situation in the cornfield, a very stable species/individuals ratio can develop in the *Miscanthus* plantation. This means that each of the species is represented by a considerably large number of individuals (increases stability), a similar situation occurs in the reeds, but the number of *ecological niches* in the cornfield is considerably lower.

The *Miscanthus* site is an open and arid biotope which could be classified similarly to extensively used greenland. This is demonstrated by the domination of the beetle *Calathus fuscipes*, which prefers xerophile, arid areas and open fields. The occurrence of species which are characteristic of wood-habitats can be explained by the form of the *Miscanthus* plantation which resembles a forest edge, thus attracting this group of animals.

The conclusions of the work of Eppel-Hotz & Jodl (1997) are that *Miscanthus* plantations have a clear higher ecological value than the cornfields. This is the case especially when the plantations are situated in a poorly structured landscape.

9.9 Landscape

Widespread cultivation of energy cropping systems might have an impact on the landscape. However, crop planting should be carried out in order to ensure that adverse landscape impacts are minimised. According to Bijl (1996) and Hartmann (1995a), a *Miscanthus* plantation may have a somewhat negative impact on the landscape as the crop does not have a great variation in structure or colour. However, a positive aspect is the softening effect of the relatively high *Miscanthus* plants swaying according to air movements, especially when panicles are present on the plants.

9.10 Conclusions

This chapter has outlined the environmental aspects of *Miscanthus* production and utilisation. In summary, *Miscanthus* is a more environmentally acceptable crop than others in terms of soil erosion, biodiversity, use of resources and nutrient leaching. In addition, the substitution of fossil fuels through the use of *Miscanthus* as a fuel can lead to reductions in greenhouse gas emissions and acid rain. It is worth noting however, that these environmental benefits will only occur if the production and conversion processes are carefully managed and guidelines are adhered to.

Bibliography

Adati, S. and Shiotani, I. (1962) The cytotaxonomy of the genus *Miscanthus* and its phylogenetic status, *Bulletin of the Faculty of Agriculture, Mie University*, **25**: pp 1–14.

Allen, J., Browne, M., Hunter, A., Boyd, J. and Palmer, H. (1997) Supply systems for biomass fuels and their delivered costs. In: Bullard, M.J. *et al.* (eds), *Biomass and Bioenergy Crops. Aspects of Applied Biology* **49**: pp 369–78.

Andersson, N.J. (1885) Description of *Miscanthus sinensis*, *Oefvers. Svensk. Vet. Akad. Forh. Stockh.* **7**: pp 165–7.

Ball, J.T., Woodrow, I.E. and Berry, J.A. (1987) A model predicting stomatal conductance and its contribution to the control of photosynthesis under different environmental conditions. In: Biggins, J. (ed), *Progress in Photosynthesis Research*, Nihjoff, Dordrecht, pp 221–4.

Bao, M., Lopez, M. J., Lamas, J. and Vega, A. (1992) Preliminary results of experimental culture of *Miscanthus sinensis* in Galicia (N.W. Spain). In: Hall, D.O., Grassi, G. and Scheer, H. (eds), *Biomass for Energy and Environment, Agriculture and Industry – Proceedings of 7th E.C. Conference. 5–9 October 1992, Florence, Italy*, Ponte Press, Bochum, Germany, pp 621–5.

Beale, C.V. (1996) *Analysis of the Radiation-, Nutrient- and Water-Use Efficiencies of the Potential Energy Crops* Miscanthus *x* giganteus *and* Spartina cynosuroides, *Grown under Field Conditions in S.E. England*, unpublished PhD thesis, University of Essex, Colchester, UK.

Beale, C.V. and Long, S.P. (1995) Can perennial C-4 grasses attain high efficiencies of radiant energy conversion in cool climates, *Plant Cell and Environment*, **18**: pp 641–50.

Beale, C.V. and Long, S.P. (1997a) The effects of nitrogen and irrigation on the productivity of the C4 grasses *Miscanthus* x *giganteus* and *Spartina cynosuroides*. In: Bullard, M.J. *et al.* (eds), *Biomass and Bioenergy Crops. Aspects of Applied Biology*, **49**: pp 225–30.

Beale, C.V. and Long, S.P. (1997b) Seasonal dynamics of nutrient accumulation and partitioning in the perennial C4-grasses *Miscanthus* x *giganteus* and *Spartina cynosuroides*. In: Bullard, M. J. *et al.* (eds), *Biomass and Bioenergy Crops. Aspects of Applied Biology*, **12**: pp 419–28.

Beale, C.V., Morison, J.I.L. and Long, S.P. (1999) Water use efficiency of C-4 perennial grasses in a temperate climate, *Agricultural and Forest Meteorology*, **96**: pp 103–15.

Bijl, G. van der (1996) Sustainability of production and use of biomass for European energy supply. In: Chartier, P., Ferrero, G.L., Henius, U.M., Hultberg, S., Sachau, J. and Wiinblad, M. (eds), *Biomass for Energy and the Environment – Proceedings of the 9th European Bioenergy Conference. 24–27 June 1996, Copenhagen, Denmark*, Elsevier Science Ltd., Oxford, **1**: pp 387–92.

Biscoe, P.V. and Gallagher, J.N. (1977) Weather, dry matter production and yield. In: Landsberg, J.J. and Cutting, C.V. (eds), *Environmental Effects on Crop Physiology*, Academic Press, London, pp 75–100.

Boelke, B. (1995) Untersuchungsergebnisse zum Einfluß der Pflanzzeit und des Termins der Stickstoffdüngung auf die Ertragsbildung von Miscanthus. In: *Symposium Miscanthus –*

Biomassebereitstellung, energetische und stoffliche Nutzung, FNR-Schriftenreihe 'Nachwachsende Rohstoffe' 4. Landwirtschaftsverlag, Münster, pp. 71–86.

Bolton, J. (1995) The potential of plant fibres as crops for industrial use, *Outlook on Agriculture* **24**: pp 85–9.

Boote, K.J. and Pickering, N.J. (1994) Modelling photosynthesis of row crop canopies, *Hort Science*, **29**: pp 1423–34.

Bullard, M.J. (1997) *Review of Economics and Markets for* Miscanthus, HMSO, London.

Bullard, M.J., Christian, D.G. and Wilkins, C. (1996) The potential of graminaceous biomass crops for energy production in the UK: An overview. In: Chartier, P., Ferrero, G.L., Henius, U.M., Hultberg, S., Sachau, J. and Wiinblad, M. (eds), *Biomass for Energy and the Environment – Proceedings of the 9th European Bioenergy Conference. 24–27 June 1996, Copenhagen, Denmark*, Elsevier Science Ltd., Oxford, **1**: pp 592–7.

Bullard, M.J., Heath, M.C. and Nixon, P.M.I. (1995) Shoot growth, radiation interception and dry matter production and partitioning during the establishment phase of *Miscanthus sinensis 'Giganteus'* grown at two densities in the UK, *Annals of Applied Biology*, **126**: pp 365–78.

Bullard, M.J. and Kilpatrick. J.B. (1997) The productivity of *Miscanthus sacchariflorus* at seven sites in the UK. In: Bullard, M.J. *et al.* (eds), *Biomass and Bioenergy Crops. Aspects of Applied Biology*, **49**: pp 207–14.

Bullard, M.J., Nixon, P.M.I. and Heath, M.C. (1997) Quantifying the yield of *Miscanthus x giganteus* in the UK. In: Bullard, M.J. *et al.* (eds), *Biomass and Bioenergy Crops. Aspects of Applied Biology*, **49**: pp 199–206.

Bullard, M.J., Nixon, P.M.I., Kilpatrick, J.B., Heath, M.C. and Speller, C.S. (1995) Principles of weed control in *Miscanthus* spp. under contrasting field conditions. In *Proceedings of British Crop Protection Conference (Weeds). November, 1995, Brighton, UK*, pp 991–6.

Campbell, G.S. (1977) *An Introduction to Environmental Biophysics*, Springer-Verlag, New York.

CEC (1996a) *The Agricultural Situation in the European Union: 1995 Report*, Luxembourg, Commission of the European Communities, Brussels.

CEC (1996b) *Energy for the Future: Renewable Sources of Energy. CEC Green Paper for a Community Strategy COM(96) 576 Final*, Commission of the European Communities, Brussels.

Christian, D.G., Bullard, M.J. and Wilkins, C. (1997) The agronomy of some herbaceous crops grown for energy in Southern England. In: Bullard, M.J. *et al.* (eds), *Biomass and Bioenergy Crops. Aspects of Applied Biology*, **49**: pp 41–51.

Christian, D.G., Lampty, J.N.L., Forde, S.M.D. and Plumb, R.T. (1994) First report of barley yellow dwarf leuteovirus on *Miscanthus* in the United Kingdom. *European Journal of Plant Pathology*, **100**: pp 167–70.

Christian, D.G., Poulton, P.R., Riche, A.B. and Yates, N.E. (1997a) The recovery of ^{15}N-labelled fertilizer applied to *Miscanthus x giganteus*. In: Bullard, M.J. *et al.* (eds), *Biomass and Bioenergy Crops. Aspects of Applied Biology*, **12**: pp 21–4.

Christian, D.G. and Riche, A.B. (1997) Uptake of nitrogen by *Miscanthus*. In: van der Bilj, G. and Biewingo, E.E. (eds), *Proceedings of Conference on the Environmental Impact of Biomass for Energy. May, 1997*. CLM, Utrecht, The Netherlands, pp 71–72.

Christian, D.G., Riche, A.B. and Yates, N.E. (1997b) Nitrate leaching under *Miscanthus* grass. In: van der Bilj, G. and Biewingo, E.E. (eds), *Proceedings of Conference on the Environmental Impact of Biomass for Energy. May, 1997*. CLM, Utrecht, The Netherlands, pp 69–70.

Clayton, W.D. and Renvoize, S.A. (1986) *Genera Graminum*, Kew Bulletin additional series X111, HMSO, London.

Clifton-Brown, J.C. (1997) *The Importance of Temperature in Controlling Leaf Growth of Miscanthus in Temperate Climates*, unpublished PhD thesis, University of Dublin, Ireland.

Clifton-Brown, J.C. and Jones, M.B. (1997) The thermal response of leaf extension rate in genotypes of the C4-grass *Miscanthus*: An important factor in determining the potential productivity of different genotypes, *Journal of Experimental Botany*, **48**: 1573–81.

Clifton-Brown, J.C., Neilson, B.M. and Jones, M.B. (1996) The potential of *Miscanthus* as an energy crop in Ireland. In: Chartier, P., Ferrero, G.L., Henius, U.M., Hultberg, S., Sachau,

J. and Wiinblad, M. (eds), *Biomass for Energy and the Environment – Proceedings of the 9th European Bioenergy Conference. 24–27 June 1996, Copenhagen, Denmark*, Elsevier Science Ltd., Oxford, **1**: pp 628–33.

Collatz, J.G., Ribas-Carbo, M. and Berry, J.A. (1992) Coupled photosynthesis-stomatal conductance model for leaves of C_4 plants, *Australian Journal of Plant Physiology*, **19**: pp 519–38.

Eghbal, K. (1993) Ertragsleistung und Biomassequalitatät von *Miscanthus sinensis* als mölicher Energie- und Selluloserohstoff, *Zeitschrift fuer Laborpraxis in Biologie und Landwirtschaft* **3**: pp 44–7.

El-Bassam, N. (1996) Performance of C4 plant species as energy sources and their possible impact on environment and climate. In: Chartier, P., Ferrero, G.L., Henius, U.M., Hultberg, S., Sachau, J. and Wiinblad, M. (eds), *Biomass for Energy and the Environment – Proceedings of the 9th European Bioenergy Conference. 24–27 June 1996, Copenhagen, Denmark*, Elsevier Science Ltd., Oxford, **1**: pp 42–7.

El-Bassam, N. (1998) *Energy Plant Species. Their Use and Impact on Environment and Development.* James & James (Science Publishers), London.

El-Bassam, N., Dambroth, M. and Jachs, I. (1992) Die Nutzung von *Miscanthus senensis* als Energie- und Industriegrundstoff, *Landbauforschung Volkenrode*, **42**: pp 199–205.

Eppel-Hotz, A. and Jodl, S. (1997) Comparative faunistic examination in *Miscanthus* (*Miscanthus x giganteus*), corn (*Zea mays*) and reed (*Phragmites australis*) expanses. Summary of the study: Muschketat, L.F. and Otte, J. (1996) Vergleichende faunistische Untersuchung in Beständen hochwüchsiger Sü(gräser (Poaceae). Unpublished.

Eppel-Hotz, A., Jodl, S. and Kuhn, W. (1998) Miscanthus: new cultivars and results of research experiments for improving the establishment rate. In: El-Bassam, N., Behl, R.K. and Prochnow, B. (eds), *Proceedings of the International Conference on Sustainable Agriculture for Food, Energy and Industry. 23–27 June 1997*, Braunschweig, Germany, pp 178–86.

Farquhar, G.D., von Caemmerer, S. and Berry, J.A. (1980) A biochemical model of photosynthetic CO_2 assimilation in leaves of C_3 species, *Planta*. **149**: pp 78–90.

Fernando, A., Duarte, P. and Oliveira, J.F.S. (1996) Bioremoval of heavy metals from soil by *Miscanthus sinensis Giganteus*. In: Chartier, P., Ferrero, G.L., Henius, U.M., Hultberg, S., Sachau, J. and Wiinblad, M. (eds), *Biomass for Energy and the Environment – Proceedings of the 9th European Bioenergy Conference. 24–27 June 1996, Copenhagen, Denmark*, Elsevier Science Ltd., Oxford, **1**: pp 531–6.

Field, C. (1983) Allocating leaf nitrogen for the maximisation of carbon gain: leaf age as a control on the allocation program, *Oecologia*, **56**: pp 341–7.

Fitter, A.H. and Hay, R.K.M. (1987) *Environmental Physiology of Plants*, 2nd edition, Academic Press, London.

Forseth, I.N. and Norman, J.M. (1993) Modelling of solar irradiance, leaf energy budget, and canopy photosynthesis. In: Hall, D.O., Scurlock, J.M.O., Bolhar-Nordenkampf, R.C., Leegood, R.C. and Long, S.P. (eds), *Techniques in Photosynthesis and Productivity Research for a Changing Environment*, Chapman and Hall, London, pp 207–19.

Gosse, G. (1995) Environmental issues and biomass. In: Chartier, P., Ferrero, G.L., Henius, U.M., Hultberg, S., Sachau, J. and Wiinblad, M. (eds), *Biomass for Energy and the Environment – Proceedings of the 9th European Bioenergy Conference. 24–27 June 1996, Copenhagen, Denmark*, Elsevier Science Ltd., Oxford, **1**: pp 52–62.

Graham, J., McNicol, R.J., Greig, K. and Van De Ven, W.T.G. (1994) Identification of red raspberry cultivars and an assessment of their relatedness using fingerprints produced by random primers, *Journal of Horticultural Science*, **69**: pp 123–30.

Greef, J.M. (1994) Development of above and below ground organs in *Miscanthus x giganteus* in Northern Germany. In: Hennik, S., van Soest, L.J.M., Pillian, K. and Hof, L. (eds), *Alternative Oilseed and Fiber Crops for Cold Wet Regions of Europe*, European Commission, Luxembourg, pp 101–12.

Greef, J.M. and Deuter, M. (1993) Syntaxonomy of *Miscanthus x giganteus*, *Angew. Bot.*, **67**: pp 87–90.

Greef, J.M. and Schondelmaier, J. (1997) Genetic diversity of European *Miscanthus* species revealed by AFLP fingerprinting. In: Bullard, M.J. *et al.* (eds), *Biomass and Bioenergy Crops. Aspects of Applied Biology,* **49**: pp 231–5.

Haase, E. and Hunsinger, H. (1995) Mitteilungen aus der Biologischen Bundesanstalt für Land- und Forstwirtschaft, Berlin-Dahlem. H. **310**: pp 178–83.

Hague, J.R.B. (1997) Biomass as feedstocks for the forest products industry. In: Bullard, M.J. *et al.* (eds), *Biomass and Bioenergy Crops. Aspects of Applied Biology* **49**: pp 455–64.

Hall, D.O. (1997) Biomass energy in industrialised countries – a view of the future, *Forest Ecology and Management,* **91**: pp 17–45.

Hansen, L.A. (1996) Etablering og dyrkning af "Elefantgræs", *Miscanthus* Sin. Giganteus 1989–1994. Rapport fra markforsøg hos danske landmænd. Terrateam Støvring, Denmark.

Harley, P.C., Thomas, R.B. and Reynolds, J.F. (1992) Modelling photosynthesis of cotton grown in elevated CO_2, *Plant Cell Environ.*, **15**: pp 271–82. QUERY 26

Hartmann, H. (1995a) Environmental aspects of energy crop use – a system comparison. In: Chartier, Ph., Beenackers, A.A.C.M. and Grassi, G. (eds), *Biomass for Energy, Environment, Agriculture and Industry – Proceedings of 8th E.C. Conference. 3–5 October, 1994, Vienna, Austria,* Elsevier Science Ltd., Oxford, **3**: pp 2250–5.

Hartmann, H. (1995b) Lagerung, Transport und Umschlag von Halmgütern. (Storage, transport and handling of strawshaped material), *Logistik bei der Nutzung biogener Festbrennstoffe (Logistics at using biomass for energy).* Schriftenreihe Nachwachsende rohstoffe **5** pp 63–76.

Harvey, J. and Hutchens, M. (1995) Progress in commercial development of Miscanthus in England. In: Chartier, Ph., Beenackers, A.A.C.M. and Grassi, G. (eds), *Biomass for Energy, Environment, Agriculture and Industry – Proceedings of 8th E.C. Conference. 3–5 October, 1994, Vienna, Austria,* Elsevier Science Ltd., Oxford, **1**: pp 587–93.

Hay, R.K.M. & Walker, A.J. (1989) *An Introduction to the Physiology of Crop Yield,* Longman Scientific and Technical, Harlow, Essex.

Heuvel, E.M.J.T. van den (1995a) *Pretreatment Technologies for Energy Crops.* Final report of NOVEM project 355300/0302, BTG, Enschede, The Netherlands.

Heuvel, E.M.J.T. van den (1995b) *Third Annual Progress Report, BTG, European Miscanthus Network,* BTG, Enschede.

Heuvel, E.J.M.T. van den (1995c) Conversion routes for energy crops: integrating agricultural and environmental opportunities in Europe. In: Chartier, Ph., Beenackers, A.A.C.M. and Grassi, G. (eds), *Biomass for Energy, Environment, Agriculture and Industry – Proceedings of 8th E.C. Conference. 3–5 October, 1994, Vienna, Austria,* Elsevier Science Ltd., Oxford, **1**: pp 587–93.

Hillis, D.M., Larson, A., Davis, S.K. and Zimmer, E. (1990) Nucleic acids III: Sequencing. In: Hillis, D.M. and Moritz, C.M. (eds), *Molecular Systematics,* Sinauer Associates, Inc. Massachusetts, pp 340–1.

Himken, M., Lammel, J., Neukirchen, D., Czypionka-Krause, U. and Olfs, H-W. (1997) Cultivation of *Miscanthus* under West European conditions: seasonal changes in dry matter production, nutrient uptake and remobilization. *Plant and Soil,* **189**: pp 117–26.

Hodkinson, T.R., Renvoize, S.A. and Chase, M.W. (1997) Systematics of *Miscanthus.* In: Bullard, M.J. *et al.* (eds), *Biomass and Bioenergy Crops. Aspects of Applied Biology,* **49**: pp 189–97.

Horvath, G. (1997) *Costs and Energy Consumption at Drying* Miscanthus. Internal report A559-942/2. Department of Agricultural Engineering and Physics, Wageningen Agricultural University, The Netherlands.

Hotz, A., Kolb, W. and Kuhn, W. (1993) Chinaschilf wächst nicht in den Himmel. *DLG-Mitteilungen/agrar-inform,* **1**: pp 50–3.

Hotz, A. and Kuhn, W. (1994) Erkenntnisse aus sechsjähriger Forschungstätigkeit mit Miscanthus. In: *Tagungsband zum 2. Fachgespräch* Miscanthus *am 1.2.1995 in Velburg,* C.A.R.M.E.N. e.V., Rimpar, Germany, pp 49–60.

Hotz, A., Kuhn, W. and Jodl, S. (1996) Screening of different *Miscanthus* cultivars in respect of their productivity and usability as a raw material for energy and industry. In: Chartier, P., Ferrero, G.L., Henius, U.M., Hultberg, S., Sachau, J. and Wiinblad, M. (eds), *Biomass for*

Energy and the Environment – Proceedings of the 9th European Bioenergy Conference. 24–27 June 1996, Copenhagen, Denmark, Elsevier Science Ltd., Oxford, **1**: pp 523–7.

Huggett, D.A. (1996) Potential aphid pests of the biomass crop *Miscanthus*. In: *Proceedings of Brighton Crop Protection Conference (Pests and Diseases)*, British Crop Protection Council, Farnham, Surrey, pp 427–8.

Huisman, W. (1995) Logistics of harvest of *Miscanthus Sinensis Giganteus*. In: Chartier, Ph., Beenackers, A.A.C.M. and Grassi, G. (eds), *Biomass for Energy, Environment, Agriculture and Industry – Proceedings of 8th E.C. Conference. 3–5 October, 1994, Vienna, Austria*, Elsevier Science Ltd., Oxford **1**: pp 361–71.

Huisman, W. and Gigler, J.K. (1997) Logistics of the biomass fuel chain. In: Bullard, M.J. *et al.* (eds), *Biomass and Bioenergy Crops. Aspects of Applied Biology*, **49**: pp 379–87.

Huisman, W., Kasper, G.J. and Venturi, P. (1996) Technical and economical feasibility of the complete production-transport chain of *Miscanthus x Giganteus* as an energy crop. In: *Proceedings of First European Energy Crops Overview Conference. 30th Sept – 1st Oct 1996*, BTG, Enschede, The Netherlands, pp 1–8.

Huisman, W. and Kortleve, W.J. (1994) Mechanisation of crop establishment, harvest and post harvest conservation of *Miscanthus Sinensis* Giganteus, *Industrial Crops and Products*, **2**: pp 289–97.

Humphries, S.A. and Long, S.P. (1995) WIMOVAC: A software package for modelling the dynamics of plant leaf and canopy photosynthesis, *CABIOS*, **11**: pp 361–71.

Iglesias, G., Bao, M., Lamas, J. and Vega, A. (1996) Soda pulping of *Miscanthus sinensis*. Effects of operational variables on pulp yield and lignin solubilization, *Bioresource Technology*, **58**: pp 17–23.

Jodl, S., Hotz, A. and Christian, D.G. (1996) Nutrient demand and translocation processes of *Miscanthus x Giganteus*. In: Chartier, P., Ferrero, G.L., Henius, U.M., Hultberg, S., Sachau, J. and Wiinblad, M. (eds), *Biomass for Energy and the Environment – Proceedings of the 9th European Bioenergy Conference. 24–27 June 1996, Copenhagen, Denmark*, Elsevier Science Ltd., Oxford, **1**: pp 517–22.

Johnson, I.R. (1993) *Plamtmod 2.0: Exploring the Physiology of Plant Communities*, Greenhat Software, Armidale.

Johnson, R.C. (1994) Genetic variation and physiological mechanisms for water-use efficiency in temperate grasses and legume germplasm, *Aspects of Applied Biology*, **38**: pp 71–8.

Jones, M.B., McCarthy, S., Keane, R. and Halbert, C. (1994) *Miscanthus* Productivity Network. In: Hall, D.O., Grassi, G. and Sheer, H. (eds), *Biomass for Energy and Industry – Proceedings of the 7th E.C. Conference. 5-9 October, 1992, Florence, Italy*, Ponte Press, Bochum, Germany, pp 101–7.

Jonkanski, F. (1994). *Miscanthus* – The future biomass crop for energy and industry. In: Chartier, Ph., Beenackers, A.A.C.M. and Grassi, G. (eds), *Biomass for Energy, Environment, Agriculture and Industry – Proceedings of 8th E.C. Conference. 3–5 October, 1994, Vienna, Austria*, Elsevier Science Ltd., Oxford, **1**: pp 372–9.

Jordan, D.B. and Ogren, W.L. (1984) The CO_2/O_2 specificity of ribulose1,5 – bisphosphate carboxylase/oxygenase. Dependence on Ribulose bisphosphate concentration, pH and temperature, *Planta*, **161**: pp 308–13.

Jørgensen, U. (1994) Course of yield, nutrient dynamics and time of harvest in *Miscanthus*. In: Jørgensen, U. and Hansen, J. (eds) *Symposium on Miscanthus*, Foulum, Denmark, Statens Planteavlsforsøg Report No. 16, pp 33–9.

Jørgensen, U. (1995) Lowcost and safe establishment of *Miscanthus*. In: Chartier, Ph., Beenackers, A.A.C.M. and Grassi, G. (eds), *Biomass for Energy, Environment, Agriculture and Industry – Proceedings of 8th E.C. Conference. 3–5 October, 1994, Vienna, Austria*, Elsevier Science Ltd., Oxford, **1**: pp 541–7.

Jørgensen, U. (1996) *Miscanthus* yields in Denmark. In: Chartier, P., Ferrero, G.L., Henius, U.M., Hultberg, S., Sachau, J. and Wiinblad, M. (eds), *Biomass for Energy and the Environment*

– *Proceedings of the 9th European Bioenergy Conference. 24–27 June 1996, Copenhagen, Denmark*, Elsevier Science Ltd., Oxford, **1**: pp 48–53.

Jørgensen, U. (1997) Genotypic variation in dry matter accumulation and content of N, K and Cl in *Miscanthus* in Denmark, *Biomass and Bioenergy*, **12**: pp 155–69.

Jørgensen, R.N. and Jørgensen, B.J. (1996) The effect of N_2O emission on the net CO_2-displacement by energy crop production. In: Chartier, P., Ferrero, G.L., Henius, U.M., Hultberg, S., Sachau, J. and Wiinblad, M. (eds), *Biomass for Energy and the Environment – Proceedings of the 9th European Bioenergy Conference. 24–27 June 1996, Copenhagen, Denmark*, Elsevier Science Ltd., Oxford, **3**: pp 1701–5.

Jørgensen, U. and Mortensen, J. (1997) Perennial crops for fibre and energy use as a tool for fulfilling the Danish strategies on improving surface and ground water quality. In: Olesen, S.E. (ed), *Alternative Use of Agricultural Land*, SP Report No. 18; pp 12–21.

Kaltschmitt, M., Reinhardt, G.A. and Stelzer, T. (1996) LCA of biofuels under different environmental aspects. In: Chartier, P., Ferrero, G.L., Henius, U.M., Hultberg, S., Sachau, J. and Wiinblad, M. (eds), *Biomass for Energy and the Environment – Proceedings of the 9th European Bioenergy Conference. 24–27 June 1996, Copenhagen, Denmark*, Elsevier Science Ltd., Oxford, **1**: pp 369–86.

Karp, A., Edwards, K., Bruford, M., Vosman, B., Morgante, M., Seberg, O., Kremer, A., Boursot, P., Arctander, P., Tautz, D. and Hewitt, G. (1996) Molecular techniques in the assessment of botanical diversity, *Annals of Botany*, **78**: pp 143–9.

Kaye, G.W.C. and Laby, T.H. (1973) *Tables of Physical and Chemical Constants*, 14th edition, Longman, London.

Keen, R.E. and Spain, J.D. (1992). Temperature and biological activity. In: Keen, R.E. and Spain, J.D. (eds), *Computer Simulation in Biology: A Basic Introduction*, Wiley, New York, pp 183–200.

Kicherer, A., Görres, J., Spliethoff, H. and Hein, K.R.G. (1995) Biomass co-combustion for the pollutant control in pulverized coal units. In: Chartier, Ph., Beenackers, A.A.C.M. and Grassi, G. (eds), *Biomass for Energy, Environment, Agriculture and Industry – Proceedings of 8th E.C. Conference. 3–5 October, 1994, Vienna, Austria*, Elsevier Science Ltd., Oxford, **2**: pp 926–35.

Kordsachia, O., Seeman, A. and Patt, R. (1992) Fast-growing poplar and *Miscanthus sinensis* – Future raw materials for pulping in Central Europe. In: Hall, D.O., Grassi, G. and Scheer, H. (eds), *Biomass for Energy and Environment, Agriculture and Industry – Proceedings of 7th E.C. Conference. 5-9 October 1992, Florence, Italy*, Ponte Press, Bochum, Germany, pp 307–16.

Kristensen, E.F. (1997) Experiences from *Miscanthus* harvesting in Denmark. In: Jørgensen, U. (ed.) *Harvest and Other Mechanical Pretreatments of Lignocellulosic Energy Crops. Proceedings of the IEA Bioenergy Workshop at CLAAS, Harsewinkel, Germany Nov. 1996*, Danish Institute of Agricultural Sciences, Foulum, Denmark, pp 37–48.

Lazenby, A. (1988) The grass crop in perspective: selection, plant performance and animal production. In: Jones, M.B. and Lazenby, A. (eds), *The Grass Crop, the Physiological Basis of Production*, Chapman & Hall, London, pp 311–54.

Leaver, D. (1991) *Forage Maize Production for Dairy Cattle, A Farm Study*, Wye College, University of London.

Lee, Y.N. (1964) Taxonomic studies on the genus *Miscanthus* (1) New species and varieties, *Journal of Japanese Botany*, **39**: pp 19–27.

Lehmann, H., Paryke, R., Pfluger, A. and Reetz, T. (1996) Sustainable land use in the European Union. In: Chartier, P., Ferrero, G.L., Henius, U.M., Hultberg, S., Sachau, J. and Wiinblad, M. (eds), *Biomass for Energy and the Environment – Proceedings of the 9th European Bioenergy Conference. 24–27 June 1996, Copenhagen, Denmark*, Elsevier Science Ltd., Oxford, **3**: pp 1727–32.

Lewandowski, I. and Kahnt, G. (1993). Tissue culture of *Miscanthus sinensis* – A potential for mass production?. In: Hall, D.O., Grassi, G. and Scheer, H. (eds), *Biomass for Energy and Environment, Agriculture and Industry – Proceedings of 7th E.C. Conference. 5-9 October 1992, Florence, Italy*, Ponte Press, Bochum, Germany. pp 696–9.

Lewandowski, I. and Kahnt, G. (1994) Einfluß von Bestandesdichte und Stickstoff Düngung auf die Entwicklung, Nährstoffgehalte und Ertragsbildung von *Miscanthus* 'Giganteus'. *Mitt. Ges. Pflanzenbauwiss*, **7:** pp 341–3.

Lewandowski, I., Kicherer, A. and Vonier, P. (1995) CO_2-balance for the cultivation and combusion of *Miscanthus. Biomass and Bioenergy*, **8**: pp 81–90.

Linde-Laursen, I. (1993) Cytogenetic analysis of *Miscanthus* 'Giganteus', an interspecific hybrid, *Hereditas*, **119**: pp 297–300.

Linke, W.F. (1965) *Solubilities: Inorganic and Metal-Organic Compounds*, 4th edition, American Chemical Society, Washington DC.

Long, S.P. (1983) C-4 photosynthesis at low-temperatures, *Plant Cell and Environment*, **6**: pp 345–63.

Long, S.P. (1985) Leaf gas exchange. In: Barber, J. and Baker, N.R. (eds), *Photosynthetic Mechanisms and the Environment*, Elsevier, Amsterdam, pp 453–500.

Long, S.P. (1991) Modification of the response of photosynthetic productivity to rising temperature by atmospheric CO_2 concentrations: Has its importance been underestimated? *Plant Cell and Environment*, **14**: pp 729–39.

Long, S.P. (1999) Environmental responses. In: Sage, R.F. and Monson, R.K. (eds), *C_4 Plant Biology*. Academic Press, San Diego, pp 215–49.

Long, S.P. and Drake, B.G. (1991) Effects of the long-term elevation of CO_2 concentration in the field on the quantum yield of photosynthesis of the C_3 sedge, *Scirpus olneyi*, *Plant Physiology*, **96**: pp 221–6.

Long, S.P. and Drake, B.G. (1992) Photosynthetic CO_2 assimilation and rising atmospheric CO_2 concentration. In: Baker, N.R. and Thomas, H. (eds), *Crop Photosynthesis: Spatial and Temporal Determinants*, Elsevier, Amsterdam, pp 69–95.

Long, S.P., Farage, P.K., Aguilera, C. and Macharia, J.M.N. (1992) Damage to photosynthetic productivity of crops. In: Barber, J., Guerrero, M.G. and Medrano, H. (eds), *Trends in Photosynthesis*, Intercept, Andover. pp 345–56.

Mangan, C.L. (1994) Non-food crops and non-food uses in EC research programs. In: Hall, D.O., Grassi, G. and Sheer, H. (eds), *Biomass for Energy and Industry – Proceedings of the 7th E.C. Conference. 5-9 October, 1992, Florence, Italy*, Ponte Press, Bochum, Germany, pp 341–7.

Marshall, D.G., Chua, A., Napoleon Keeling, P.W., Sullivan, D.J., Coleman, D.C. and Smyth, C.J. (1995) Molecular analysis of *Helicobacter pylori* populations in antral biopsies from individuals patients using randomly amplified polymorphic DNA (RAPD) fingerprinting, *FEMS Immunology and Medical Microbiology*, **10**: pp 317–24.

McCarthy, S. and Mooney, M. (1995) European *Miscanthus* Network. In: Chartier, Ph., Beenackers, A.A.C.M. and Grassi, G. (eds), *Biomass for Energy, Environment, Agriculture and Industry – Proceedings of 8th E.C. Conference. 3–5 October, 1994, Vienna, Austria*, Elsevier Science Ltd., Oxford, **1**: pp 380–8.

Min, H. and Hengzhong, T. (1988) *Experiment and Practices in the Manufacture of Printing Papers with Amur silver grass* BKP, Yueyang Paper Mill, Yueyang, Hunan and Paper Industrial Research Institute, Ministry of Light Industry, Beijing.

Mitchell, C.P. (1995) Resource base. In: Chartier, Ph., Beenackers, A.A.C.M. and Grassi, G. (eds), *Biomass for Energy, Environment, Agriculture and Industry – Proceedings of 8th E.C. Conference. 3–5 October, 1994, Vienna, Austria*, Elsevier Science Ltd., Oxford, **1**: pp 115–28.

Molenaar, J.A., Huisman, W. and Venturi, P. (1996) Energy consumption and costs of the production chains of *Miscanthus x giganteus*. In: Chartier, P., Ferrero, G.L., Henius, U.M., Hultberg, S., Sachau, J. and Wiinblad, M. (eds), *Biomass for Energy and the Environment – Proceedings of the 9th European Bioenergy Conference. 24–27 June 1996, Copenhagen, Denmark*, Elsevier Science Ltd., Oxford, **2**: pp 867–72.

Moller, F. and Schwarz, K.U. (1996) Natural sandwich material: The use of *Miscanthus x giganteus* as core material. WKI Short report 17. [Uffe Jørgensen] Frauenhofer Wilhelm-Kluditz-Institut für Holzforschung, Braunschweig, Germany.

Monteith, J.L. (1965) Light distribution and photosynthesis in field crops, *Journal of Experimental Biology*, **29**: pp 17–37.

Monteith, J.L. (1973) *Principles of Environmental Physics*, Edward Arnold, London.

Monteith, J.L. (1977) Climate and the efficiency of crop production in Britain, *Philosophical Transactions of the Royal Society of London*, **281**: pp 277–94.

Monteith, J.L. (1978) Reassessment of maximum growth rates for C3 and C4 crops, *Experimental Agriculture*, **14**: pp 1–5.

Monteith, J.L. and Unsworth, M.H. (1990) *Principles of Environmental Physics*, 2nd Edition, Edward Arnold, London.

Nellist, M.E. (1997) Storage and drying of arable coppice. In: Bullard, M.J. *et al.* (eds), *Biomass and Bioenercy Crops. Aspects of Applied Biology*, **49**: pp 349–60.

Nie, G.Y., Long, S.P. and Baker, N.R. (1992). The effects of development at suboptimal growth temperatures on photosynthetic capacity and susceptibility to chilling-dependent photoinhibition in Zea-Mays, *Physiologia Plantarum*, **85**: pp 554–60.

Nielsen, P.N. (1987) The productivity of *Miscanthus* sinensis 'Giganteus' on different soil types, *Tidsskrift für Plateval*, **91**: pp 275–81.

Nix, J. (1997) *Farm Management Pocketbook* (27th edition). Ashford, Imperial College at Wye, p 256.

Norman, J.M. (1980) Interfacing leaf and canopy light interception models. In: Hesketh, J.D. and Jones, J.W. (eds), *Predicting Photosynthesis for Ecosystem Models*, CRC Press, Boca Raton, FL., pp 49–67.

O'Neill, N.R. and Farr, D.F. (1996) *Miscanthus* Blight, a new foliar disease of ornamental grasses and sugarcane incited by *Leptosphaeria* sp. and its anamorphic state *Stagonospora* sp., *Plant Disease*, **80**: pp 980–4.

Papatheofanous, M.G., Koukios, E.G., Marton, G. and Dencs, J. (1996), Characterization of *Miscanthus sinensis* potential as an industrial and energy feedstock. In: Chartier, P., Ferrero, G.L., Henius, U.M., Hultberg, S., Sachau, J. and Wiinblad, M. (eds), *Biomass for Energy and the Environment – Proceedings of the 9th European Bioenergy Conference. 24–27 June 1996, Copenhagen, Denmark*, Elsevier Science Ltd., Oxford, **1**: pp 504–8.

Parnell, J. and Waldren, S. (1996) Detrended correspondence analysis in the ordination of data for phenetic and cladistics, *Taxon*, **45**: pp 71–84.

Penman, H.L. (1948) Natural evaporation from open water, bare soil and grass, *Proceedings of the Royal Society of London*, **193**: pp 120–45.

Petersen, K. and Holme, I.M. (1994) Induction of callus and regeneration of plants from different tissues of *M. x ogiformes* 'Giganteus'. In: *Abstracts of the 8th International Congress of Plant Tissue and Cell Culture Firenze, June 12–17*, p 187.

Pierik, J.T.G. and Curvers, A.P.W.M. (1995) Logistics and pretreatment of biomass fuels for gasification and combustion. In Curvers, A.P.W.M.: *Energy from Biomass: An Assessment of Two Promising Systems for Energy Production*. ECN-C–95-038, p 63.

Pignatelli, V., Nanna, F., Cardinale, G., Zimbardi, F. and Cappelletto, P.L. (1995) *Nuovi prodotti e tecnologie per l'industria della carta: produzione di pasta di cellulosa da* Miscanthus sinensis *mediante trattamento di steam explosion*. ENEA Technical Report No. RT/INN/95/06, Roma, Italy.

Pignatelli, V., Nanna, F., Cardinale, G., Zimbardi, F. and Cappelletto, P.L. (1996) Produzione di pasta di cellulosa da *Miscanthus sinensis* mediante trattamento di steam explosion, *Carta e Cartiere*, **7**: pp 10–18.

Pignatelli, V., Viggiano, D., Zimbardi, F. and Cappelletto, P.L. (1995) Steam explosion pretreatment of *Miscanthus sinensis* for pulp and paper production. In: Chartier, Ph., Beenackers, A.A.C.M. and Grassi, G. (eds), *Biomass for Energy, Environment, Agriculture and Industry – Proceedings of 8th E.C. Conference. 3–5 October, 1994, Vienna, Austria*, Elsevier Science Ltd., Oxford, **2**: pp 1234–46.

Reynolds, J.F., Chen, J.L., Harley, P.C., Hilbert, D.W., Dougherty, R.L. and Tenhunen, J.D. (1992) Modelling the effects of elevated carbon dioxide on plants: extrapolating leaf response to a canopy, *Journal of Agricultural Forest Meteorology*, **61**: pp 69–94.

Roberts, M.J., Long, S.P., Tieszen, L.L. and Beadle, C.L. (1993) Measurement of plant biomass and net primary production of herbaceous vegetation. In: Hall, D.O., Scurlock, J.M.O.,

Bolhar-Nordenkampf, H.R., Leegood, R.C. and Long, S.P. (eds), *Photosynthesis and Production in a Changing Environment: A Field and Laboratory Manual*, Chapman and Hall, London, pp 1–21.

Rodrigues, A., Ferreira, L.J., Fernando, A.L. and Oliveira, J.S. (1996) Co-compostagem de resíduos lenho-celulósicos com lamas de ETAR. In: Borrego, C., Coelho, C., Arroja, A., Boia, C. and Figueiredo, E. (eds) *Actas da 5ª Conferência Nacional sobre a Qualidade do Ambiente (Proceedings of the 5th National Conference on the Quality of the Environment), 10–12 Abril, Aveiro, Portugal*, 2nd Volume, pp 1143–54

Ryan, M. and Buckland, M. (1997) *Farm Wood Fuel and Energy Project – Crop Performance Monitoring* ETSU B/W2/00199/REP, ETSU, Harwell, UK.

Schaal, B.A., Leverich, W.J. and Rogstad, S.H. (1991) A comparison of methods for assessing genetic variation in plant conservation biology. In: Falk, D.A. and Holsinger, K.E. (eds), *Genetics and Conservation of Rare Plants*, Oxford University Press, Oxford.

Schwarz, H. (1993) *Untersuchungen zu einer bedarfsgerechten Nährstoffversorgung und Optimierung weiterer steuerbarer Produktionsfaktoren bei* Miscanthus sinensis *'Giganteus'*. Dissertation der Universität für Bodenkultur, Wien, Austria.

Schwarz, H. (1994) *Miscanthus sinensis* 'Giganteus' production on several sites in Austria, *Biomass and Bioenergy*, **5**: pp 413–19.

Schwarz, H. and Liebhard, P. (1995) Fertilization effects on production of *Miscanthus sinensis* 'Giganteus'. In: Chartier, Ph., Beenackers, A.A.C.M. and Grassi, G. (eds), *Biomass for Energy, Environment, Agriculture and Industry – Proceedings of 8th E.C. Conference. 3–5 October, 1994, Vienna, Austria*, Elsevier Science Ltd., Oxford, **1**: pp 523–9.

Schwarz, H., Liebhard, P., Ehrendorfer, K. und Ruckenbauer, P. (1993) Ertragsverlauf von *Miscanthus sinensis* 'Giganteus' auf zwei unterschiedlichen Ackerstandorten in Österreich, *Die Bodenkultur – Journal für Landwirtscharfliche Forschung*, **44**: pp 253–63.

Schwarz, H., Liebhard, P., Ehrendorfer, K. and Ruckenbauer, P. (1994) The effect of fertilization on yield and quality of *Miscanthus sinensis* 'Giganteus', *Industrial Crops and Products*, **2**: pp 153–9.

Schwarz, K.-U., Murphy, D.P.L. and Schnug, E. (1994) Studies of growth and yield of *Miscanthus* x *giganteus* in Germany, *Aspects of Applied Biology*, **40**: pp 533–40.

Schwarz, K.-U., Greef, J.M. and Schnug, E. (1995a) Untersuchungen zur etablierung und biomassebildung von *Miscanthus giganteus* unter verschiedenen umweltbedingungen, *Landbauforschung Völkenrode Sonderheft* 155.

Schwarz, K.-U., Schnug, E. and Greef, J.M. (1995b) Yield development and fixation of energy and CO_2, *Natural Resources and Development*, **41**: pp 50–63.

Sharkey, T.D. (1985) Photosynthesis in intact leaves of C_4 plants: physics, physiology and rate limitations, *Botanical Review*, **51**: pp 53–105.

Speller, C.S. (1993) Weed control in *Miscanthus* and other annually harvested biomass crops for energy or industrial use. In: *Proceedings of Brighton Crop Protection Conference* (Weeds), British Crop Protection Council, Farnham, Surrey.

Squire, G.R. (1990) *The Physiology of Tropical Crop Production*, CAB International, Wallingford.

Stülpnagel, R. (1997) Dry or humid biomass from agriculture for energy. In: El Bassam, N., Bacher, W., Korte, A.M. and Prochnow, B. (eds), *Abstracts of International Conference on Sustainable Agriculture for Food, Energy and Industry. June 1997*, Federal Agricultural Research Centre, Braunschweig, Germany.

Tack, F. and Kirschbaum, H.G. (1995) Verfahren und Technik der Lagerung von *Miscanthus*, In: Fachagentur Nachwachsende Rohstoffe e.V. (eds), *Symposium* Miscanthus, *Biomasse-bereitstellung, energetische und stoffliche Nutzung. 1994 Dresden*, Schriftenreihe 'Nachwachsende Rohstoffe' 4, Landwirtschaftsverlag GmbH, Münster. pp 129–41.

Tang, Y.H., and Washitani, I. (1995) Characteristics of small-scale heterogeneity in light availability within a *Miscanthus sinensis* canopy, *Ecological Research*, **10**: pp 189–97.

Tanner, C.B. and Sinclair, T.R. (1983) Efficient water-use in crop production: research or re-search? In: Taylor, H.M., Jordan, W.R. and Sinclair, T.R. (eds), *Limitations to Efficient Water Use in Crop Production*, Am. Soc. Agron., Madison, Wisconsin, pp 1–27.

The Plant Names Project (1999) *International Plant Names Index*, published on the Internet, http://www.ipni.org (accessed 28 August, 2000).

Thomas, H. (1994) Diversity between and within temperate forage grass species in drought resistance, water use and related physiological responses, *Aspects of Applied Biology*, **38**: pp 47–55.

Thornley, J.H.M. and Johnson, I.R. (1990) *Plant and Crop Modelling*, Oxford University Press, Oxford.

United Nations (1996) *Energy Statistics Yearbook*, New York, United Nations.

Venturi, P., Huisman, W. and Molenaar, J. (1996) *Cost Calculations of Production Chains of Miscanthus Giganteus*. Internal Report A559 – 942/1. Department of Agricultural Engineering and Physics, Wageningen Agricultural University, The Netherlands.

Vos, P., Hogers, R., Bleeker, M., Reijans, M., Van de Lee, T., Hornes, M., Frijters, A., Pot, J., Peleman, J., Kuiper, M. and Zabeau, K. (1995) AFLP: A new technique for DNA finger-printing, *Nucleic Acids Research* **23**: pp 4407–24.

Warwick, S.I., Phillips, D. and Andrews, C. (1986) Rhizome depth: the criticalor in winter survival of *Sorghum halepense* (L.) Pres. (Johnson grass), *Weed Research*, **26**: pp 381–7.

Welsh, J. and McCelland, M. (1990). Fingerprinting genomes using PCR with arbitrary primers, *Nucleic Acids Research*, **18**: pp 7213–18.

Werf, H.M.G. van der., Meijer, W.J.M., Mathijssen, E.W.J.M. and Darwinkel, A. (1993) Potential dry matter production of *Miscanthus sinensis* in The Netherlands, *Industrial Crops and Products*, **1**: pp 203–10.

Wiesler, F., Dickmann, J. and Horst, W.J. (1997) Effects of nitrogen supply on growth and nitrogen uptake by *Miscanthus sinensis* during establishment, *Zeitschrift für Pflanzenernährung und Bodenkunde*, **160**: pp 25–31.

Wilkins, C. and Abrutat, P.H. (1995) Growing energy crops on land contaminated by heavy metals. In: Chartier, Ph., Beenackers, A.A.C.M. and Grassi, G. (eds), *Biomass for Energy, Environment, Agriculture and Industry – Proceedings of 8th E.C. Conference. 3–5 October, 1994, Vienna, Austria*, Elsevier Science Ltd., Oxford, **3**: pp 2269–74.

Wilkins, C. and Redstone, S. (1996) Biomass production for energy and industry in the far south west of England. In: Chartier, P., Ferrero, G.L., Henius, U.M., Hultberg, S., Sachau, J. and Wiinblad, M. (eds), *Biomass for Energy and the Environment – Proceedings of the 9th European Bioenergy Conference. 24–27 June 1996, Copenhagen, Denmark*, Elsevier Science Ltd., Oxford, **1**: pp 799–805.

Williams, J.G.K., Kubelik, A.R., Livak, K.J., Rafalski, J.A. and Tingey, S.V. (1990) DNA polymorphisms amplified by arbitrary primers are useful as genetic markers, *Nucleic Acid Research*, **18**: pp 6531–5.

Wüllerstorff, B. von. (1994) Demonstration activities in the community, in particular for biodiesel. In: Hall, D.O., Grassi, G. and Sheer, H. (eds), *Biomass for Energy and Industry – Proceedings of the 7th E.C. Conference. 5–9 October, 1992, Florence, Italy*, Ponte Press, Bochum, Germany, pp 108–16.

Yamashita, S., Nonaka, N., Doi, Y. and Yora, K. (1985) *Miscanthus* streak virus, a geminivirus in *Miscanthus sacchariflorus* Benth et Hook, *Annals of the Phytopathological Society of Japan*, **5**: pp 582–90.

Yi-ming, W. and Yu, Q. (1987) *The Characteristics of Miscanthus sacchariflorus Kraft Cooking and Using for Process Control*, Tianjin Institute of Light Industry, Department of Chemical Engineering, Tianjin.

Yuanlu, L. and Zaizhong, P. (1984) *Preliminary Study of Amur Silver Grass CMP During High Consistency Refining*, Yunnan Institute of Technology, Yunnan.

Zaussinger, A. and Dissemond, H. (1995) *Trocknung von Miscanthus. Bericht aus Energie- und Umweltforschung* 9/95, Bundesministerium für wissenschaft, Forschung und Kunst, Wien 1995.

Index